COMPARATIVE METHODOLOGY

COMPARATIVE METHODOLOGY

Theory and Practice in International Social Research

edited by
Else Øyen

SAGE Studies in International Sociology 40
Sponsored by the International Sociological Association/ISA

First published 1990

SAGE Publications Ltd
28 Banner Street
London EC1Y 8QE

SAGE Publications Inc
2111 West Hillcrest Drive
Newbury Park, California 91320

SAGE Publications India Pvt Ltd
32, M-Block Market
Greater Kailash – I
New Delhi 110 048

British Library Cataloguing in Publication data

Comparative methodology: theory and practice in
   international social research. – (Sage studies in
   international sociology; v. 40).
   1. Comparative sociology. Methodology
   I. Øyen, Else
   301.01

ISBN 0–8039–8325–5
ISBN 0–8039–8326–3 pbk

Library of Congress catalog card number 90–61356

Typeset by Photoprint, Torquay, Devon
Printed in Great Britain by Dotesios Printers Ltd,
Trowbridge, Wiltshire

Contents

Preface

This is the second book published by the Research Council of the International Sociological Association. The first was *Sociology: The State of the Art* (1982), edited by Tom Bottomore, Stefan Nowak and Magdalena Sokolowska. The initiative to present an integrated view of the work of the many ISA Research Committees was taken by the late Professor Sokolowska, who was then Chair of the Research Council. The resulting volume became the official book for the Tenth World Congress of Sociology, held in Mexico City in 1982.

The forty-two Research Committees are the backbone of the ISA. This is an empirical as well as a political statement. While the World Congress is the most important event of the ISA, it occurs only once in every four years. In the periods between World Congresses the Research Committees are the lively arenas for joint research projects, local workshops, regional symposia and international meetings, the publications of newsletters, papers and books, and the creation of innumerable informal contacts leading to new research and the consolidation of professional networks. All this activity has only kept on increasing, as has the number of Research Committees, Working Groups and Thematic Groups. Other important initiatives are the creation of the International Sociological Institute, with a Summer School and a Research Forum for the use of all the Research Committees, located at Ljubljana in Yugoslavia, and the Oñati International Institute for the Sociology of Law, located at Oñati in the Basque country in Spain.

However, the professional power of the Research Committees is not sufficiently reflected in the organizational structure of the ISA. Each Research Committee is entitled to send a delegate to the Research Council, which in turn acts as a coordinating and supportive body for the Research Committees and their interests. Little formal power is embodied in the Research Council. Of the sixteen representatives on the ISA Executive Committee, the Research Council elects only five, and the procedures for the elections of president and vice-presidents have as a consequence that the Research Council is not in a position to elect its own Chair. Proposed amendments to the Statutes in order to change this situation have been forwarded to the ISA Council.

In the Preface to the first book of the Research Council it was stated that, 'Beginning in the early 1950s, the various research committees were among the first organizations to develop comparative research, and they remain a stimulus to the advancement of sociology in various parts of the world.' At a Research Council symposium in 1988 the Research Committees were invited to present papers on the methodology of comparative research. The time had come to review the achievements of sociology within this area and assess future directions.

As a result of the discussion, the Research Council decided that a book on comparative methodology would be valuable. Most of us have never been taught how to conduct cross-national studies. We were trained in universities where the main focus was on sociological methodologies for studies within our own culture. Much of the discussion at the Research Council symposium centred on this issue, and it seemed as though we had all been through the lonesome journey of trial and error in learning how to do cross-national research on our own.

An ideal publication would have been a comprehensive book dealing with the state of the art in comparative sociological methodology. But such a book may not yet be ready to be written. For a long time we assumed that the knowledge and skills in cross-national research would accumulate at the same speed as the increase in the number of comparative studies. Now we know this is not so. This new cognition lies in the knowledge of the limitations of comparative sociological methodology, and it is on this cognition that progress may be made. It now seems as if we are ready to move into a new stage of comparative research, where optimism has yielded the ground to realism.

This book reflects this attitude. The contributors were not asked to furnish the ordinary presentations of a successful piece of comparative research. These presentations are available elsewhere. Instead, our aim has been to make visible some of the important choices we were faced with when engaging in cross-national studies, thereby displaying pitfalls to be avoided and improving our awareness of available strategies and their limitations. We have also made an effort to emphasize and demonstrate weaknesses and strengths of using concepts, theories and methods within cross-national contexts, as opposed to what is ordinarily found within one-nation studies. Doing this has not always been an easy task. The authors have had to call on all their pedagogical skills. Although the aim of the project was neither to write a handbook showing how to do comparative research step by step, nor to do a book for those sophisticated comparativists who have been in the game for a long time, we have wanted to produce a book which at the same time points to some of the difficulties and potentials of cross-national methodology, directs the readers to available literature on comparative research and stimulates a debate about comparative methodology that involves a wider audience of sociologists than has been the case so far.

The authors have been recruited mainly from the Research Council. On purpose, no attempt has been made to represent certain research traditions or include topics which seem to be a must in most anthologies these days. The contributions have been selected for their quality and the variety of insight they give into methodological issues of cross-national research.

My sincere gratitude goes to my colleagues who helped write the book, to the members of the Research Council who participated in the discussions and to the many members of the Research Committees who through their comparative studies have furnished us all with the wealth of data and analytical insights upon which the future of comparative sociological research will be built.

Else Øyen
Chair of the ISA Research Council

Notes on the Contributors

RUDOLF ANDORKA is Professor of Sociology and Head of the Department of Sociology of the Karl Marx University of Economic Sciences, Budapest. Previously he worked at the Demographic Research Institute of the Central Statistical Office, and at the Department of Social Statistics of the Central Statistical Office. His major books include *Determinants of Fertility in Advanced Societies* (1978); *Socio-occupational Mobility in Hungary and Poland* (1980) (with K. Zagorski); *Agricultural Population and Structural Change; A Comparison of Finland and Hungary* (1987) (with M. Alestalo and I. Harcsa); *Modernization in Hungary in the Long and Short Run Measured by Social Indicators* (1988) (with I. Harcsa). Research fields are: determinants of fertility in advanced societies, social stratification and mobility, time budget and deviant behaviour. He is now President of the ISA Research Committee on Social Stratification.

DANIEL BERTAUX is Directeur de recherche at the French Centre National de la Recherche Scientifique. He was initially trained and worked in the natural sciences (mathematics, physics, aeronautical engineering, artificial intelligence) before changing to sociology. His books include *Destins personnels et structure de classe* (1977); *Biography and Society* (1981); *La mobilité sociale* (1985). He is founder and President of the ISA Research Committee on Biography and Society, and since 1986 a member of the Executive Committee of the ISA where he has been organizing the new project Worldwide Competition for Young Sociologists. His current research interests cover such topics as social mobility, family forms, the processes of production of human energy or 'anthroponomy', social movements, intellectuals.

FERNANDO CALDERON is Executive Secretary of the Latin American Council on the Social Sciences (CLACSO). He has a Ph.D. in sociology from the Ecole Pratique des Hautes Etudes in Paris. He is currently working on social movements and the changing relationships between state, society and economy. He has been Visiting Lecturer at the University of Texas, Austin, the University of Buenos Aires, Argentina, and the University of Barcelona, Spain. His major books are: *La Política en las calles* (1983); *Urbanizacion y etnicidad: El caso de La Paz* (1984); *La mina urbana* (1985); *Busquedas y bloqueos* (1987).

EVA ETZIONI-HALEVY is Professor at the Department of Sociology and Anthropology, Bar-Ilan University, Israel, and Reader at the Department of Sociology, the Faculties, the Australian National University. She is the author of *Social Change* (1981); *Bureaucracy and Democracy* (rev. edn, 1985); *The Knowledge Elite and the Failure of Prophecy* (1985); *National Broadcasting under Siege* (1987); and *Fragile Democracy* (1989). She is a Fellow of the Academy of the Social Sciences in Australia.

VINCENZO FERRARI is Professor of Sociology of Law at Bologna University, Italy. He has a degree in Law from Milan State University, and is a practising lawyer in Milan. Until 1983 he was Professor in Sociology of Law at Cagliari University. He is Joint Editor-in-Chief of *Sociologia del diritto*, Vice-President of the ISA Research Committee on Sociology of Law and member of the board of the Oñati International Institute of Sociology of Law. His books include *Successione per testamento e trasformazioni sociali* (1972); with R. Boniardi and N.G. Velicogna, *Assenteismo e malattia nell'industria* (1979); *Funzioni del diritto* (1987), 2nd edn, 1989).

JOHAN GALTUNG has had an international academic career spanning thirty years, five continents, and he has held a dozen major positions and forty Visiting Professorships, has written fifty books and published more than 1,000 articles. In 1959 he set up the International Peace Research in Oslo, Norway. He is currently Professor of Peace Studies at the University of Hawaii, USA, working on comparative civilization theory, development theory and a new approach to economics which can more comfortably accommodate such major goals as peace, development, human growth and ecological balance. His publications range from *Gandhi's Political Ethics* (1955), four volumes on methodology and six volumes of *Essays in Peace Research* (1974–88), to *There Are Alternatives* (1984) and *Hitlerism, Stalinism, Reaganism* (1984).

JAN-ERIK LANE is Professor of Public Administration. He holds a temporary research position in Public Policy located to the Department of Economics at Lund University. He has published widely in the fields of political theory, comparative politics and public policy, including books like *Politics and Society in Western Europe* (1987, with Svante Ersson); *Contemporary Political Economy* (forthcoming, 1990), also with Svante Ersson); and *Institutional Reform* (1990). He is Co-editor of the *Journal of Theoretical Politics* and Chairman of the Committee on Conceptual and Termino-logical Analysis (COCTA). Lane has taught as Visiting Professor at Northwestern University and at the University of California at San Diego. He has edited two Sage volumes: *State and Market* (1985); and *Public Choice* (1987).

KARL M. VAN METER is doing research in the social sciences with the French Centre National de la Recherche Scientifique. He has degrees in social science and pure mathematics from the United States, Great Britain and the University of Paris. He has been working with the Ministry of Justice, the Ministry of Culture and the Ministry of Research and Technology, and since 1985 as an independent consulting expert with the Health Directorate of the Commission of the European Communities. In 1983, he founded and continues to direct the quarterly scientific review, *BMS – Bulletin de Méthodologie Sociologique*. Since 1986, he has been Secretary of the ISA Research Committee on Logic and Methodology and is currently Chair of the ISA Ljubljana Committee responsible for the Research Forum and the Summer School within the International Sociological Institute.

ELSE SJØRUP ØYEN is Professor of Social Policy at the University of Bergen, Norway. She is the retiring Vice-President of the International Sociological Association and Chair of the ISA Research Council, former President of the ISA Research Committee on Poverty, Social Welfare and Social Policy, and member of the Executive Committee of the International Social Science Council. She has been a Visiting Professor at the Australian National University, Canberra, and at the University of California, Santa Barbara, and a Visiting Fellow at the Zentrum für Interdisziplinäre

Forschung, Bielefeld. Major works include *Sosialomsorgen og dens forvaltere* (1974 and 1978); *Taushetsplikten i den sosiale sektor* (1980, with A. Kjønstad); *Sosiologi og ulikhet* (ed.) (1976, 1983, 1990); *Comparing Welfare States and Their Futures* (ed.) (1986). Current research interests lie within comparative social policy.

ALEJANDRO PISCITELLI is Deputy Secretary to the Latin American Council on the Social Sciences (CLACSO). He has a Master of Social Science degree from the University of Louisville, Kentucky. He is involved in sociology of innovation and the linguistic behaviour of organizations. Among his main papers are contributions to constructivist epistemology, the sociology of sociology and paradigmatic analyses of substantive social theories. He is actively involved in building up computer networking for the social sciences throughout Latin America.

ERWIN K. SCHEUCH is Professor of Sociology at the University of Cologne. There he is also Director of the Zentralarchiv für Empirische Sozialforschung and Co-director of the Institute of Applied Social Research, which he originally founded as the Institute for Comparative Research, and of the Seminar für Soziologie at the School of Economics. He holds degrees in economics, statistics and sociology. For a time he held a position at the Department of Social Relations in Harvard. Scheuch has spent a substantial part of his life in countries other than his native West Germany, most frequently working in the United States, but also as a Visiting Professor at Auckland University, New Zealand, Stockholms Universitet, the Grande Ecole en Sciences Sociales in Paris and the Collège de l'Europe in Brügge, Belgium. Scheuch combines his primary interests in quantitative methodology with an internationalist orientation into studies in comparative social research.

HENRY TEUNE is Professor of the Political Science Department at the University of Pennsylvania. He has been involved in cross-national research on India, Poland, Yugoslavia, the USA, Thailand, Malaysia and the Philippines. His authored or co-authored comparative focused books include *The Integration of Political Communities* (1964); *The Logic of Comparative Social Inquiry* (1970); *Values and the Active Community* (1971); *The Developmental Logic of Social Systems* (1978); and, most recently, *Growth* (1988). He has held research or teaching appointments in India, Japan, the Netherlands and Yugoslavia. In 1981 he was President of the International Studies Association and currently serves as Vice-President of the Research Committee on Social Ecology of the ISA. He is now engaged in comparative projects on revenue systems and 'new urban forms'.

RALPH H. TURNER is Professor of Sociology at the University of California, Los Angeles. He is a former President of the American Sociological Association, Vice-President of the International Sociological Association, President of the Society for the Study of Symbolic Interaction, and Editor of *Sociometry* and of the *Annual Review of Sociology*. Books include *Collective Behavior* (1957, 1972, 1987; with L. Killian); *The Social Context of Ambition* (1964); *Robert Park on Social Control and Collective Behavior* (1967); *Family Interaction* (1979); and *Waiting for Disaster: Earthquake Watch in California* (1986; with J. Nigg and D. Paz). His current research interests include the theory of social roles, especially dynamic processes and the relationship between role and person and the social self; collective behaviour, including social movements; and the history of sociology.

PART I

COMPARATIVE RESEARCH AS A SOCIOLOGICAL STRATEGY

1

The Imperfection of Comparisons

Else Øyen

There is no reason to believe there exists an easy and straight-forward entry into comparative social research. All the eternal and unsolved problems inherent in sociological research are unfolded when engaging in cross-national studies. None of the methodological and theoretical difficulties we have learned to live with can be ignored when we examine critically such questions as what is comparative research, how we go about doing comparative work, and how we interpret similarities and differences in countries compared. The problems are more likely to be exacerbated when another analytical level, filled with unknown variables, is added to our investigations. Yet, more cross-national studies than ever before are being carried out, and the need as well as demand for comparisons across countries is formidable.

The call for more comparative studies has its roots in very different kinds of forces. Some of these forces are located outside the arena of sociological research, and some are located inside the field of sociology. Since the former kind of forces seem to be far more powerful than the latter, questions may be raised as to whether the external forces are more instrumental in directing the development of comparative research than are the internal forces.

The major external force is, of course, the growing international-ization and the concomitant export and import of social, cultural and economic manifestations across national borders. Labour and people flow between countries in ways we have never seen before, and the establishment of international organizations having no country as their natural base increases steadily. This globalizing trend has changed our cognitive map. While some cultural differences are diminishing, others are becoming more salient. Comparative research may have to shift its emphasis from seeking uniformity among variety to studying the preservation of enclaves of uniqueness among growing homogeneity and uniformity (Sztompka, 1988: 215).

The globalization of problems is another key concept, which the World Commission on Environment and Development helped put on the agenda through the Brundtland Report on *Our Common Future* (1987). A national crisis is seldom merely national any more. The air we breathe is polluted from faraway sources. An understanding of poverty in the Third World cannot be isolated from a consideration of the wealth accumulated in the rich countries. The suppression of minorities becomes public property throughout the world when caught by television. Within such a perspective the use of countries as units in comparative research may not appear to be the most fruitful approach. However, the world is divided according to these administrative units, and since much of the infrastructure available for comparative research is tied to the territories enclosed by national boundaries, it becomes seductively convincing to use such units in comparative studies.

Also, many of the external actors initiating comparisons are based within a national context and may have vested interests in studies which compare their country to other countries. So far, national research councils and funding agencies have given preference to research which includes their own country. Politicians are calling for comparisons which increase their understanding and mastery of national events, while accepting that intuitive comparisons form a basis for the major part of the decision-making. Bureaucrats make extensive use of national and international statistics for comparisons, and industry and business are constantly comparing the social context of national and foreign markets. The need for more precise, reliable comparisons has become part of a political and economic reality which is a driving force behind the demand for more cross-national comparisons, most of which apply to specific problems and are fairly limited in scope.

In a historical account of the development of comparative social research Scheuch shows how the commercial institutes for market and opinion research went into cross-national comparisons as early as in the thirties. But for a long time the spill-over effect into a comparative social science was limited. In the fifties social science institutions started forming around the polling agencies, which opened up for large international surveys and laid the foundation for the national and international data archives as we see them today. With the advancement of new technology, in particular computers, new techniques and methodologies were developed for handling the enormous masses of data, most of which were collected and processed in the industrialized countries. Much of the present comparative research has its roots in the networks of those social scientists who took over the tools of a commercial and political enterprise and transformed them into an international exchange system of comparative knowledge. Part of the heritage also is the strong emphasis on technical issues involved in cross-national studies, while theoretical matters have been more of secondary interest (Chapter 2).

Teune elaborates on the history of comparative research and paints a fairly pessimistic picture of the contributions by the social scientists so far. The aim of cross-national research is to reduce unexplained variance and find patterns and relationships, but the variance-reducing schemes presented in the studies do not often yield the relationships which are suitable as a foundation for building theoretical explanations. Throughout the period during which we have been struggling with comparative research, one lesson learned is that whatever we do in the way of cross-national comparisons must be theoretically justified –`and cutting into countries theoretically is a complex process, of the beginning of which we have only caught a glimpse. Methodologically, Teune makes as one of several points, that cross-sectional analysis, looking at countries at a single point in time, and cross-time analysis give artefactual results because of problems of aggregation and disaggregation. And after having critically examined some of the major cross-national studies, he concludes that any set of categories established will create biases in the observations. Although our sensitivity to the problems has increased, most of the problems still lie unsolved (Chapter 3).

At the same time, however, sociologists increasingly seem to be drawn towards a return to more holistic models, taking on new challenges without having fully confronted the old ones in a satisfying manner. Macro-sociological analysis used to be the focus of sociological analysis and theory. One of the arguments is that it is still within this framework that theories from the many different sub-fields of sociology can be tested, and that macro-sociology offers the best arena for sociologists to examine their skills as sociologists (Eisenstadt and Curelaru, 1977). Another argument is that cross-national research provides an especially useful method both for the further development of sociological theory, and for establishing the generality of findings and the validity of interpretations derived from studies of single nations (Kohn, 1989b: 77). If this is so, then sociology as a science stands to gain from the extended development of cross-national research.

What is Comparative Social Research?

For most sociologists the very nature of sociological research is considered comparative, and thinking in comparative terms is inherent in sociology. All empirical observations must be related to some kind of theoretical construction, and no theoretical construction has any value unless it bears some relation to empirical observations. When sociologists choose to observe only part of the surrounding social realities the choice always represents a comparison of the selected phenomenon under observation in relation to other social phenomena, whether this choice is made explicitly or implicitly. Normal behaviour and norms cannot be studied without acknowledging deviations from the normal. Actually, no social phenomenon can be isolated and studied without comparing it to other social phenomena. Sociologists engage actively in the process of comparative work whenever concepts are chosen, operationalized or fitted into theoretical structures. Trying to understand and explain variation is a process which cannot be accomplished without previous reflections on similarities and dissimilarities underlying the variation.

The whole discussion on explicit and implicit comparisons is an integral part of a scientific world, and the discourse is particularly well developed within the philosophical and literary traditions. The debate has solid roots in social anthropology and political science, but has left as many unanswered questions there as it has in the sociological discussion on the issue, which received new and vigorous attention in the 1970s and 1980s.

One of the main questions, in the present context, is whether comparisons across national boundaries represent a new or a different set of theoretical, methodological and epistemological challenges, or whether this kind of research can be treated just as another variant of the comparative problems already embedded in sociological research. Quite another kind of question is whether doing comparative research involving two countries is any different from research involving three or more countries, and how different the countries to be compared can be allowed to be before they are no longer comparable. Answers to the latter kind of questions are usually referred to the limited theoretical context within which the variables are selected, because only within such a framework do these questions seem meaningful. But the search for answers also reaches beyond theoretical fragments and joins the eternal search for basic patterns of human behaviour which transcends all cultural influences. The only logical terminal point for such world-wide comparisons – and terminal it may be – is the discovery of all-embracing 'social laws' which either bend towards still higher levels of abstraction or portray fundamental humanistic behaviour in such a way that we are forced to ask whether the results should rather be interpreted as a result of basic biological needs.

Sociologists are not a very homogeneous group, and they vary in the way they relate to basic issues in sociology, as they vary in their approaches to comparative research. When going through the very extensive literature written on comparative studies, it looks as if at least four different ways of conducting cross-national studies can be identified.

One group of sociologists – let us call them the purists – stand firmly in the belief that conducting comparative research across national boundaries is no different from any other kind of sociological research. Therefore they include no special discussion on problems encountered in cross-national studies, but refer to theoretical and methodological considerations involved in doing multilevel research. At heart we are all purists.

On the other hand we find those sociologists – shall we call them the ignorants – who pursue their ideas and data across national boundaries without ever giving a thought to the possibility that such comparisons may add to the complexity in interpreting the results of the study. Such behaviour may not be as unforgivable as it sounds. Most of us have sinned in this respect, either directly in our own research, or indirectly by uncritically importing research results or theories developed in another country and implanting them into our own analysis. As a matter of fact, in our education as sociologists this is much the tradition in which we have been brought up.

The third group of sociologists, the totalists, are only too well aware of the many problems of doing cross-national research in a world of complex interdependencies. They consciously ignore the many stumbling blocks of the non-equivalence of concepts, a multitude of unknown variables interacting in an unknown context and influencing the research in question in unknown ways. And they deliberately ignore the scientific requirements regarding the testing of hypotheses in settings which do not and cannot meet the conditions for such testing. If they were to take all these unmanoeuvrable problems into consideration, the totalists would be paralysed and have to leave the field of cross-national comparisons. Instead they go ahead, opting for compromises and trying to make the tools of sociological analysis provide new insights (Øyen, 1986a; 1986b).

Then there are the comparativists who acknowledge the points of view held by the purists and the totalists, but argue that in order to advance our knowledge about cross-national research it is necessary to raise questions about the distinctive characteristics of comparative studies. Ragin, for example, states that one of the differences between the comparativists and the non-comparativists is that the former by a conscious choice define the macro-social units as real, while the latter tend to treat these units as abstractions that need not be operationalized and made explicit. Another distinction of comparative social science is 'its use of attributes of macrosocial units in explanatory statements' in order to reach 'the twin goals of comparative social science – both to explain and to interpret macrosocial variation' (Ragin, 1987: ch. 1).

Alapuro and his colleagues distinguish between endogenous and exogenous models for comparisons. In the endogenous model both the possible causes and the possible effects are seen as located within the country being compared. The 'utilization of general concepts makes one object of study in a basic sense comparable to others' (1985: 22). In the exogenous model the countries are viewed as a system of interdependent units, and the position of a country within this larger system is considered an external factor affecting the processes under study.

Kohn identifies four kinds of cross-national research on the basis of the different *intent* of the studies. Here countries can be (1) the *object* of the study – that is, the investigator's interest lies primarily in the countries studied, (2) the *context* of the study – namely, the interest is primarily vested in testing the generality of research results concerning social phenomena in two or more countries, (3) the *unit* of analysis – where the interest is chiefly to investigate how social phenomena are systematically related to characteristics of the countries researched, and (4) *trans-national* – namely, studies that treat nations as components of a larger international system. Kohn proceeds to show how the theoretical implications of the different kinds of studies are distinguishable (1989a: 20–4).

Ragin elaborates on this classification within a two-dimensional matrix. Along one dimension is placed the number of countries included in the comparative studies. Along the other dimension is presented the nature of the explanatory statements of the studies, such as the intrinsic qualities of the countries, general features of the countries, and features of a larger unit of which the country/ countries form part. Within the nine cells formed by cross-tabulating the two dimensions Ragin also places the types of comparison described by Kohn. One of the gains of the matrix is the addition of the single-country study – the assumed uninteresting case for cross-national research – and the demonstration of its usefulness when the emphasis is on explanatory statements based on character- istics of the country and the analysis is either of a more general nature or can be fitted into studies done in other countries. As a demonstration of the power of his classification Ragin places examples of different studies within the nine cells. The seemingly different studies have as a major commonality that 'characteristics of macro-social units appear in explanatory statements in all nine types', which to Ragin is a key, unifying feature of comparative social science (1989: 65–8).

The vocabulary for distinguishing between the different kinds of comparative research is redundant and not very precise. Concepts such as cross-country, cross-national, cross-societal, cross-cultural, cross-systemic, cross-institutional, as well as trans-national, trans-societal, trans-cultural, and comparisons on the macro-level, are used both as synonymous with comparative research in general and as denoting specific kinds of comparisons, although the specificity varies from one author to another. The confusion reflects the point that national boundaries are different from ethnic, cultural and social boundaries. Within all countries, even the very old and fairly homogeneous ones, we may find several sub-societies which on some variables may show greater variation than comparisons across national boundaries can demonstrate: that is, within-variation may sometimes be greater than between-variation. Good examples may be found in the history of India (Oommen, 1989), and in recent changes in Eastern Europe and the Soviet Union, where conflicts between cultural, social and national norms form the basis for the demands for changes of administrative and country borders to accommodate the different identities.

Calderon and Piscitelli stress the double-sided relationship of the Latin American region which at the same time has its own identity, different from the rest of the world, and also embraces a set of different cultural identities within the region. This leads the authors 'to presume the existence of a complex, uncomfortable and enthralling relationship between the Latin American identity and the methodological levels of analysis focusing on it' (Chapter 5). Teune shows the different implications of using nation versus country as unit of analysis for comparative studies (Chapter 3), while Scheuch points out that only in the most ideological form does the nation-state assume a sameness among its citizens (Chapter 2). Therefore, a mere cleaning up of the ambiguities built into the different concepts only meets the problem halfway, as the complexity embedded in the social realities still remain to be accounted for.

The term 'cross-country' in this volume is synonymous with 'cross-national' (notwithstanding the reservations made by Teune, as the English language does not provide an adjective for 'cross-countrial' studies). At the Vienna Centre, for example, the trend has moved towards the use of the term 'trans-national' research, thereby signalling that the focus now is on the macro-structures in the countries to be compared (Charvat et al., 1988).

In the following the use of the terms 'cross-cultural', 'cross-societal', 'trans-cultural' and 'trans-societal' are rather a result of the different authors' preferences and educational tradition than being a reflection of substantive realities. The terms have much the same content and imply that the level of analysis is below that of the level of country. The term 'cross-historical' contains the ambiguity of pointing both to a certain methodological approach in comparative research (see Etzioni-Halevy, Chapter 7), and to the more diffuse meaning of making comparisons of social phenomena over time. The terms 'cross-institutional' and 'cross-systemic' simply mean what they signal; namely, comparisons of the same kinds of institutions or systems in different countries.

Theoretical Poverty of Comparative Research

If we accept that comparative research, whether it is carried out as cross-national studies or as comparisons on a lower level, has as its major aim to verify social theories, then the attention is directed towards the present state of social theory. Nowak argues that the development of sociological theory has for a long time been neglected, and that much of what today is called sociological theory is formulated in such a way that it makes empirical verifications of hypotheses or theorems 'difficult or even impossible'. Given that Nowak is right, then the major building block for conducting comparative studies is missing. More will be gained by developing sociological theory in general, hereunder also specifying the relationship between the different levels of analysis, be the studies cross-national or comparative on a lower level. Only through such a process, says Nowak, can we begin to close the gap between what comparativists pretend to do and what they actually are doing (1989). The term 'theory' here refers to 'possibly unambiguous sets or systems of laws, or to broad lawlike generalizations, integrated on the basis of a common unifying principle, with clearly stated topological and (or) historical conditions of their validity' (Nowak, 1989: 40).

Presumably, part of the problem is that to many comparativists this very definition of a sociological theory does not constitute their point of departure, but the *intent* of their research, and conducting cross-national studies, incorporating the historical dimension, are their instruments for arriving at broad, law-like generalizations.

The chapter by Ferrari is a meticulous attempt to establish one of the basic building blocks that Nowak is calling for; namely, that of translating a concept from one cultural context into another cultural context, without distorting the content and meaning of the concept, and without losing valuable and characteristic information through the translation (Chapter 4). This is probably the area in which the social anthropologists have wrestled the longest, trying to interpret their observations in 'native' societies within the native system of explanation and without undue interference from their own Western culture. At the same time the observers face the challenge of communicating the original and interpreted observations back to a Western framework of understanding, *and* relating the observations in a meaningful way to observations in the Western countries. Only through such a process can concepts be developed and more general theories be formed so as to explain the behaviour in the original observations as well as in the observations from the Western cultures (see, for example, Bohannan, 1963). Step by step Ferrari takes us through the deliberations sociologists of law go through when trying to arrive at meta-theoretical clarifications for the sake of comparison. As an example he uses the central concept of *law*, which spans the range between official state law and intuitive folk law. The legal systems in which the concept originates reflect not only different national cultures and local traditions, but also different kinds of power structures and doctrinal style of interpretations. Therefore, Ferrari says, law should not be defined as a static concept, but should reflect the normative content and the interaction between the social actors involved in the process of limiting the range of behaviour in a community. Although the ultimate goal has always been that of building a common and unambiguous lexicon of concepts as an instrument for comparative research, part of the sociological reorientation is to acknowledge that a concept can also be a variable among variables.

Calderon and Piscitelli give evidence of the failure of an entire theoretical tradition in sociology which was uncritically translated and exported from the 'central' countries to the 'peripheral' countries (Chapter 5). Cross-national research was revived and took a new direction when the Third World made its way on to the political agenda of the industrialized countries in the fifties and sixties. Theories of development and modernization, in sociology as well as in political science and economics, zoomed in on the 'undeveloped' countries and paved the way for an analysis coined in the terms of the Western countries. While comparative research in general may have benefited, as more refined and differential approaches to macro-societal analysis surfaced (Eisenstadt and Curelaru, 1977: ch. 2), social science in peripheral countries experienced a serious setback. In Latin America social scientists in good faith were instrumental in adapting ideas embedded in theories of development and modernization for political implementation. The analysis and the conceptual tools proved inadequate, theoretically as well as politically. As a consequence, Latin American social scientists are now very conscious of the processes involved in transforming sociological approaches and concepts generated outside the region, even the local region, within which the research is carried out. The notion of syncretism has become a central and necessary element in revitalizing the research strategies.

The strategy for a comparative social science stretching towards a universal social science, for which Galtung is a proponent, takes as its point of departure that much of what is being presented as sociological theory might just as well be labelled story-telling or meditation, while sociologists who follow the textbook prescription for theory construction run the risk of presenting only the static reality of the past. Requirements of a good theory are not only that the theory reflects the enormous complexity of the present social reality, the course of which is constantly being changed by its own actors. It should also make possible the incorporation of the social realities of an unforeseen future, and include a meta-theory which reflects on the social and political consequences of the ideology underlying the theory (Chapter 6). The linkage to the fate of the theories of development and modernization in Latin America is evident here. No single theory can meet all these requirements, and Galtung therefore argues for working simultaneously with a multi-tude of theoretical approaches, none of which should ever be completely believed or disbelieved on its own merit. This is the classical ideal, forgotten in the empire-building of sociological schools. The analysis is carried into a discussion of the linkage between the micro-level and the macro-level in comparative research, although Galtung prefers the term 'space' to 'level', in order to avoid the causal explanations and reductionism inherent in the idea of lower and higher levels within a social system. People live in spaces (nature, personal, social, world), experience spaces, have images of spaces; and the spaces in their turn interact in many other ways than hierarchically ordered levels, including the level of nation. Of course, questions may be raised as to whether this reordering really escapes causality and reductionism. However, in the present context the importance of the contribution lies in the pregnant questions raised about the use of traditional concepts, models of thought and research strategies.

The Art of Methodological Compromises

The question of whether cross-national research has qualities different from sociological research in general may now be repeated as we enter the discussion on the methodology of cross-national studies. Is it possible to distinguish a specific comparative methodology, other than that of adding to the complexity of the analysis as an additional level is introduced? Again, there is little consensus on the matter.

Also the issue is muddled by the fact that cross-national research becomes part of a

> built-in transition from internationality to interdisciplinarity: it is simply difficult to establish acceptable comparisons between countries and cultures without bringing in broader ranges of variables than those of only one discipline. . . . We find a variety of attempts at interdisciplinary bridge-building in works of theory and methodology but only very few signs of a corresponding recognition of the need for interdisciplinarity in the actual programmes of training or research: at that level, there is much greater stress on disciplinary identities, on the demarcation of boundaries. (Rokkan, 1978: 5)

This implies that participating in cross-national research may require knowledge and the use of methodological skills which sociologists are not familiar with, and more or less have to learn as they go along.

Although Nowak (1989) and Galtung (Chapter 6) disagree on the goals and the theoretical framework for cross-national research, they join hands in defending the premise that basic rules of scientific analysis must be applied. Classical skills such as those of carefully constructing concepts and typologies, and securing ties between data and theory, as well as making use of inference, remain indisputable virtues. The studies presented by Etzioni-Halevy (Chapter 7) and Turner (Chapter 8) are good examples of this tradition.

In the study of parliamentarians, by Etzioni-Halevy, the research problem is comparative in the sense that the questions asked cannot be answered unless data from different countries are compared. The theory calls for countries which are well-established democracies with similar parliamentary systems. Thereby one level of analysis is given, and the range of countries limited. The choice of countries to be included in the study was finally determined by the fact that the researcher had easy access to data and familiarity with these two countries in question. Such compromises form part of the research process, but can at the same time yield windfall solutions, as the familiarity with a country provides additional information, increasing the value of the explanatory statements. The question of equivalence is particularly pertinent in the present project, where the comparisons focus not only on people's actual patterns of action, but also on their norms and standards, their definitions of the situation, and of their own roles. The problem becomes even more prominent where the 'something' to be compared is as elusive as semi-corruption. The choice of two countries with a very similar background may meet some of the difficulties involved in the quest for equivalence. But the researcher is thrown back into the struggles of interpretation when differences and similarities occur within the same group of interviewees (Chapter 7).

Turner uses corporation biographies in a study of mobility patterns. The project fits into a larger research scheme concerning differences in the British–American cultures, so the choice of countries is self-evident. The challenge of equivalence when comparing documents from different countries is countered through the establishment of national validation panels, a procedure well-known in social psychology but not in comparative content analysis. Two panels of judges, chosen from British and American business and industry, were presented with a questionnaire listing verbs and verb expressions identified in the biographies as describing job change. The judges were asked to give their opinion on the meaning of these expressions when used in different kinds of contexts. Practical problems made it difficult to construct the panels according to the original intentions. Content analysis can be used to make inferences about public opinion, attitudes, values or the nature of social structure, and many forms of written documents can serve as objects of such analysis. Disadvantages of the method lie in the sampling and the indirectness of the observations which assume knowledge about the translation from the observable. Advantages of the method lie in the unobtrusiveness which eliminates interaction between the investigator and the data producer, and that inferences can be made about non-observable phenomena. Turner concludes that national validation panels are a valuable instrument for reducing the impact of cultural differences in the judgement process, a method which can be further improved and made adaptable also to comparative studies in countries which do not share the same language (Chapter 8).

In a critical review of the progress of comparative research, Sztompka proposes a paradigmatic shift for cross-national studies. He argues that the models of comparative work have been outdated by the rapid changes in the social realities. 'Galton's problem' (cf. the discussion by Scheuch, Chapter 2) is more problematic than ever, and the dubious logic of quasi-experimentation is even less feasible in a world which has grown into an interdependent and interlinked global system. We need more variety in our comparative approaches, and in a two-dimensional matrix Sztompka offers six such approaches, each of which requires a different methodology. If we accept that the goal for comparative inquiry is that of formulating propositions about society, then one dimension in the matrix is the focus of comparative research (respectively modifying the scope of applicability, changing the scope of objects and altering the scope of predicates). The other dimension is the direction of comparative research (seeking uniformity versus seeking uniqueness). The emphasis used to be on comparisons seeking uniformity and attempting to establish generality of findings across national borders, in 'an attempt to imitate the logic of experiment'. Now the time has come, he says, to search for uniqueness and comparisons that point to the peculiarities of a country, to single out a certain category of people by contrasting them with other people, and to search for attitudes and beliefs thåt are atypical. To reach this goal a reorientation towards history and the humanities is necessary (Sztompka, 1988). The implications of such a shift also point to a revival of theories of deviation, and will certainly provoke a discussion in epistemological terms.

Bertaux has written his contribution much within the same comparative framework, although *ex post facto*, as the research was carried out before the investigators became aware of the paradigm advanced by Sztompka. With a 'wide-angle vision' the early commitment to the students' movements of the sixties was analysed in six countries, through the life stories of selected persons who were close to the movements from the beginning. One of the research questions was why these very people were to become the first activists. Life stories are in-depth accounts of personal experiences which sociologically can be used not only to study the subjective side of social life but also to understand structural relationships. The wealth of the data collected is complex and diverse, and 'it takes a sociological eye' to analyse a particular experience and to understand what is universal about it. Sociological thinking has to be present at every step of the research process, and part of the sociological imagination is to perceive processes that transcend nations and cultures. The goal is to generate hypotheses that can be exposed to the critique of the sociological community. Bertaux stresses that the process of generating hypotheses, and the process of testing them, are two processes which should not be confused. The emphasis in comparative research on the latter is killing off the sociological imagination necessary for the former (Chapter 9).

Whereas the populations studied by Bertaux were highly visible, Van Meter directs his research towards populations that are hidden or in hiding from public attention. Surveys and descending methodologies do not capture these groups, some of which are also very small. Through the snowball technique one or two persons in the hidden population are approached, and via their networks still more persons are identified. The process is repeated over and over again, until the point of saturation and the entire population is identified. This ascending methodology can be used for numerical purposes and for intensive data collection which can be linked together in a cross-classification analysis, incorporating data from various countries. Comparative studies of (for example) drug use in different major

European cities seem to yield valid results which could not have been obtained otherwise (Chapter 10).

Some will label the methods used by Bertaux and Van Meter as qualitative, although Bertaux does not adhere to the term, and Van Meter rejects the discussion about qualitative versus quantitative research as outdated and not tenable in concrete comparative research projects. Others may refer to the methods as empirically intensive.

This is a methodological discourse which has been carried over from general sociology, and at times has obscured issues about comparative methodologies as such. One of the most significant contributions to sorting out the analytical dimensions involved in using empirically intensive and empirically extensive methods in comparative studies has been done by Ragin (1987; 1989). He develops a research strategy, described as Boolean methods of qualitative comparisons, which is an attempt to bridge the gulf between the case-oriented approach and the variable-oriented approach, while incorporating the strength of both methodologies. This is not the place to develop the argument or the objections. It is more relevant to direct attention to his thorough discussion of causal complexity and the questions it raises for comparative reasoning (1987: ch. 2), and the conflicting logic underlying case-oriented comparative methodologies (1987: ch. 3).

The chapter by Lane is a demonstration of methods which can be labelled empirically extensive. Here the efforts at turning the enormous masses of data stored in the many national and international social science data archives into meaningful comparative research are presented, exemplified by the use of data archives in political sociology. The studies introduced range from comparative modelling to semi-comparative work with comparative implications. Lane examines critically advantages and disadvantages of using the archives for cross-national research, and directs our attention to the selective procedures whereby data find their way into the archives. The contents of the archives are forceful in determining the direction of comparative studies, and research on political behaviour is one of the fields which have benefited the most. In the future it is important that theoretical considerations play a larger part in influencing the composition of the data in the archives. But it is also important that a wider variety of theoretical interests be reflected in the data collected (Chapter 11).

The project presented by Andorka on time series is among those studies which would have benefited greatly, had comparable data on the use of time series been available in the national social science archives, and had they been categorized in such a way that equivalence in time units could have been incorporated. Instead, the social indicators had to be developed through comprehensive surveys and national statistics which were not tailored to the research in question. Andorka and his colleagues ask the kind of political questions that are being asked widely after the many recent events in Eastern Europe; namely, what did a socialist model mean for the development of a country compared to a capitalist model? This kind of question can only be answered within a comparative perspective (Chapter 12). And the driving force behind the demands for such comparisons is not only researchers, but now also politicians, bureaucrats and people in general who are trying to grasp the social realities of a rapidly changing world.

Organizing for Comparative Research

It can be assumed that much research, comparative or otherwise, is guided by the principles of least resistance or invitation by opportunity. One of the central research strategies, although not much discussed, seems to be the preference given to available data and methodological tools, and the leaning towards accessible networks and easy funding. Many comparative projects would never have surfaced, had they not adopted such a strategy. Organizing for comparative research, involving two or preferably more countries, and taking into account as many of the theoretical and methodological considerations mentioned above as possible in order to carry through a high-quality study, demands resources of such a magnitude in terms of money, time and personnel, that only relatively few sociologists will ever have the opportunity to control such funds. The pristine goal of sociological research as a guiding principle for our choices in cross-national research may for most of us have to stay pristine.

Another kind of barrier to a well-composed comparative investigation can be found in the social context for the project. In his review of the activities of the Vienna Centre Berting notes a development of a culture which favours a research strategy

> emphasising the influence of 'traditional' and other system-specific differences, of decision-making by political and economic elites and of intended and unintended consequences of human actions upon the direction of societal development . . . the projects are lopsided in a specific way: cultural variables . . . are treated as dependent variables which can have a significance in their own right in a process of explanation. . . . [The projects] tend to neglect social phenomena which are indicative of collective protest movements and conflicts in relation to societal change, . . . and the research designs are seldom of a diachronistic type. (1988: 75–7)

Political barriers to certain research topics are not unknown, and within Unesco, for example, some countries exempt themselves from the participation in certain kinds of comparative studies. Sociology is not a globally recognized field of inquiry, and as noted earlier, comparative studies can also be used as political instruments.

So far most of the cross-national studies have been located in Western Europe and North America. This is also where we find most of the sociologists, the sociological institutions, the data banks, the agencies for funding basic and applied research, and the infrastructure for conducting social investigations. The climate for using social research in policy-making is milder here than in most other places, and we find that a discussion of comparative methodology can also be tied to questions as to what methodologies yield the best understanding of how social policies can be improved (Higgins, 1986; Lawrence, 1986).

From their strongholds social scientists from developed countries have reached into the developing countries with comparative studies. The time of the 'native' social scientists feeding their 'educated' counterpart undigested data, to be processed and analysed in a foreign context, has passed. Now there is a widespread understanding, legitimated ethically as well as methodologically, that cross-national studies profit from being conducted in close cooperation with researchers based in the respective countries, and collaborating during all the phases of the project. Familiarity with the national history and culture is now considered a prerequisite, as it provides an interpretation of the results which cannot be obtained by an outsider. Some will argue that close collaboration with a country-based social scientist is necessary merely in case-oriented comparisons where local knowledge helps tie together the intensive data in a meaningful way. Others will argue that neither can the results from the variable-oriented comparisons, based for example on data derived from national archives, be interpreted by an outsider (compare the earlier discussion of equivalence and the renewed emphasis on cross-historical approaches).

Informal and formal networks link sociologists together in groups which are used for producing comparative research. Not much is known about how these networks are formed, how they are transformed into productive units of research, what the criteria and critical mass for research production is, and who the participants are. By looking at the end result of the production, the publication of comparative studies, it becomes evident that, for example, women seem to participate less in comparative investigations than do men. Does that mean that women are less interested in cross-national studies than men, or do they not get invited to join the networks? Have women leaned towards micro-sociological studies, or are they alienated in the male-dominated arena of statistical analysis and mathematical modelling which is growing out of the data banks? Have women oriented themselves towards research problems which do not attract sizeable funding, or do they not gain entrance into the networks which have access to the funding agencies? Or are cross-national studies simply so time- and energy-consuming that they are incompatible with the combined role of mother, wife and comparativist? Let it suffice to pose the questions.

Social scientists in the Third World have formed networks of their own, partly as a reaction to the networks of 'central' scholars, partly to stimulate social science in their own region, ask different questions, and help develop the region. In Latin America, for example, networks were formed around the non-governmental institution of CLACSO (the Latin American Council on Social Sciences). The network functions as a multi-purpose instrument, fulfilling the aims of the Council to train social scientists from the region and to encourage regional research, and as a bank of knowledge for comparative studies. The explicit ideology has been to incorporate younger scholars, avoid elitism and make information accessible throughout the entire network. Given the enormous distances and the scarcity of travel funds, a project is under way to develop electronic networking (Piscitelli, 1989).

The loose and the somewhat more formalized networks developed by the Research Committees within the ISA are another important instrument for comparative research, embedded in which is the promising potential for becoming a central vehicle for future world-embracing studies.

References

Alapuro, R., M. Alestalo, E. Haavio-Mannila and R. Vayrynen (eds) (1985) *Small States in a Comparative Perspective*. Norwegian University Press.

Asher, Herbert A., Bradley M. Richardson and Herbert F. Weisberg (1984) *Political Participation: An ISSC Workbook in Comparative Analysis*. Frankfurt: Campus.

Berting, Jan (1988) 'Research Strategies in International Comparative and Cooperative Research: The Case of the Vienna Centre', in F. Charvat, W. Stamatiou and Ch. Villain-Gandossi (eds) (1988) *International Cooperation in the Social Sciences: 25 Years of Vienna Centre Experience*. Bratislava: Publishing House of the Technical Library.

Bohannan, Paul (1963) *Social Anthropology*. London: Holt, Rinehart & Winston.

Bottomore, Tom, Stefan Nowak and Magdalena Sokolowska (eds) (1982) *Sociology: The State of the Art*. London: Sage.

Charvat, F., W. Stamatiou, and Ch. Villain-Gandossi (eds) (1988) *International Cooperation in the Social Sciences: 25 Years of Vienna Centre Experience*. Bratislava: Publishing House of the Technical Library.

Eisenstadt, S.N. and M. Curelaru (1977) 'Macro-sociology: Theory, Analysis and Comparative Studies', *Current Sociology*, 25 (2): 1–112.

Higgins, Joan (1986) 'Comparative Social Policy', *Quarterly Journal of Social Affairs*, 2 (3): 221–42.

Kohn, Melvin L. (1989a) 'Introduction', in Melvin L. Kohn (ed.), *Cross-national Research in Sociology*. Newbury Park: Sage.

Kohn, Melvin L. (1989b) 'Cross-national Research as an Analytical Strategy', in Melvin L. Kohn (ed.), *Cross-national Research in Sociology*. Newbury Park: Sage.

Kulcsár, Kalman (1988) 'Problems of Comparison, Problems of Cooperation: An International Comparative Project on Law and Dispute Treatment', in F. Charvat, W. Stamatiou and Ch. Villain-Gandossi (eds), *International Cooperation in the Social Sciences: 25 Years of Vienna Centre Experience*. Bratislava: Publishing House of the Technical Library.

Lawrence, John (1986) 'Comparative Study of Social Policy: Conceptual and Methodological Issues', *International Journal of Sociology and Social Policy*, 6 (3): 1–12.

Nowak, Stefan (1989) 'Comparative Studies and Social Theory', in Melvin L. Kohn (ed.), *Cross-national Research in Sociology*. Newbury Park: Sage.

Oommen, T.K. (1989) 'Ethnicity, Immigration, and Cultural Pluralism: India and the United States of America', in Melvin L. Kohn (ed.), *Cross-national Research in Sociology*. Newbury Park: Sage.

Øyen, Else (ed.) (1986a) *Comparing Welfare States and Their Futures*. Aldershot: Gower.

Øyen, Else (1986b) 'The Muffling Effect of Social Policy: A Comparison of Social Security Systems and their Conflict Potential in Australia, the United States and Norway', *International Sociology*, 1 (3): 271–82.

Piscitelli, Alejandro G. (1989) 'Network Development, Research and Training: The Latin American Council on the Social Sciences (CLACSO) Experience', Paper presented at the International Forum on Network Experiences in Development Research and Training. Buenos Aires: CLACSO.

Ragin, Charles (1987) *The Comparative Method: Moving Beyond Qualitative and Quantitative Strategies*. Berkeley: University of California Press.

Ragin, Charles (1989) 'New Directions in Comparative Research', in Melvin L. Kohn (ed.), *Cross-national Research in Sociology*. Newbury Park: Sage.

Rokkan, Stein (1978) 'A Quarter Century of International Social Science: Papers and Reports on Developments 1952–1977', *Publications of the International Social Science Council*, 19: 3–15.

Sztompka, Piotr (1988) 'Conceptual Frameworks in Comparative Inquiry: Divergent or Convergent?', *International Sociology*, 3 (3): 207–18.

World Commission on Environment and Development (1987) *Our Common Future*, Geneva.

2

The Development of Comparative Research: Towards Causal Explanations

Erwin K. Scheuch

With few exceptions the social sciences rely on observational data; even in his time John Stuart Mill saw this as a necessity. This causes many difficulties in interpretation. Usually a *tertium comparationis* is desirable in deciding whether observations at specific times and places have importance. Time series and comparisons across localities are obvious ways to cope with this difficulty. Why are such comparisons not more commonplace in empirical social research, and why should there be a speciality 'methodology of comparative research' at all?

The Unstable Interest in Comparative Research

Empirical social research developed in the nineteenth century in a variety of industrialized and industrializing countries, but it was only in the United States that it was institutionalized, complete with method courses and textbooks as early as the late twenties.

Social research in the USA was problem-oriented, beginning with the founding of the American Social Science Association in 1866. The purpose of the research was the exact description of social ills as a basis for social reform and social engineering – all this understood as problems of American society.[1] In the Chicago School of the twenties and thirties the founding fathers asked young social scientists to look upon the city of Chicago as a social laboratory of great cultural diversity. Together with the preferred mode of explanation – namely, social psychological mechanisms – this was to mean that one could compare and yet stay at home.

The Chicago School dominated the developing discipline of sociology, and it was perhaps only rivalled by Columbia University – both young institutions representing the American spirit of the times. And social problems were understood as specific in time and space. The period between the two great wars was everywhere a time of preoccupation with one's own national state. It was only in the turmoil of World War II that a significant number of American social scientists became internationally oriented again, trying to understand how regimes such as those in Germany and Japan were possible, and attempting to influence the economic and social development of the Third World.

Of all the social sciences, sociology is probably the discipline least international in outlook and research. Nevertheless, the 1950s were a period with important internationally comparative projects, mostly initiated by American scholars. Examples are the contributions by Ruth Benedict, Daniel Lerner, Alex Inkeles, Hadley Cantril, Maurice L. Farber, Natalie Rogoff Ramsøy, Frederick W. Frey, Kurt W. Back and Mayone Stycos.

Many of these important comparative projects in basic research are in retrospect remarkable for their ingenuity. An early example is the UNESCO tensions project headed by Otto Klineberg. Several technical innovations were used, such as self-anchoring scales, and the notion of functional equivalence rather than identity of stimuli was already advanced then. Another important set of international projects initiated by UNESCO was the comparison of rates of political participation, led by Stein Rokkan. Gabriel Almond's comparative study on the appeals of communism should not be forgotten, nor Cantril's international investigation on the appeals of extremism. All these projects were multilateral comparisons.

And yet Robert M. Marsh found that, of all the American dissertations in sociology submitted during the 1950s, only 12 per cent used any data from outside the United States.

Interest in comparative data waned in the later fifties in the USA, and the US *Public Opinion Quarterly* terminated its section on world polls. Hadley Cantril's attempt at a world-wide collection of public opinion material over the period 1935–46 found no successor. All of these initiatives were largely forgotten by the mid-sixties when a new generation with different experiences dominated the methodological scene, spearheaded by Stein Rokkan and later Sandor Szalai. The organizational nuclei then changed to the International Social Science Council (ISSC), and later to some of the newly established Research Committees of the International Sociological Association.

The Contribution of Commercial Survey Research

During these pioneer times the more general and sustained advances in expertise occurred with commercial survey organizations. This is understandable, as commercial survey organizations had a head start. Parallel to the developments in America in the thirties, some institutes had been started in Europe as well. The knowledge of sampling was absent there, and inferior techniques were used. But interviewing techniques were developed, as were forms of panels, and even the use of systematic observational techniques. In 1936 the BBC in London started a panel-like procedure for continuous observation, and, with the encouragement by Bronisław Malinowski, Mass Observation was started in 1937 as an institute that used techniques developed by ethnologists. In Germany, the still existing Gesellschaft für Konsumforschung was begun in 1937, relying primarily on a panel of experts, stratified according to population proportions. Perhaps the most interesting scholarly organization was the Institut Français de l'Opinion Publique (IFOP), founded in 1938 by the social psychologist Jean Stoetzel, which only three years after the founding of *Public Opinion Quarterly* published the first European journal on polling, *'Sondage'*.

As the war ended, the ground was prepared for a rapid development of survey research as a new international service. Institute after institute was started: in 1944, Service de Sondage in France (Max Barioux); in 1945 in Norway (Leif Holbak Hansen); in 1945 in Hungary (Paul Shiller); in 1945 in Czechoslovakia Institute of Public Opinion (Adamec and Viden); in 1945 in the Netherlands NIPO (De Jong and Jan Stapek); 1946 in Italy DOXA (Luzzato Fegiz); in 1945–47 in Germany EMNID (von Stackelberg), and DEMOSKOPIE (Noelle-Neumann). Further institutes were founded in rapid succession. In several Western European countries government-sponsored survey agencies were developed, the most famous of which was probably in France INSEE (Institut National de la Statistique et des Etudes Economiques) (Levy Bruhl), and in Britain the Social Survey (C.A. Moser).

This expansion of national survey facilities was accompanied by attempts to organize international connections. The World Association for Public Opinion Research (WAPOR) was founded in 1948, although for many years it was not a very important network. In 1949 a 'European Society for Opinion and Market Research' (ESOMAR) was started, and WAPOR gained strength as its two component organizations (ESOMAR and AAPOR) increased their importance – a sort of model of a bipolar Atlantic community. By the early sixties the number of institutes for market and opinion research outside of the United States numbered approximately 200.

Early on several opinion researchers saw a permanent market for international service, and organized chains of opinion research institutes.[2] In 1945 various institutes in the USA, South America and Europe formed a chain under the name International Research Associates (INRA), and George Gallup followed in 1947 with his International Association for Public Opinion Institutes. These chains have a somewhat varied history. The largest volume of research was generated nationally and the internationally comparative studies never became a matter of economic value for any of the institutes.

Why was there not more of a market for international survey research? In part because international consumer research became important for some firms. The largest potential clients of such chains created their own international networks. Examples were the British American Tobacco Company, Royal Dutch Shell and Unilever.

These were by no means all the forms of corporation on an international scale. As a matter of fact, from around 1960 the morphology became more complicated. Thus in Europe there were several international chains of advertising agencies, which cooperated in specifying research topics and supervising analysis. Clearly, international survey facilities paralleled the internationalization of consumer good markets.

Polling public opinion in various countries became relevant as an international force at a much slower pace. No country was probably more tuned to changes in public opinion abroad than the USA. Consequently, the US Information Agency has remained as one of the largest consumers of international research facilities.[3] The office of the Japanese Prime Minister has become another important client of comparative research. The public relations department of the High Authority of the Common Market conducts surveys in all member countries twice a year through the Gallup chain.

With the sizeable volume of research of a cross-national character going on, it is surprising that (1) this did not penetrate more widely into the awareness of social scientists; (2) that more substantive information has not been used; and (3) that this research has not contributed more to methodological knowledge in academic training. In most countries for a long time the relation between commercial research and academics remained distant.

Institution-building for Comparative Research

The picture changed in the USA during the 1940s. Some key figures in empirical social research served as bridge-builders to commercial polling. Princeton was the location where fascination with the new tool, the representative survey, brought together George Gallup, Elmo Roper and Archibald Crossley from commercial polling with the social psychologist Hadley Cantril. This led to institution-building, of which some had a lasting importance.

Hadley Cantril was the moving spirit behind the invitation of survey researchers from several countries to a conference on public opinion research in 1946 in Colorado. A year later the *International*

Journal of Opinion and Attitude Research was started in Mexico City by Laszlo Radvanyi, and was until its untimely death in 1951 the world's leading journal in survey research methodology.[4] Many of the methodological observations in comparative projects are as relevant today as they were then. In 1947 the World Association for Public Opinion Research (WAPOR) was founded, and as soon as one year later counted 129 members from eighteen countries. At that time there was a deliberate balance between academics and directors of commercial agencies. And last but not least, UNESCO opened a Social Science Division and established in turn in 1952 the International Social Science Council (ISSC). There were expectations of 'world polling' as a regular report on a developing world society.

In routine investigations, empirical social research tends to be a snapshot of a particular place at a particular time. Until quite recently it was technically difficult to proceed otherwise. One of the first scholars who realized the new possibilities and needs for time series was Hadley Cantril. As a source for such comparisons Cantril published a monumental volume of surveys around the world between 1936 and 1946. Cantril thought of this as the first volume of a 'Princeton Index', to be established as a regular undertaking by WAPOR.[5]

At about the same time Elmo Roper conceived the idea of a data archive serving the same purpose even better. Since the official founding of the Roper Center in 1957, the model spread. At the time of writing there is an International Federation of Data Organizations (IFDO) linking these data resources for secondary analyses of machine-readable data in more than a dozen countries.

In several countries 'General Social Surveys' have become an institution. These are national sample surveys that are meant to serve any qualified researcher as a freely available facility. Since 1985 the organizers of these General Surveys in by now thirteen countries have agreed to construct an internationally comparative 'module' of questions every year. By this means it becomes possible to use comparative data without going through a process of difficult data collection. Together with the facilities available through IFDO it is now possible to do cross-national comparisons with little effort across time and locations. We have become data rich – however, without an equivalent advance in methodology.

The Role of International Organizations in Advancing Methodology

Of course, there had been important methodological discussions of the specific problems and promises associated with international comparisons. Yet, there has been a strange lack of continuity, and repeatedly the wheel of cross-cultural methodology was reinvented. This is all the more remarkable as the debate after World War II, when empirical research spread world-wide, was encouraged and supported by international organizations, and organizations tend to have memories. However, the methodological discourse remained dependent on the initiative of a small number of scholars, usually driven by problems in their own empirical studies. When these groups satisfied their intellectual curiosities, they left the field – later being succeeded by a new group, driven by a new research problem.

A case in point is the fate of 'Project Demoscope', which came about as an effort to prevent a collective amnesia about issues already clarified. In the early phase after World War II there had been some discussions of the volume of quantitative comparative work reaching back until the twenties, but there had never been an attempt to summarize the experiences. The new Social Science Division of UNESCO was persuaded to award WAPOR a contract to remedy this forgetfulness. For the period between 1925 and 1955 Stuart Dodd and Jiri Nehnevasja compiled 1,103 entries on comparative work. The final report of the 'Project Demoscope' was only circulated in mimeographed form, and is now forgotten as though it had never existed.

In the 1960s and for most of the 1970s, the initiative in furthering comparative research shifted to Western Europe. As early as 1952 the International Social Science Council (ISSC) had been founded in Paris as an administrative and intellectual base for continuous interdisciplinary and internationally comparative work. However, until its reorganization in 1961 the ISSC did not have much impact. Then Stein Rokkan took the initiative to call a meeting at La Napoule in 1962, and under his leadership a number of projects, conferences and publications materialized that for a decade shaped the development of comparative research and its methodology.

By the beginning of the sixties, methodological reflection had shifted to academic researchers and to Western Europe. In two major international conferences it was attempted to summarize the state of the art in comparative research, both with respect to methodology *sensu stricto* and for research technology. In 1964 at Yale the leading scholar was Sandor Szalai from Hungary, and the proceedings concentrated on macro-studies such as the *World Handbook*, the Yale Political Data Program and the Human Relations Area File. In general, the accent was on the research philosophy, including the interrelation between research design and the objective of the comparison.

In the second of the conferences in 1972 in Budapest, many of the same researchers came together again. The main agenda was a *post mortem* on five large-scale comparative studies: the Time Budget Project; Juvenile Delinquency and Development; Images of the World in the Year 2000; the Jacobs and Jacobs study on leadership values; and the Verba and Nie Project on political participation. All these projects were based on survey research. This time, basic discussions on design alternated with exchanges of management experiences in actually carrying out comparative research, and on available technology.[6]

The proceedings of both conferences can still be considered as major compendia. However, their impact on the teaching of methodology, and on the practice of comparative work, has been limited. There has been little progress since the sixties, when a high level of methodological refinement had already been reached: an example is the international comparative study for the WHO on the utilization of medical care facilities 1968–69, with 48,000 interviews in twelve research sites.

Perhaps the more lasting impact of the activities supported by the International Social Science Council was the development of a network of researchers for comparative work. Stein Rokkan had organized a Standing Committee on Data (1966–77) and a Standing Committee for Comparative Research (1967–78) of the ISSC. These Standing Committees were the meeting ground for preparing international conferences, and in spreading the idea of data archives.[7]

In the meantime data centres were established in Norway, in the Netherlands and in the Federal Republic of Germany, with the understanding that they would be part of an international exchange system. It was here that the idea of IFDO was developed. The Standing Committee on Data was decisive in preventing an attempt by the Roper Center to concentrate all data-archiving in the United States.[8]

The most important activities of the Standing Committee for Comparative Research were training conferences in comparative social research: altogether seven international workshops and seminars plus three European Summer Schools for training in comparative research, beginning in 1971. In these training courses the format of a data confrontation seminar as a new form of transmitting skills was developed: comparing publications with the data on which the publications were based, much as an aspiring painter copies old masters. In elaborating this data confrontation concept, the Standing Committees commissioned four so called 'workbooks' where a data tape and codebooks could be related to exercises and specimen analysis of the material.[9] This programme of the Standing Committee for Comparative Research was guided by the assessment that by now the major problem was no longer training in the collection of data but rather in the skills in analysis and especially in interpreting results.

After the early death of Alexander Szalai and then of Stein Rokkan, the centre of activities shifted again. A major reason for this lack of continuity might have been the disappointing substantive pay-off of the major efforts during the fifties in the USA and in Europe in the sixties and most of the seventies. Another reason was a change in the character of the ISSC.[10]

Two other institutions now became central for increasing the scope of comparative research and its methodology; on a European scale the Vienna Centre for Social Sciences Information and Documentation,[11] and the International Sociological Association. It is a characteristic of this field that the cluster of researchers active through these institutions largely overlapped. During its World Congress in 1970 in Varna, the International Sociological Association (ISA) had institutionalized the 'Research Committees' as a regular part of its programme. Very soon the Research Committees became the most important part of the operations of the ISA, and also an international one. They offered opportunities to reach agreements for international cooperation. Especially in the eighties a number of important comparative studies were completed in this setting, such as the Mega Cities project.

The network of Research Committees of the ISA is still the most important infrastructure for comparative work. Within this framework the emphasis has shifted from individual projects by leaders in the field to broad participation in comparative studies in the specialized fields of sociology. Here, the expected pay-off is not the breakthrough in the understanding of contemporary societies or in general theory, but rather the analysis of specific problem areas through broadening the base of observations.

Towards the end of the sixties and the beginning of the seventies the methodological literature on comparativism had grown to such proportions that international institutions again commissioned major bibliographies. The International Sociological Association requested Robert Marsh to prepare an overview of the literature since 1950. The International Social Science Council had asked that such a biography be concentrated on survey research, and subsequently the Vienna Centre issued a contract for an update. Limiting the studies to English language journals only and also somewhat the scope of subject matter, Frederick W. Frey from the Center of International Studies of MIT compiled an annotated bibliography with 1,600 individual entries.

In the eighties, a number of books have been published, such as

1984 *How to Compare Nations* by Mattei Dogan and Dominique Pelassy, and in the same year appeared Manfred Niessen, Jules Peschar and Chantal Kurilsky (eds), *International Vergleichende Sozialforschung*, the latter again an initiative of the Vienna Centre. Melvin Kohn used his Presidency of the American Sociological Association for a world-wide stocktaking. The contributions to the presidential session in 1987 can be read as a demonstration that the comparative approach is now a permanent aspect of empirical social research. It is our considered judgement that in terms of methodology *in abstracto* and on issues of research technology, little has been added in recent years.

The Central Problem is not Technical but Theoretical

In textbooks and during conferences the additional problems of research carried out comparatively were predominantly discussed as technical problems. Indeed, such additional problems are difficult to handle. However, the major problem is one of design and of theory. Why does one need to be comparative? What do different settings stand for? Failure to clarify this leads even a master in the logic of explanation in empirical work such as Emile Durkheim to risk research artefacts.[12]

Evans-Pritchard considered it to be typical for the school of the Annales to argue by way of *petitio principii*.[13] The influential essay on kinship classifications by Durkheim and Mauss is certainly a case in point. Durkheim and Mauss maintain that there is a correspondence between the social structure of societies (in reality their kinship structure) and the forms of symbolic classification (in reality kinship terminology), and that thus the social origin of classification systems as mirrors of social structure is proved. Even if one sets aside for a moment the fact that the societies that did not fit the thesis were ignored, a correspondence between one element of social structures and the symbolic classifications does not explain 'that the society is the cause or even the model of the classification'.[14]

A recent variant of the very same *petitio principii* is the use of the Human Relations Area File. Reports on more than 500 'cultures' were coded: that is, descriptions were translated into variables. Subsequently, correlations between traits were computed, as for example between types of economies and kinship systems. As with Durkheim, but on a more general scale, cases that did not fit were bypassed. In the Human Relations Area File the units of comparison were 'cultures' – within-culture variation (as is frequent in cross-cultural comparisons) being bypassed as an irritant. But the Human

Relations Area File is yet another prime example of problems of inferences in cross-cultural comparisons.

With world-wide communication systems, unprecedented levels of international trade, and a volume of cross-border travel exceeding the level of 400 million movements per year, international diffusion is evidently a major factor in culture change.[15] However, while the magnitude may be something unique, the phenomenon is not new at all. It was already specified around the turn of the century by the famous statistician Galton, as part of the controversy about cultural diffusion.

'Galton's problem' is the issue whether a given culture can be thought of as 'causing' something, or whether the something is instead the result of diffusion across cultures. The issue is given the name 'Galton's problem', as it was first raised by him during a meeting of the Royal Anthropological Institute in 1889. Galton, at that time already a famous statistician, is quoted as having remarked in discussing a paper by Tylor,

> It was extremely desirable for the sake of those who may wish to study the evidence for Dr Tylor's conclusion, that full information should be given as to the degree in which the customs of the tribes and races which are compared together are independent. It might be, that some of the tribes had derived the customs from a common source, so that they were duplicate copies of the same original. (cited in Tylor, 1961: 23)

During the first spell of popularity that comparative research enjoyed following the end of World War II, the preferred tool had been the survey – if possible, representative for a country. The purpose of comparisons was to demonstrate numerically the uniqueness of the countries surveyed – such as Germany or Japan as aberrant cases of industrialized countries.[16] In their study of 'political culture', Almond and Verba assumed they knew that properties that could be shown as being peculiar to the USA could be used to define a democratic political culture, those peculiar to Mexico as denoting an incompletely integrated system, and those specific for (Western) Germany as an indication of a non-democratic milieu.

It is characteristic in this use of comparisons that a country is merely used as a dummy variable for all of the data collected in that area. To proceed this way appeals to common sense, but it is objectionable on grounds of principle. Whether the nation-state as a relatively recent form of political aggregation did in fact succeed in integrating social structures and neutralizing older mediating levels differs by country and also by domain.

In the frequent comparative surveys, including the four Scandinavian countries – the most important one is the Welfare Survey, directed by Eric Allardt – Finland is often the odd case. This proved to be true again in an investigation of the incidence of various illnesses. In particular, coronary heart disease has a much higher incidence in Finland than in neighbouring Sweden. An analysis of the survey data by subregion rather than only by country showed that this high incidence was entirely due to the concentration of that ailment in the northern, much more rural half of Finland; values for the southern, more developed part – where one would otherwise expect higher incidences – were identical with rates for Sweden, Denmark and Norway. The currently accepted explanation for the concentration of coronary heart diseases in rural northern Finland is the combined effect of life under conditions of duress for farmers and especially lumber workers, and the high levels of alcohol consumption. It was not 'Finland' as a nation-state, culture or society that could account for the odd values, but Finland as an administrative unit included a setting with aberrant living conditions.

Since the mid-sixties, protest movements have become a routine element in the politics of Western Europe. There are cross-national differences and similarities, but the factors explaining differences are primarily not national but cultural. Those movements have become an as yet uninstitutionalized institution parallel to insti-tutionalized politics, and as such are a characteristic of Protestant Europe, and within that context weaker in Lutheran areas. Maybe that is true only as a description, and to turn the descriptive correlations into an explanation is premature. Is it really something in Protestantism, as a religious culture; or is it at least in part the consequence of its younger clergy? Or is it mainly the consequence of a tension between the desire for individual moral/religious commitment, and the waning of institutionalized religion in a society with high functional differentiation? Or is it an inter-relation of all those factors? All this is currently unclear. What is clear is the fact that the explanandum cuts across the administrative bound-aries of nation-states. States that include both Protestant and Catholic territories – that is the case in West Germany – offer an opportunity for a check as to which factor is the stronger: religious culture or nation-state. Both are relevant, but religious culture appears to be more important.[17]

While nation-state, culture or society may be too large a unit for a causal attribution (such as the Finnish example) or too small (as in the case of protest movements), it may also be too weak a context to account for differences observed with individual data. True, in its most ideological form the nation-state assumes a basic sameness among its citizens. However, all industrial societies are pluralistic – and if material well-being and the political system permit this, they are so pluralistic that often within-country differences are larger than between-country differences.

Since the seventies, the High Commission for the Common Market has carried out comparative surveys in all member states twice a year, the EuroBarometer.[18] One does observe differences in percentage point distributions. However, variations for many attitudinal data rarely exceed 10 per cent between the countries high and low on a measurement scale. Obviously, when between-country variances are smaller than within-country variations then it is quite improbable that references to countries can be understood as explanations. In such pluralistic societies, survey research can usually be treated as observation under differing conditions and not as a test of the meanings and effects of a culture, of a society or of a polity.

One influential type of comparative research can be labelled 'global studies'. This approach is characterized by using the largest number of countries possible – as is true in ethnological research for the Human Relations Area File, and the Cross-Polity-Survey treating the countries as black boxes being simultaneously congruent with societies, cultures and nations.

Beginning with the Yale Political Data Handbook, Global Studies attained a certain importance, especially in political sociology. Even though the use of countries in the YPDH was severely criticized as early as the early sixties, the argument affected neither the project nor other Global Studies.[19] Ted Gurr and David Singer started a 'school' relating incidences of violence – a typical aggregate property for within-nation violence – to global properties of nations. More central for sociology has been the World Systems approach by Immanuel Wallerstein. It became a veritable research paradigm, possibly because of its ideological appeal. A related 'school' started by Peter Heintz understand this comparison of the largest feasible number of nation-states as an attempt to test propositions in a quasi-experimental design.

By using partial regressions for the largest possible number of countries computing relations between input and output variables, one eliminates all third factors as in an experiment. But it is just this that makes this 'largest numbers of black box countries' approach unsociological. If theoretical-sounding terms are used by the Wallersteiners and their terms 'centre', 'periphery', or 'dependencia' or 'World System', they are undefined and/or used meta-phorically.[20] Taken as an approach, Global Studies are probably more responsible for research artefacts than any other comparative approach.

Alternative Meanings of Comparative Research

Observation under differing conditions is the aim of social research. This accepted, it is necessary to consider the central difference between observational data and data from experiments. In experiments, 'third factors' intervening between the assumed dependent and independent variables are controlled *ex ante* through design. For observational data this control is largely *ex post* through appropriate statistical techniques. Data from comparative survey research are thus more difficult to analyse and interpret than experimental data.

There are two major reasons for these difficulties. First, if one maintains that a high-order unit – especially if one uses a nation-state – is a 'cause' of a lower-order unit, the chains of inferences can become very long. This increases the likelihood that third factors intervene between the presumed cause and the effect. Second, many higher-order units – and certainly 'nations' or 'cultures' – have the character of systems where the parts are interrelated. Technically this means that the explanandum would be over- and under-determined.

The prevailing kind of comparative research is in practice a cross-level design with an unsatisfactory understanding of the highest of the levels. To understand this better, and to gain insight of what this means for analysis and interpretation, it is useful to recall a distinction proposed by Stein Rokkan: cross-national, cross-cultural and cross-societal comparisons.[21]

Usually, the nation-state is the geographical frame for sampling. Subsequently, the data collected in various nation-states are used as if the comparisons are cross-cultural and cross-societal as well. Whether the three meanings that the geographical sampling frame could have – namely, nation, culture and society – do in fact coincide is in any particular case a substantive issue.

Table 2.1 *Use of Context*

Purpose of comparisons	Context is treated as a 'real' thing	Context is treated as a set of variables
Find identicals	(1) Identification of 'universals'	(2) Show the universality of a statement
Show differences	(3) Specify the unique property of a society	(4) Specify time-space coordinates for a phenomenon

Depending on the goal of the comparisons, completely different designs are indicated. Table 2.1 is intended to facilitate the understanding of differences in design and explanation.[22] An example of comparison in Type 1 is the use of the Human Relations Area File by Murdock, as mentioned earlier. His one 'universal' is the generality of the incest taboo. Indeed, if this taboo is observed in all societies known, and if these societies are as different as the cases in the HRAF, then a very strong case has been established. In this instance, it is not very risky to use cultures in explanations as black boxes.

Comparisons of Type 3 are very frequent in survey research – for instance, Almond and Verba – and in cultural sociology. Max Weber's comparative studies of world religions are an impressive case in point. His argument that the rationality characteristic for Western music, Christian theology and a capitalistic mode of production is a unique cultural product is very much strengthened by comparing very different cultures, these being treated as unique systems.

The comparisons of Type 2 were the dominant form in comparative research by academics. Whiting's study of the post-partem sex taboo is a very distinct example. In these comparisons, the various cultures were to represent different strengths of the variable 'regularity of food supply'. The length of the post-partem sex taboo was considered to be a form of birth control. The causal relation between the climatic conditions of countries and various lengths of post-partem sex taboo was thus: the more irregular the sufficient food supply, the more restrictive the birth control.

Survey research in comparisons is often a variant of Type 4 comparisons. When Alex Inkeles compared responses from various countries, these countries were understood to be systems with different prevalences of situations, in which the workforce produced under varying conditions of modernity. In this approach it is quite difficult to control third factors, especially the effect of country-specific institutions. A recent case are the attempts of Ronald Inglehart to relate the time of the beginning and the volume of wealth to the growth in the share of 'post materialists'. Here, too the difficulties in excluding third factors, and abstracting from the system characteristics of countries are obvious.

Notes

This chapter is partly based on some of the material from Erwin K. Scheuch, 'Theoretical Implications of Comparative Survey Research', *International Sociology*, 4 (2) (1989): 147–68.

1. See Young, 1939 – especially her description of the survey movement around the turn of the century.

2. A representative source for the perspective of that time is: Surveys of World Opinion, in Second International Conference on Public Opinion Research, Williamstown, MA, 2–5 Sept. 1947, published by NORC/Chicago, 1948, p. 126.

3. The core of the 'USIA studies' are the XX series of four nations (UK, FRG, Italy and France). This series contains about 20 separate timepoints that begin in 1953 and continue until 1972; beginning in 1965 the series was expanded into World Surveys, including the original four nations and an additional five to ten nations from around the world.

4. Radvanyi's death coincided with the McCarthy harassment of many social scientists. Foundations and other donors were intimidated, and therefore funds for the journal dried up.

5. See Noelle-Neumann, 1979: 279f.

6. Of special importance here is the chapter by Szalai in Szalai and Petrella, 1977: 49–93.

7. The activities of the Standing Committees were regularly reported in the official journal of the ISSC, *Social Sciences Information*. In the early phase of the Standing Committees, data were seen as the prerequisite for an expansion of comparative research cf. Rokkan, 1966.

8. The Roper Center had enlisted the assistance of major American polling agencies to persuade their European partners to turn over their data only to the repository in the USA. European social researchers would then have to rent back data collected in Europe from the US archive. This was considered necessary by the Americans as a source of income since funds from the USA proved to be insufficient for maintaining the Center.

9. Four workbooks (ISSC Workbooks in Comparative Analysis) have been published: (1) Thomas Herz, *Social Mobility*. Frankfurt: 1986; (2) Andrew S. Harvey, Alexander Szalai, David H. Elliott, Philip J. Stone, and Susan M. Clark, *Time Budget Research*, Frankfurt: 1984; (3) Stein Rokkan, Derek Urwin, Frank H. Aarebrot, Pamela Malaba, and Terje Sande, *Centre-Periphery Structures in Europe*, Frankfurt: 1987; (4) Herbert A. Asher, Bradley M. Richardson and Herbert F. Weisberg, *Political Participation*, Frankfurt: 1984. All books were published by Campus, but can also be procured via the member institutes of IFDO.

10. Originally, the ISSC was a body that appointed representatives from the various social science disciplines (social sciences by UNESCO definition). It was then changed to be a federation of the international disciplinary organizations. Then, in the late seventies, the various national research councils formed a Standing Committee within the ISSC, and the centre of attention changed.

11. The Vienna Centre was at the time of its founding in 1963 a subsidiary of the ISSC, and we included some of its activities in the passages dealing with the ISSC. At least since the mid-seventies the Vienna Centre has been in practice an independent institution concentrating on comparative research that crosses the political division between Eastern and Western Europe.

12. Masterful in his *Le Suicide* (1895) where he ingeniously separated anomic suicide from other causes of suicide.

13. Thus the criticism of Claude Lévi-Strauss in *Totémisme aujourd'hui*, Paris, 1962, p. 102.

14. Rodney Needham in his introduction to the publication of 'De quelques formes primitives . . .'; in English: *Primitive Classification*, 1963, p. XXV. See also Andreski, 1963: 67 *et passim*.

15. On tourism as a vehicle of international diffusion, see Scheuch, 1981, especially p. 1109 ff. Also Cohen, 1979.

16. Thus the criticism of Claude Lévi-Strauss in *Totémisme aujourd'hui*, Paris, 1962, p. 102.

17. Erwin K. Scheuch, 1989.

18. The data and machine-readable code-books are available to the social science community directly through the Zentralarchiv at the University of Cologne, or indirectly through data archives that are members of the International Federation of Data Archives (IFDO).

19. Merritt and Rokkan, 1966, is largely a detailed methodological critique of the black box approach of the Global Studies as exemplified by the YPDH.

20. Michael Hechter points to this in his review in *Contemporary Sociology*, vol. 1 (1975), pp. 217–22. The lack of distinctiveness in using the term 'world system' is criticized by Arthur L. Stinchcombe in a review in the *American Journal of Sociology*, 87 (1982): 1389–95.

21. Compare Rokkan, *Citizens, Elections, Parties*, Oslo, 1970. The taxonomy was in part inspired by Talcott Parsons' distinction between a social system, a cultural system and the polity.

22. A more detailed discussion of this typology can be found in Scheuch, 1967, especially p. 677.

References

Allardt, Eric (1966) 'Implications of Within-Nation Variations and Regional Imbalances for Cross-national Research', in Richard Merritt and Stein Rokkan (eds) *Comparing Nations: The Use of Quantitative Data in Cross-national Research*. New Haven, CT: Yale University Press.

Almasy, Elina, Anne Balandier and Jeanine Delatte (1976) *Comparative Survey Analysis – an Annotated Bibliography 1967–73*. Beverly Hills, CA: Sage Professional Papers.

Almond, Gabriel (1954) *The Appeals of Communism*. Princeton, NJ.

Almond, Gabriel and Sidney Verba (1963) *The Civic Culture*. Princeton, NJ.

Andreski, Stanislav (1963) *The Uses of Comparative Sociology*. Berkeley, CA.

Asher, Herbert A., Bradley M. Richardson and Herbert F. Weisberg (1984) *Political Participation: An ISSC Workbook in Comparative Analysis*. Frankfurt.

Barnes, Samuel H. and Max Kaase (eds) (1979) *Political Action*. Beverly Hills, CA: Sage Publications.

Bollen, Kenneth (1983) 'World System Position, Dependency, and Democracy', *American Sociological Review*, 48: 468–78.

Buchanan, William and Hadley Cantril (1953) *How Nations see Each Other*. Urbana, IL.

Cantril, Hadley (ed.) (1951) *Public Opinion 1936–1946*, Princeton, NJ.

Cantril, Hadley (1958) *The Politics of Despair*. New York.

Cantril, Hadley and L.A. Free (1962) 'Hopes and Fears for Self and Country', *American Behavioral Scientist*, 6 (2), supl. pp. 4–30.

Cohen, Eric (ed.) (1979) 'Sociology of Tourism', *Annals of Tourism Research*, special issue vol. 6 (Jan. and April).

'Comparative Sociology 1950–1963', special issue of *La Sociologie Contemporaine*, XIV (2). The Hague: Mouton, 1966.

Dodd, Stuart C. and Jiri Nehnevasja (1956) *Techniques for World Polls – a Survey of Journal Articles on Cross-Cultural Polling, 1925–1955*. Paris.

Dogan, Mattei and Dominique Pelassy (1984) *How to Compare Nations*. Chatham, NJ: Chatham House.

Durkheim, Emile (1903) 'Les quelques formes primitives de classification: contribution à l'étude des représentations collective', *Année Sociologique*, VI: 1–72.

Durkheim, Emile (1912) *Les Formes élémentaires de la vie religieuse.*

Frey, Frederick W. with Peter Stephenson and Katharine Archer Smitz (1969) *Survey Research on Comparative Social Change*. Cambridge, MA: MIT Press.

Glock, Charles V. (1954) 'The Comparative Study of Communication and Opinion Formation', in Wilbur Schramm (ed.), *The Process and Effects of Mass Communication*, University of Illinois, Urbana, IL.

Gurr, Ted Robert (1968) 'A Causal Model of Civil Strife – a Comparative Analysis Using New Indices', *American Political Science Review*, 62: 1104–24.

Gurr, Ted Robert (1970) *Why Men Rebel*. Princeton, NJ.

Gurr, Ted Robert (1974) 'The Neo-Alexandrians', *American Political Science Review*, 68: 243–52.

Harvey, Andrew S., Alexander Szalai, David H. Elliott, Philip J. Stone and Susan M. Clark (1984) *Time Budget Research. An ISSC Workbook in Comparative Analysis*. Frankfurt.

Heintz, Peter (1969) *Ein soziologisches Paradigma der Entwicklung*. Stuttgart.

Heintz, Peter (1973) *The Future of Development*. Berne.

Heintz, Peter (1982) *Ungleiche Verteilung, Macht und Legitimität*. Dissenhofen.

Herz, Thomas A. (1986) *Social Mobility: An ISSC Workbook in Comparative Analysis*. Frankfurt.

Hechter, Michael (1975) Review Essay of Wallerstein, Immanuel: 'The Modern World System: Capitalist Agriculture and the Origins of the European World Economy in the 16th Century', *Contemporary Sociology*, 4: 217–22.

Inglehart, Ronald (1989) *Cultural Change*. Princeton, NJ.

Inkeles, Alex and David H. Smith (1974) *Becoming Modern: Individual Change in Six Developing Countries*, Cambridge, MA.

Jacobs, Philip and Betty Jacobs (eds) (1971) *Values and the Active Community*. New York: Free Press.

Klineberg, Otto (1950) *Tensions Affecting International Understanding*. New York: Social Science Research Council, Bulletin 62.

Kohn, Melvin L. (ed.) (1989) *Cross-national Research in Sociology*. London.

Kohn, Robert and Kerr L. White (eds) (1976) *Health Care*. Oxford: Oxford University Press, especially chapter 3.

Lévi-Strauss, Claude (1962) *Totémisme audjourd'hui*, Paris.

Lijphart, Arend (1975) 'The Comparable Cases Strategy in Comparative Research', *Comparative Political Studies*, 8: 158–77.

Madge, John (1962) *The Origins of Scientific Sociology*. Glencoe, IL, ch. 4.

Manaster, Guy J. and Robert J. Havighurst (1972) *Cross-national Research*. Boston.

Marsh, Robert M. (1962) 'Training in Comparative Research in Sociology', *American Sociological Review*, 27: 147–9.

Meckstroth, Theodore W. (1975) 'Most Different Systems and Most Similar Systems – a Study in the Logic of Comparative Inquiry', *Comparative Political Studies*, 11 (8): 132–57.

Merritt, R.L. and Stein Rokkan (eds) (1966) *Comparing Nations: The Use of Quantitative Data in Cross-national Research*. New Haven, CT: Yale University Press.

Murdock, George P. (1949) *Social Structure*. New York.

Naroll, Raoull (1961) 'Two Solutions to Galton's Problem', *Philosophy of Science*, 28: 15–39.

Naroll, Raoull (1965) 'Galton's Problem: The Logic of Cross-cultural Research', *Social Research*, 32: 428–51.

Needham, Rodney (1963) *Primitive Classification*, Chicago.

Niessen, Manfred, Jules Peschar and Chantal Kurilsky (eds) (1984) *International Vergleichende Sozialforschung*, Frankfurt: Campus Verlag.

Noelle-Neumann, Elisabeth (1979) 'International and Interdisciplinary Perspectives', in Stein Rokkan (ed.), *A Quarter Century of Social Science*, New Delhi, pp. 279–80.

NORC/Chicago (1948) 'Surveys of World Opinion', in *Second International Conference on Public Opinion Research*. Williamstown, MA, 2–5 Sept. 1947 (published 1948), p. 126.

Olivia, Carl (1987) 'Die Vernachlässigung der Bedeutung internationaler Regionen in Datenanalyse und Theoriebildung', *Kölner Zeitschrift für Soziologie und Sozialpsychologie*, 39: 531 f.

Przeworski, Adam and Henry Teune (1970) *The Logic of Comparative Social Inquiry*, New York.

Przeworski, Adam (1983) 'Methods of Cross-national Research 1970–1983 – an Overview', Paper delivered at the Wissenschaftszentrum, Berlin, p. 17.

Przeworski, Adam (1989) 'Comparing, Miscomparing and the Comparative Method', Mimeo (Dec.).

Ragin, Charles C. (1987) *The Comparative Method*, Berkeley, CA.

Rokkan, Stein (1960) 'Citizen Participation in Political Life', *International Social Science Journal*, 12: 1–99.

Rokkan, Stein (ed.) (1962) *Approaches to the Study of Political Participation*. Bergen.

Rokkan, Stein and S. Høyer (1962) 'Comparative Research in Citizen Participation in Politics', *International Social Science Journal*, 14: 351–63.

Rokkan, Stein (ed.) (1966) *Data Archives for the Social Sciences*, Paris.

Rokkan, Stein (1970) *Citizens, Elections, Parties*, Oslo.

Rokkan, Stein (ed.) (1979) *A Quarter Century of International Social Science*, Paris.

Rokkan, Stein (1979) 'The ISSC Programme for the Advancement of Comparative Research', in Stein Rokkan, 1979, op. cit., pp. 17 f.

Rokkan, Stein, Derek Urwin, Frank H. Aarebrot, Pamela Malaba and Terje Sande (1987) *Centre–Periphery Structures in Europe: An ISSC Workbook in Comparative Analysis*, Frankfurt.

Rokkan, Stein, Sidney Verba, Jean Viet and Elina Almasy (1969) *Comparative Survey Analysis*, Paris: Mouton.

Russett, Bruce M., Hayward R. Alker, Karl W. Deutsch and Harold D. Lasswell (1964) *World Handbook of Political and Social Indicators*. New Haven, CT: Yale University Press.

Scheuch, Erwin K. (1967) 'Entwicklungsrichtungen bei der Analyse sozialwissenschaftlicher Daten', in René König (ed.), *Handbuch der empirischen Sozialforschung*, 2nd edn, vol. 1, Stuttgart.

Scheuch, Erwin K. (1981) 'Tourismus', in *Die Psychologie des 20. Jahrhunderts*. Zurich: Kindler Verlag.

Scheuch, Erwin K. (1989) *Argumentationsfeld Volkszählung 1987 – Pro und Contra soziologischer Aspekte*. Stuttgart.

Scheuch, Erwin K. (1990) 'From a Data Archive to an Infrastructure for the Social Sciences', *International Social Science Journal*, February.

Schweizer, Thomas (1978) *Methodenprobleme des interkulturellen Vergleichs*. Köln: Böhlau, especially ch. 5.

Singer, David and M. Small (1972) *The Wages of War 1816–1965*. New York: Wiley.

Smith, Tom (1988) 'The Ups and Downs of Cross-National Survey Research', *IASSIST Quarterly*, (Winter): 18–24.

Stinchcombe, Arthur L. (1982) Review essay of Wallerstein, Immanuel: 'The Modern World System II: Mercantilism and the Consolidation of the European World Economy, 1600–1750', *American Journal of Sociology*, 87: 1389–95.

Szalai, Alexander in collaboration with Philip E. Converse, Pierre Feldheim, Erwin K. Scheuch and Philip J. Stone (eds) (1972) *The Use of Time*. The Hague: Mouton.

Szalai, Alexander and Ricardo Petrella (eds) (1977) *Cross-national Comparative Survey Research*. Oxford: Pergamon Press.

Tylor, E.B. (1961) 'On a Method of Investigating the Development of Institutions Applied to Laws of Marriage and Descent', originally 1889, reprinted in F.W. Moore (ed.), *Readings in Cross-Cultural Methodology*, New Haven, CT: Yale University Press.

Verba, Sidney and Norman Nie (1973) *Participation in America*. New York: Harper.

Wallerstein, Immanuel (1974) *The Modern World System*. New York.

Wallerstein, Immanuel (1980) *The Modern World System II*. New York.

Wallerstein, Immanuel (1984) *World Tables 1984*, Washington.

Whiting, B.J. (1968) 'Methods and Problems in Cross-cultural Research', in Gardner Lindzey and E. Aronson (eds), *Handbook of Social Psychology*. Rev. ed., vol. 2, pp. 693–728.

Whiting, B.J. (1969) 'Effects of Climate on Certain Cultural Practices', in A.P. Vayda (ed.), *Environment and Cultural Behavior*, Garden City, NY, pp. 416–55.

Young, Pauline V. (1939) *Scientific Social Surveys and Research*, New York.

3

Comparing Countries: Lessons Learned

Henry Teune

Comparing countries, or legally recognized 'states', is but one type of comparison of human systems. Countries, with claims to significant levels of autonomy, or even effective sovereignty, are presumptively rewarding entities by which to learn about general principles or laws of change. Comparing countries also can be a way of understanding the 'best' forms of political organization to realize general values, such as achieving secular goals of human development or designing policies to solve problems.

All disciplines use 'temporal and/or spatial logics of comparison': literature, art, language, biology, psychology, medicine, law. It is one of several 'logics' pursued to unify fields of knowledge and disparate experiences; others include moral purposes (godly or human betterment), the methodology of science (principles of knowing), quantitative analysis (organization of discrete observations), and ecology (conflict and system equilibrium). None has been successful as an integrator. Knowledge continues to fragment, boggling some, and convincing others of the folly of the efforts of past scholars and scientists. As the history of visual representations instructs, social science is in a 'normal' state of confusion.

Social science disciplines compare countries: sociologists, for example, compare the relationship between societies and political systems; social psychologists, for instance, patterns of national values and political behaviour; anthropologists, culture (especially when it appears coterminous with national boundaries) and institutional change; psychologists, perceptions and language; and economists, national economies (market and non-market ones). Humanistic interpretations are based on understanding experiences as they relate to country in art, literature, music, architecture. Historians have been among the most persistently comparative, and have addressed, for example, the formation of cultures, empires, nations and countries.

This assessment of what has been learned from comparing countries, legally defined as many things, but certainly including organization of authority for peoples living in a recognized, bounded territory, will be limited to research since World War II, when almost all of mankind was brought in to one of the now 150 or so country niches.

Nation is less specifiable than country. The combinations of referents of the former are complex, excepting shared law and territorial monopoly. Nation refers to birth, and it has taken on several dimensions: linguistic, social, cultural, political, as well as special psychological attachments, including loyalty. Although nationalism was perhaps the most significant modern force of change, in contrast to country, it no longer attracts much contemporary research. During the wars of the 1930s and 1940s nationalism became associated with human differences and the denial of human qualities, justifying action to prove superiority through domination. Since the end of the independence movements, when nationalism symbolized equal human worth rather than invidiously attributed distinctiveness, nationality took on other meanings. Almost all countries today are multi-ethnic and not at all forceful in eroding older, or indeed new, social, economic and political identities. Country embodies the meaning of the legal concept of state. Most countries, however, can be characterized neither as nations nor states in the Western sense, other than by courtesy.

To survey what has been learned theoretically from comparing countries is selective. Choices include legislatures, constitutions, bureaucracies; families, religions, communities, enterprises, unions, research; and many other things – as it were, some set of volumes entitled *Macro Comparative Social Science*. The vast bulk of research in political science, sociology and the other social sciences remains micro, focused within countries and without pretence to being general. Furthermore, comparative research is often treated as a thing apart, residing in disciplinary sub-fields, such as comparative politics or sociology (Ragin, 1987).

General lessons have been learned from the comparative study of countries that tried to make macro-generalizations about human systems of the following type: 'In competitive electoral political systems, two-party systems have greater capacity to change policy directions than multi-party ones.' These kinds of generalizations are often separate from research based on countries historically or comparatively that is directed to learning from the experiences of others, whether it be Canadian health care or the applicability of the Yugoslav self-management system.

Social theory will be the focus of this evaluation. 'Macro' necessarily implies 'micro'. Together they constitute a relational concept, just as 'left' is relational to 'right'; both depend on where one stands. The comparison of cities within countries, for example, uses the same logic as cross-country comparisons of size and participation. And since all social systems by definition involve principles of super- and sub-ordination, they all have levels, hierarchical structures (Teune, 1984a). At the moment there are no countries without multiple levels of authority. Cross-level generalizations across systems constitute macro-theory in the social sciences: to be theories of change, they also must be cross-time or historical.

Country comparisons underpin much of the empirical foundations of contemporary macro social, economic and political theory. They dominate how we think about political and social systems – groups, firms and organizations within countries or any other kind of human organization – and our effort to discipline ideas. In this sense we also talk about comparative methods, referring to research about the impact of any kind of macro or more encompassing systems on micro ones, and vice versa.

An Overview of the Comparison of Countries

What is learned as general principles or laws comes from the study of differences or variance. These differences are something to be explained, as J.S. Mill over a century ago argued (1843; 1961). And Western social science disciplines, with their marks of self-conscious, systematic comparisons, are only a little over a century old.

The giants who established modern social science were both macro and historical, and without much self-proclamation, systematically comparative, including those among countries. Durkheim, Marx, Weber, Spencer, and others addressed differences and asked why. Their comparisons, unlike so many today, were closely tied to macro developmental and historical theory about change and the future.

The 1930s turned Europe and North America inward because of the problems of the Great Depression. Many researchers felt a moral obligation to do something about these problems. One consequence was an increase in empirical national research and new techniques to improve its quality and extensiveness. Comparative political studies, however, still involved West European and North American countries, while comparative sociology moved to abstract formulations of Weber and Marx or empirical studies about urban life, often tinted by Darwinism under the label of human ecology (Smelser, 1976; Teune, 1988b).

The new world political order formulated after 1945 made comparative research on newly independent states a necessary part of the US government's commitment to a decolonized and decentralized world order. International relations would take on a central role in international studies, dominated by the USA. Because of the outcome of war, the US-originated and -supported research was heavily influenced by ideologies of US democracy, and its Capitol's immediate needs to know. Eastern Europe and the Soviet Union were priority areas, but also the Middle East, Asia and Africa. US government-sponsored research at first turned to area scholars, many of whom had particular political perspectives, such as immigrants from Eastern Europe, or people with strongly divided views on certain countries, such as China. Later, social scientists from other countries would become involved in this research, but they too would carry a variety of biases about how to create social change in the former colonial areas. The comparison of countries became dominated by the United States, and there were many unspecified theories of change.

In the forty or so years of comparing countries on a world-wide basis, much had to be done with little knowledge to build on. And much has been learned – or, more importantly, discarded. Hundreds of thousands of 'man'-years were given to covering the globe; many millions of dollars were spent. In most areas, because of colonial practice, there were few social scientists. Later they would grow in numbers, collaborating with Western researchers or reacting with hostility towards them.

The Country as the Engine of Development

Most comparative research after 1945 accepted the country as its main point of departure – building nations outside Western Europe and North America and completing the development of the older states. National development, the creation of effective states, was expected to overcome divisions based on religion, ethnic identity, language and region, and was still a problem for Europe and North America. From one perspective the consequences of the Industrial Revolution had created economic classes in the West that divided countries. From another, they would act as a new force for class-based international solidarity along with the possible unpleasant side-effect of violence.

The state was assumed to be an instrument of change, a focal point for unifying peoples and transcending what divided them. And different theoretical orientations led to contending views on whether economic change would be the basis of state formation and political change or whether the state would have to be built before economic change could be expected (Lipset, 1960; Holt and Turner, 1967).

What has been learned from comparative research since 1945 is

that governments of countries have limits as institutions of homogen-
ization. In most of Third World countries, ethnic, religious and
regional conflicts persist. In some older countries ascriptive identities
of birth re-asserted themselves in the 1960s. Few can be confident
that they will not from time to time re-emerge in conflict.' Class
identities in the new states did not abolish traditional cleavages or
cut across the borders of countries. Class has transcended neither
ethnicity nor country. Indeed, in some areas, religions have militantly
challenged the secular state.

One of the first systematic comparative research projects undertaken after 1945 addressed the question of class versus nation in a
population survey in several West European countries (Buchanan
and Cantril, 1953; 1972). Samples within countries were asked
whether they identified more with, or felt closer to, their fellow
countrymen or to others of similar class in other countries. The
results helped answer an important political question of the time
and were somewhat surprising, given the contemporary fears about
post-war Europe. Strong national identification compared to class
remained. Experience since then with Euro-communism, Italian
communism, and other internationally based political ideologies
indicate that class economic interests have been insufficient to break
the hold of country or other identities.

Another question, in European-based comparative research, was
why cleavages within European countries endured (Lipset and
Rokkan, 1967). Several research programmes on this issue, primarily
within Western Europe, focused on why, after so long a period of
relatively well-financed state intervention, the peripheries and the
centre were so different and the state had survived these differences
rather than overcome them (Rokkan et al., 1970). Part of this
research found its way into what was to be called social and political
ecology, where the unit of analysis was usually local governments.

Instability in Third World countries, even with substantial growth,
was obvious. Civil wars broke out, religious violence erupted, and
in some areas governments rapidly changed by force. The concept
of political development following growth was challenged. Economic
development was defined as a national phenomenon and, hence
proceeded national economic plans. Ideas about infrastructure and
'take-off' continued in the face of persistent evidence of inequality
and poverty (Rostow, 1960). What was true of one region of a
country – for example, the relationships between capital investments
and growth – could not be found in others. And in some cases social
and regional differences created conflicts that broke up or threatened
to break up countries (Migdal, 1988).

Despite incomplete state formation in the West and weak states elsewhere, where national institutions were built on top of mosaics of social patterns, the number of new states continued to increase until the late 1960s. Now few believe as strongly as before that the state tied to growing urbanization will be the cutting edge for change and the focal point for national integration. In recent years the emergence of a global political economy seems to have replaced the country as the developmental focus, challenging many countries' assertions to sovereignty and capacity to direct change. Indeed, the 'opening up' of national economies is now a strategy for development.

Country Groupings and Quantitative Comparisons of States

One scientific objective is to reduce variance or variety into general categories or to put it under general relationships. Over time certain peoples spread territorially or their cultures and ideas became diffused. The juxtaposition of geography with culture gave rise to area studies. In the nineteenth century the term 'oriental' took on a huge part of the world with the idea that the area possessed something in common. Buddhism created geographical unity.

A principle of science is generality. The belief in science which was spreading among social scientists in the United States after 1945 developed into a tension between area specialists, who were convinced that social scientists knew little specific about anything and social scientists, who countered that area specialists were tellers of stories of little general relevance (Ward, 1964). Most of that conflict has now quieted down, with each group favouring their own associations and journals.

A more complicated version of this argument between 'area' specialists was that most countries were too different to be compared fruitfully. This led to the quest of social scientists for typologies or groupings of countries on dimensions asserted to be theoretically significant: wealth, democracy, size, culture, socialism and so on. This effort to categorize countries in order to reduce variance tried to use similarities that cut across culture and history.

The 1960s was a decade of exponential growth in quantitative comparisons of countries. The research projects were numerous, and one result was a number of world handbooks listing data (for example, Taylor and Hudson, 1976). In contrast to typologies using regional and political (OECD) principles, but with few exceptions, the inclusionary principle was legal recognition by the UN and some registration of data in some of their offices.

Both typological and quantitative approaches were flawed. Selecting a type to reduce variance made it impossible to find out what difference the category of inclusion meant. Thus, if being democratic or wealthy has consequences, it is necessary to look at some cases of being non-democratic or poor. In addition, most categories provide less information than quantities: how rich or how democratic. If one has quantitative information, why throw it away in a crude category? Further, some of the groupings by area that were used by scientifically committed comparative researchers, such as for Western Europe or Latin America, obscured altogether what was significant theoretically about those countries, other than being close to one another, relatively speaking.

Quantitative comparisons of countries became easier as international organizations collected more data, although not too many questions were asked about their quality (for example, deaths by group violence), and computers became more powerful with faster capacities to print. But there are also problems with the inclusion of all countries so named on political grounds. First, an assumption made is that the countries selected are 'significant' variance reducers; that is, the variance within them is less than that among them – for example, GNP per capita. There is greater variance within Yugoslavia by region, for instance, than between it and many other countries. This is less of a problem when comparing variances within countries, such as income disparities. But even then those differences must be connected to the structures of country. An isolated, poor area is unlikely to have much impact one way or another on national military expenditures. Second, the country must be free to vary on the attributes being examined; that is, be able to take on those characteristics or vary. If a country has no capacity to invade its neighbours, it should not be credited with peaceful or unwarlike behaviour.

Another questionable practice in quantitative comparisons that attribute properties to countries involves looking for patterns among entities 'A' but selecting a different set of objects. Examples are studying wars, but making them attributes of countries, thus giving the Netherlands a victory in World War II; or studying political parties but sampling countries or party systems (for example, Singer and Small, 1972; Janda, 1980).

Recent methodological demonstrations strongly indicate that cross-sectional examination of countries at a single point in time, and cross-time analysis yield artefactual results because of problems of aggregation and disaggregation. The arguments are complex (Kramer, 1983). Another side of this problem is the attribution of meaning to a particular year (when data are available) or to particular time intervals (looking at yearly military budgets as arms build-up). Different years and time intervals have different meanings for different countries and activities; for example, in the manufacturing of weapons or in buying them from exporters.

What we have learned from all of this is that selecting countries and time points should be *theoretically justified*. The same holds true for single or pair-wise country case studies. If they are embedded in a theory, they are potentially theoretically relevant. Examples are comparisons of Poland and Mexico with single parties and difficult processes of political co-option, or Nigeria and Brazil with state-owned development corporations. And countries do not have to be compared at the same time point. Nigeria before 'privatization' can be compared with Brazil today.

But this conclusion is tantamount to saying that we would not select inappropriate or weak cases if we knew what we were doing. But at least we now understand that the countries chosen have to be justified theoretically. The 'barefoot' experiences of area study empiricism or looking at everything have been instructive but not theoretically productive. Indeed, even single-country case studies, if theoretically framed, can be used to support generalizations – for example, the relationship between labour–management conflict and economic growth – rather than just to establish a specific historical fact – for example, a strike in Sweden. Such cases also can be important first steps to selecting other relevant cases to elaborate a theoretical problem or, indeed, to test a proposition.

An understanding of the role of theoretical designs in case studies has given them a new life (Eckstein, 1975). Their added value is enhanced quality of data. There is the hard and soft case. In the first case, if it is true that the level of economic development is a strong condition for democratic practices, then India should not have even limited democratic practices. Research in depth could examine the extent to which development has been underestimated for India or its democratic practices much exaggerated. If it is true that growth leads to economic inequality – indeed, that inequality is a necessary condition for growth in order to reward risks for making innovations – then the USSR can be examined in order to determine whether it has weak labour-intensive growth or strong technology-based growth whatever its patterns of inequality. In the second case, if it is true that at a certain point of affluence, democratic decision-making can be extended to firms, then the United States must be a hard case for, despite its wealth, it disclaims practices of economic democracy. But then might it be that the extension of participation to production is really related to uncertainty in the production processes (services or developing a new technology) rather than general national affluence?

Projection of the West

With the dominance of the United States after 1945 and its policy of de-colonization and a decentralized world order – a world society made up of many independent states – one research problem became political stability and how to achieve it in the context of American political ideology. The two main features of that ideology were that the individual counts morally and that economic abundance would free individuals and yet involve them in new networks of democratic relationships. The question was how to achieve stability based on democracy in the Third World. What would that take?

The answer was a change in individual values compatible with economic growth and democratic practice. Looking at the cases of democratic stability, the values needed were modern, secular, Western ones, based on material interests. Such values were hypothesized to be embedded in education, urbanization and industrialization.

In the 1960s, when American social scientists were unleashed on to the world to test this grand hypothesis, a number of versions of individual modernization comparative studies were launched. The general ideas of growth and stability were elaborated in government research programmes. The question was initially articulated in Lerner's *The Passing of Traditional Society* (1958). The process of modernization involved literacy, urbanization and industrialization. With those were associated a particular range of values: materialism, action, equality, mastery of one's destiny and the like. Cantril compared aspirations and expectations; Verba and others, modes of participation, following up an earlier comparative study of political culture and citizen involvement in politics (Cantril, 1965; Verba et al., 1971; Almond and Verba, 1964). Jacob examined the values of action, equality, economic development, national orientation and participation (Jacob et al., 1971). The most extensive of these was Inkeles' study of modernization (Inkeles and Smith, 1974). He concluded that modern man was everywhere the same. Many remained sceptical about such an individual, behavioural approach to social change and nation formation.

Since then, studies have pointed to problems with such a 'theory' of social change, and the modernization idea has almost completely faded away. Growth values and stability in the world could not help explain the growth of India in the 1970s, the recent rapid economic expansion of China, the length of authoritarian rule in urban, literate Chile. Indeed, one of the modifications of the straight line between values, change and stability was that change in these values will stimulate increased expectations and aspirations which governments could not meet, leading to instability (Davis, 1963). In any event, the gross modernization hypothesis was a poor guide to answer the question of what range of values will lead to what kinds of change. It does appear, however, that democratic practice is not associated with the national dominance of the Islamic religion, whatever the economic growth.

Many patterns of values appear to be compatible with growth and change. Being poor does not inhibit India from holding elections, whether or not they are respectful of popular will or minorities. The processes of change to modern production in agriculture and industry may be compatible with diverse cultures and values in a global political economy. But that does not say much about the possible resulting homogeneity of values in the longer run.

Variance Reducing Theoretical Schemes

The main research target in comparing countries for theoretical ends is variance, practically the full range of human experience. What can be done to reduce the variance and to find patterns and relationships? This problem is less serious if one has some general theories; for example, one stating that deprived people support (vote for) political instrumentalities of change. An even more general theory could be that those components that are more integrated, enmeshed in social and political systems, will tend to behave in negative feedback (stabilizing) ways rather than positive (destabilizing) ones. But what if the perspective is that there is a vast array, an almost infinite human diversity? The strategy for some is to invent categories to sort it out.

Anthropologists have been looking at human differences longer than other social scientists. They developed a theoretical perspective called 'functional analysis', which became attractive as a variance reducer. Although societies could do certain things in many ways in order to survive, they had to reproduce, transmit values to younger members, and the like. There were, however, many versions of survival functions, including 'requisite' functions (Levy, 1952). Much research within this scheme ended up sterile. The structural-functional categories as adopted from anthropology by sociology and political science were little more than a set of categories with implied instructions to go and look for functions of ritual, for example, or other structures that met those functions.

A political science adaptation of this was the functions of political systems – making rules, adjudicating and implementing them (Almond and Coleman [eds], 1960). Those functions need not be met by governments. They would, however, be attended to somewhere in the political system. There were other functions of political systems, like those of societies, such as interest articulation and aggregation. These also were clearly Western concepts, ignoring ideologies of political systems that rejected interests as legitimate.

One alternative to system-level theoretical schemes to reduce variance observed within social, political and economic systems was to anchor the constants in the universals of being human (Czudnowski, 1975). The choices available are many: human needs, human nature, human development, as well as special ones, such as need to achieve, dominate and affiliate (McClelland and Winter, 1969). These carried ideological perspectives that confronted belief in human variety. The research on human nature also was in a stage of asserting ever more flexibility and adaptability. It is now more likely than before that some of this research will find some individual universals, based on a secular material view of human beings and their development (Teune, 1988c).

Neither the universal functions of social or political systems nor the constants of human nature have yet helped very much to reduce variance. The question posed was, how do societies meet these functions or needs for collective or individual survival. The answer was, in a great variety of ways. Although certain research questions were and can be coded within such schemes, they do not yield relationships, which are the foundation for building theoretical explanations. It is not how the needs for food and shelter are met or how a society socializes its members, but why it is done this way rather than others. What was enhanced with the term theory – structural-functional or Parsonian theory – was little more than a set of categories for making some kind of order. The human needs of Maslow, for example, served political goals of welfare states better than theoretical ones of explanatory research. Today, after having received so much attention, they are hardly used.

What we have learned is that there is no substitute for theory and that any set of categories will create biases in observations. There are no easy roads to theoretical knowledge. Few new such variance-reducing schemes have been proposed. The experience with categories has been one of learning about the promises of theory.

Cutting into Countries Theoretically

Once a decision has been made that there is sufficient 'system-ness' or connectedness in a country or its society and economy, the next step is where to look. Establishing 'systemness' is not easy, as indicated earlier. A country may be a country for certain kinds of things – sports, for example – but not for others – social order, perhaps. Either the behaviour is determined by systems outside it – multinational corporations or other countries – or some systems, such as regions or localities, within a country are largely autonomous. The macro characteristics of country must be used theoretically to explain something within it.

If it is demonstrated that Polish society or its local governments are systems, what does research on the Polish family or local governments tell? Possibilities include Polish society, the Polish political system, the 'former' German territories or Baltic influence. Generalizations within countries or societies are the object of comparing systems and making inferences made about them. This goal is often avoided through a diversion: saying that 'in Poland, but in France'. But this kind of description conveys little theoretically about systems. The problem is that of a theoretical leap: making connections between observations within a country and the country as a system.

One way to strengthen the probability that observing something within a system is in fact an observation of the 'whole' is a macro-theoretical context within which different types of systems, even those radically different, can be compared. For example, for a 'number of reasons', one of the possible 'benefits' of decentralization is more local political innovation and diffusion of ideas and practices with increasing political integration of the system decreasing the time taken for diffusion (Reed, 1983). One proposition from this theoretical 'context' is that more decentralized systems (at T1) will have higher levels (at T2) of local political innovation, and the more integrated they are, such as might be indicated by associations of local officials, the more rapidly those innovations will die or be diffused. Comparing highly centralized systems and very decentralized ones gives opportunities to observe what is predicted, making credible claims for having observed a system level relationship. Another example, would be increasing centralization (cross-time) and conflicts between local governments and the citizens (the 'responsiveness' of local governments). Still another would be a relationship between centralization (level and process) and quality of provisions of services. The greater the predictions from the system level property to components within them and the better the observations conform to what changes were predicted, the stronger the basis for claims to have observed system 'effects'.

Contrast theoretical comparison with observing families in two or more countries. In France, this was found; but in India, that. The only acceptable conclusions are that there are differences that should have been expected or that the differences are artefacts of research instrumentation. And the number of observations, the sample size, taken within each country is of no help.

What is the 'best' observational 'cut' or slice of a country in order to tap its political system or society? These include national elites of various kinds; local governments; the people; political institutions, such as political parties or associations; bureaucracies; or special groups, including religious and ethnic ones (Teune, 1984b). If a case can be made theoretically, then of course it is not necessary to have the 'same' cut across the countries to be compared: defining elites in studying political conflict in highly centralized systems could focus on the executive and in federated systems, on local governments. Of course, with weak theories, reliance is put on apparent similarity as a substitute for theoretical equivalence, and that could be like comparing voter turn-out in the United States and Bulgaria.

One general rule is that the more 'enmeshed' within the system the component is, the greater the chances that its characteristics and behaviour will manifest characteristics and changes of the system as a whole. But this is an empirical question. For example, comparing US and Soviet families about what are considered to be good and proper family relations is likely to be far less instructive about the US political system than about the Soviet Union. In the US family, norms are more likely to be social, a result of local practice, ethnic heritage and religion. That, however, may be changing, but unevenly, with the spread of new laws regulating family relations.

Related to the theoretical problem of cutting into countries for comparisons is the more empirical one of the units or levels of analysis. Countries as political systems, as suggested, are characterized by superordination or hierarchy over territory. Within almost all countries today there is a remarkable 'similar' structure of authority: locality (city and country), province and state, with an urban and rural sector. For years governments have been collecting data on these territorial units, sometimes also social ones (the Lapps in northern Sweden). And these data became a target of opportunity for comparing countries by looking at local or intermediate political units and groups.

The problem of levels of analysis is like that of country. For political and social institutions and structures assumptions are made about their theoretical meanings and they are specified for research. What are cities, for example, other than legally recognized components of states, or regions, except some territorial aggregations of similarities, distinguishing them from geographical neighbours? Cities as the social organization of access through proximity can also be interpreted as political organizations for 'community' or economic entities for production and consumption. Regions are often defined as social, historical residues of time/cost/distance functions for exchange and conflict and may be viable entities for planning.

Territorial aggregations of data have been extensively used, sometimes under the label of social and political ecology. Both require some support for proximity-conformity hypotheses – people tend to behave like their neighbours in voting, for example. From early studies of urbanization until the present, patterns of aggregation and disaggregation within countries are interpreted as macro indicators of change (Brown, 1988; Teune, 1990).

Since the time when modern social science was organized, the national and city were welcomed as the cutting edges of change. The state was growing in authority, especially as it began to tax and distribute the surpluses of industrial production, and cities grew as efficient aggregations of labour tied to sources of centralized energy supplies. Regional differences were diminished by both. In recent years research has found some shifts. Cities in industrialized countries, largely because of changes in technology, are no longer ascendant aggregators of people and activities. The opposite is true in the Third World (Teune, 1988a). Since the 1970s almost every wealthy country has decentralized to some (often a slight) degree, often in response to a declining ability to appropriate higher percentages of GNP for welfare. Cities are becoming disaggregated into 'neighbourhoods', and new regional entities, some spilling over national boundaries, have emerged, such as the North Sea area of Europe and the Pacific Rim. Just as national indicators were used to demonstrate the strength of nations, such as wealth, resources and people, today the relevance of levels of aggregation within countries as well as the country itself must be 'proved' empirically. And general changes are now pointing to a more complex state of affairs regarding levels: small units (neighbourhoods or residential areas); regions both smaller and larger than 'older' ones; and, of course, still the city and nation; and now perhaps the world.

Comparing Nations, Development, and the World System

Questions have been raised as to what happened to the Soviet, Chinese, Western or other 'models' of development. From the very beginning of modern social science, macro comparative studies were juxtaposed with some more encompassing, temporally framed developmental theories of change. The countries were seen as more or less advanced in terms of these developmental 'models', sometimes crudely marked in terms of fuzzily defined stages. These 'models' were deeply embedded in views of human nature and the meaning of the human experience, sometimes criticized as historicism or 'iron laws'. The focusing of change on countries, of course, posed many questions, including their capacity to develop.

In one part of the world, arguments centred on the question of one or many paths to socialism, still believed by some to be a higher order of human development, however defined. In another, the questions centred on 'convergence' theory: that because of the imperatives of technology and organization of production, very different countries would over time become more alike. Tied to these ideas were some kinds of inevitable forces for change and the various ideologies they carried. These debates too have faded, as almost all that are framed in simple 'either-or' terms eventually do.

Most comparative studies of countries in the 1950s and 1960s assumed that countries were sufficiently closed to allow for autonomous development and political direction of change. The challenge to closed, autonomous theories of change was formulated long ago in anthropology as Galton's problem (Naroll, 1976). How much of what is in a culture is due to its own autonomous dynamics and how much to diffusions of cultural items from others – whether there are single or multiple origins of ideas, such as monotheism? If there was one, it could be attributed to either the unique characteristics of a particular event or to accident there. If several, then some common conditions rather than a particular event must be used for explanation: that is, if those conditions were obtained anywhere, the probability of something new but similar being created and adopted would increase.

But what about development? The post-1945 concept applied to both new and old states was Western. If development means only increasing output of material goods per person on a continuing basis, are there many paths to industrial production or do alternative paths all end up on the same road, but at different speeds? Are there many kinds of hierarchical political control or only a limited range of alternatives for organizing constitutional governments – for example, parliamentary and presidential?

By the end of the 1960s, recognized by academics a few years later, development had shifted away from the country and had become global. The argument continues over effective state sovereignty, with the international 'system' being primarily the consequence of countries pursuing their separate interests. In this, as all such debates, the questions are simplified.

In fact, international organizations are becoming influential in setting world-wide norms about social, political and economic rights – what a country and the world are morally obligated to do; some countries have half or more of their GNP in international trade; international associations have grown exponentially with increasing control over standards and information; multinational enterprises are penetrating almost every country; and a few cities are 'world' cities influenced more by what is happening outside their national borders than within them. Countries that opened up, grew (for example, China); Those which remained closed stagnated (such as the USSR and Burma). Cities initiated 'international relations' and became part of an international division of labour. Countries shifted from being controllers of change to managers of exchanges and transactions within a global political economy.

State monopolies of military means became internationalized in treaties and systems of military production and procurement, even for those countries with sufficient capacity to do it alone (the United States). National processes of development, even those integral to state security, are now a part of a world system.

Observations of pieces of a global political economy stimulated new theories, one of which, 'dependency theory', in various formulations, addresses development (or underdevelopment) in global rather than national terms (Frank, 1980). By the early 1970s the consequences of change had been translated into simplistic world models (Meadows et al., 1974). The 'global political economy' became a new field of research. Rather than comparing countries, a few researchers looked at the world as a system in areas such as the environment, economic growth, technology, population and values. For most others the country as the unit of analysis for development remained the focus. They were locked into explaining change as a process where national borders trigger radical discontinuities in human behaviour.

A world system orientation towards development added intellectual vigour and attracted younger scholars to the debates about the future, much as the developing nations had done a few decades earlier. We have learned that things change and whether the global system as a theoretical alternative to national development will persist for long is an open question. Most social science experience with new avenues of enlightenment is that they soon dim. But today any comparisons of countries must take the international-global system into account and consider the vulnerability of countries to penetration from transnational human organizations as well as the world physical and biological 'environments'.

Equivalence

Encounters with diversity in comparing countries heightened awareness of the problem of equivalence across systems. In order to compare something across systems it is necessary to have confidence that the components and their properties being compared are the 'same', or indicate something equivalent. The variance-reducing schemes previously discussed attempted to address this problem. The message was: do not look at institutions called 'legislatures' and expect that they 'function' as legislatures. The basic idea was that of 'functional equivalence', structures that have the same role in the political system. Of course, the theoretical questions are, why must there be a legislative function and what does that mean?

Two things were learned. First, establishing credible equivalence is difficult, as 'meaning' is contextual. Second, a great deal of observational flexibility must be used to get into the systems so that comparisons can be made. Beyond that, little was learned, although sensitivity to the problem has slightly increased.

The respondent survey, or questionnaire, seemed the most comparable way of looking at countries, for example, attitudinal comparisons. We learned about its problems. First, the assumption is that individuals are differentiated, separate from the group or system, and have acquired values, attitudes and other attributes that differ from others. This is widely disputed. Values, for example, are often not acquired characteristics of individuals that influence their behaviour but, rather, emanate from the system (such as an ideology), or from situation (such as crises). Second, it is likely that social development or a culture determines individual differentiation, which defines the 'normal' distribution, or bell-shaped curve, of individual characteristics found in some countries. In any event, the strategies for assessing equivalent properties have become pragmatically flexible, adapting to context (Kuechler, 1986).

Other than with 'ratio' scale variables, based on 'zero', such as the number of people there are or years lived, it is very difficult to compare how much of any property measured in one system there is as against how much in another. Crimes, anti-social acts, voting, all must be contextually assessed. Even those most valued social science measures, GNP and income, must be adjusted. When currency exchange rates can change by 40 per cent or more in a year, as the dollar–yen did in late 1985, or estimates of 'black' or underground economic transactions are as high as 20 per cent of the reported GNP, massive contextual adjustments must be made, as the Italian government did recently, estimating upward its world ranking. The per capita income of Indians certainly would have led to early death in other contexts, but income does not mean the 'same' (Kravis et al., 1975).

One way to reduce the equivalence problem is to compare relationships and change over time within and across systems. The problem of saying how much is side-stepped by not having to know how the magnitudes are related to zero in each country. And in fact, many comparisons among countries are now of relationships within them, such as wealth and health within local governmental units. This partially solves the problem of establishing equivalence.

Another approach is to seek out theoretical equivalence in comparing the behaviour of whole systems – that is, relationships among a set of theoretically specified variables, such as those among the openness of country, the international demonstration effect (presence of what is foreign), changes in aspirations and expectations, and political instability. It is possible to introduce 'unique' or system-specific variables that would lead to predictions of different outcomes for different countries. For example, it could be predicted that countries with inclusionary and competitive political parties can manage the destabilizing consequences of aspirations for greater material income by allowing for non-material satisfaction of belonging to the system through joining a politically legitimate queue of a minority party. Countries with exclusionary political parties would be predicted to provide little alternative to violence or corruption. Such system-level predictions would have to use both cross-system and cross-time comparisons. The measure selected for the variables of the theory would gain some 'validity' because of their status in that theory (Teune, 1981). Unfortunately there are few such system dynamic theories in the social sciences other than in economics, where they appear to become less robust as national economies adjust to global developments.

Macro-theoretical Comparisons

Comparing countries is one kind of system comparison to create and establish macro-theories. Theories address change and require predictions (and retrodictions). The core problem in achieving this is logical: how to develop theories for systems characterized by changing relationships and the emergence and demise of components. Political parties emerge, they change, and their relationships with other components of the political system also change. In contrast, theories of other kinds of systems can practically assume that neither the components nor the relationships among them change (mechanical systems) or that the components increase in number and on occasion may mutate (a description rather than an explanation of an event). But the basic relationships among them either do not change or change very slowly (biological systems). Social and political systems are dominated by structural change (positive feedback), mechanical and biological ones by equilibrium process (negative feedback). None the less, the goal of social science –

theoretical prediction – must be pursued or else we will have 150 odd country and society histories or stories or a world history in which national histories are a part. And in fact, major theoretical attempts have been made, many not very convincing and a few not well pursued.

Marxist theory is a macro-theory of change with ambiguous and deficient components. Neo-Marxists have made amendments to bring the 'state' back in. Within such a theoretical framework, histories have been rewritten (Anderson, 1984). Most departed from the scientific principle of observability, and often a set of relationships is reified into a thing or process – labour, the state, struggle and so on. The state, for example, is defined as a 'bundle' of relationships (Skocpol, 1979). Relationships are properties of systems, their components and other relationships. (For example, integration is a general property of a number of other relations, such as political ones – that is, the integration of a political system.)

Empirically 'grounded' theories attempt theoretical constructions that are heavily event-oriented, making it difficult to extract the major components and their relationships and how they interact over time. Thus, it is difficult to formulate system dynamics in a general enough way so that their theoretical equivalents can be examined in other countries. One example is European state formation with a feudal history, compared to the United States without one. Another is the perspective of historical junctures. The United States in the late nineteenth century was faced with a national government that relied primarily on import taxes but had efficient and politicized manufacturing industries, which were committed to a strong navy to protect exports. The resolution of the crisis was a national income tax to substitute for reductions of import revenues to increase trade by lowering tariffs and to pay for a navy. What is being done, perhaps hopelessly poorly, in comparing political systems using either several countries or one (case study) is to develop macro-theories of change. The danger in such empirical studies is in fitting the countries to the theory rather than testing it.

A beneficiary of recent increased macro-theoretical thinking is the country case study. Its logic can be applied to other countries in terms of 'what, if . . .'. What if a country, given the opportunities of an international market and a strong comparative advantage in a commodity, decided to dedicate its resources to exploiting that commodity rather than to industrialization, such as Argentina did more than fifty years ago (Smith, 1969)? The case study has been the prime vehicle for elaborating corporatism where conflicting interests are brought together either to share in new wealth or to take advantage of others.

There are a few empirically based 'models' of macro-change,

designed within a theoretical context and tested on a few countries. One looked at politicization of the population, government taxes and expenditures, and support for the government over time in two countries (Brunner and Brewer, 1971). There have been few follow-ups of this 'model', or studies of contending cases.

A major problem is to identify the main dynamics of change within particular systems which are measurable with enough time periods and which also have some equivalence to other systems. Take the example of political systems that base their legitimacy on both participation and improved living standards and that have socialized 'the means of production' but use the markets for distribution. The implied dynamic is that in order to make participation credible, it is necessary to increase the equality of the participants; but in order to increase production that will compete in the market, it is necessary to reward differentially, often dramatically so, if improved productivity is to come from innovation which requires risk-taking. What might be predicted in a relatively precise way is a 'zig-zag' between equality campaigns in taxation and welfare and declining productivity, leading to political destabilization (for example, labour unrest), responded to by relaxing controls on private and organizational accumulation, which leads to increased output but also to cynicism about participation. It might be a run-down system (Lydall, 1989). This equality, productivity, instability dynamic might work well for Yugoslavia and it would be an interesting case of one type of a basic political dynamic, but where else could it be applied?

Tight and Loose Systems: Rediscovering Historical Social Science

The issue here is that of historical laws versus historical junctures. The first assumes necessary conditions, such as modes of production and technological prowess; the second, historical uniqueness from paths chosen when choices were taken, such as opening up or becoming a hermit country when forced to decide. World system 'theory', of course, exemplifies the former; most contemporary historians, the latter. Immanuel Wallerstein (1974) represents the former; Robert Higgs (1987), the latter. The 'in-between' position is that there are historically necessary 'sequences', but variations on what specifically follows. These are the main differences between tight and loose theoretical interpretations of change.

Not much has been learned from the shifting quagmire of change in the nineteenth and twentieth centuries about the future. What we think we know comes from a few relatively firm extrapolations: the US portion of recorded world economic production has and will continue to decline; multinational corporations will grow; more people will travel internationally. But social change is abrupt in direction, if not time. Established definitions of urbanization must be reassessed; the meaning of family re-conceptualized; defence and deterrence, restated. The reality is that concepts and theory today are aimed at rapidly changing phenomena.

Useful Comparisons: Public Policy

Political leaders, or so it is assumed, learned from the experiences of other countries. In fact, since the beginning of Western writings on social and human behaviour (Aristotle being a credible starting point), the question of what one wilful political community can learn from another has been central to human change. The problem is the multivaried contexts of countries. If the United States adopts socialized medicine, will Canada's experiences of better health care for the less wealthy obtain? Or can federal political systems survive in the long run, or what about polities that rely on law and have little or no 'policy' separate from it?

In comparing polities and policies, the goal is lessons rather than creating or testing theory. Countries that are similar are more likely to borrow from one another, even if those similarities are an illusion of doing better in one area (Teune, 1973). Indeed, historical experiences were critical to justifying the designing of polities, as exemplified by the US venture into constitutional government in 1789. The questions to ask in comparing policies are, why did governments adopt such positions, why their particular nature, and what are the consequences in both the long and short term?

Comparing countries so as to determine the efficacy of various policy alternatives is mired down in national politics and beliefs about good and bad, and winners and losers. But just as perplexing is sorting out conditions under which policies operate, what was intended, and what other policies have an impact on the one compared. What has been learned about health, education, employment, retirement and other collective efforts is that those countries that can afford them adopt them (Wilensky, 1975; Dierkes et al., 1987) with debatable costs and consequences. Theoretically based predictions rather than extrapolations are needed; none the less, politicians use experiences of other countries to support their positions and to validate their arguments.

Human Nature: Source of Universals?

What we know, but comparative social researchers have not yet learned, is that knowledge about human beings is advancing in credibility, building upon ideas of human needs that have been the foundation of the formation of the welfare state in the twentieth century. It is likely that this knowledge will focus the research agenda on questions of how to allow for better expression of what is inherent in us all.

It is now generally accepted that the genetic evolution of our species comes from a 'single source' and that we emerged rather than evolved about 100,000–300,000 years ago. In addition to recent discoveries of male–female differences and the identification of the sex gene, there is robust evidence for the following: the acquisition of languages is neurologically 'tightly wired', that is, it is nearly impossible to prohibit humans from communicating; humans teach others – that is, have a moral sense about what is right and wrong; humans respect possession of space – that is, defer to prior occupancy – even when the occupier is not present; and although humans beg and give like other primates, they minimize that behaviour in favour of asserting rights of all kinds, including 'fair' exchange (Teune, 1988c).

In addition, our directions in perception and information-processing are common: we see from right to left, and we screen in and out information that is compatible with the sensor we select for a general area of information – for example, what a particular political party 'means'. The latter has substantial implications for 'models' of rationality which have influenced comparative research.

The big issue, however, is that the size of the human brain, comparative to body size (extraordinarily large), has not increased for nearly 50,000 years, yet the pace of social evolution – its complexity – is increasing exponentially. At the moment human beings appear to have no limit to social growth, and indeed, the potential technologies of super-conductivity, ceramics, water agri-culture, resins, not to mention improvements in computing and communications will increase the rate of change. What appeared again as material limits to growth in the 1970s may be replaced by genetic limits to social complexity. If so, comparative country research will again give ground to the international or world system as it did to environmental issues in recent decades.

The Rise of International Social Sciences

Perhaps the most important influence on research comparing countries has been the emergence of communities of social science scholars. Participation in international social science associations and their activities has increased exponentially since the 1950s. This process has been inclusionary, with costs in terms of credibility and fragmentation. But this experience conforms to those of the growth of any new voluntary enterprise. The risks are many but the hope is that criteria of selectivity will evolve, as they have in certain areas of national academic societies. One benefit has been theoretical diversity, although much of that is not well articulated.

The rise of international social science has been the result of certain individuals' leadership – that of Stein Rokkan and Philip Jacob, to give only two examples – and much work by many others. The data base for comparing nations has been dramatically improved since the 1950s, if judged only by their extension. The need for very costly cultivation of area experts with language skills has been spread out in an international division of labour. Few would compare countries today without drawing on their expertise. We have learned about the ways of collaboration, often after terrible mistakes, and have evolved norms of reciprocity, however deficient they may still be.

Much could be written about international social science; some has been, and much more will be. But over the years the capacity to compare nations has been improved, one of the results of many people learning a lot of little things. The question is whether that capacity will be well used. At the moment the potential considerably exceeds the product.

Note

This chapter is an enlarged version of a paper presented to the Twenty-seventh Annual Convention of the International Studies Association, April 1987, with another presented to the Research Council of the International Sociological Association, September 1988.

References

Almond, G. and J. Coleman (eds) (1960) *The Politics of Developing Areas.* Princeton, NJ: Princeton University Press.

Almond, G. and S. Verba (1964) *The Civic Culture.* Boston, MA: Little Brown.

Anderson, P. (1984) *Lineages of the Absolutist State.* London: Verso.

Brown, T. (1988) *Migration and Politics.* Chapel Hill, NC: University of North Carolina.

Brunner, J. and G. Brewer (1971) *Organized Complexity.* New York: Free Press.

Buchanan, W. and H. Cantril (1953; 1972) *How Nations See Each Other.* Westport, CT: Greenwood Press.

Cantril, H. (1965) *Patterns of Human Concern.* New Brunswick, NJ: Rutgers University Press.

Czudnowski, M. (1975) *Comparing Political Behavior.* Chicago, IL: Aldine-Atherton.

Davis, J. (1963) *Human Nature in Politics.* New York: Wiley.

Dierkes, M., H. Weiler, and A. Antol (eds) (1987) *Comparative Policy Research: Learning from Experience.* New York: St Martin's Press.

Dogan, M. and D. Derivry (1988) 'France in Ten Slices: An Analysis of Aggregate Data', *Electoral Studies*, 7 (3): 251, 267.

Eckstein, H. (1975) 'Case Study and Theory', in F. Greenstein and N. Polsby (eds), *Handbook of Political Science*, vol. 2. Reading, MA: Addison Wesley.

Frank, A. (1980) *Crisis in the World Economy*. London: Heinemann.

Higgs, R. (1987) *Crises and Leviathan: Critical Episodes in the Growth of American Government*. New York: Oxford University Press.

Holt, R. and J. Turner (1967) *The Political Basis of Economic Development*. Princeton, NJ: D. Van Nostrand.

Inkeles, A. and D. Smith (1974) *Becoming Modern*. Cambridge, MA: Harvard University Press.

Jacob, P. et al. (1971) *Values and the Active Community: A Cross-National Study of the Influence of Local Leadership*. New York: Free Press.

Janda, K. (1980) *Political Parties: A Cross-National Survey*. New York: Free Press.

Kohn, H. (1962) *The Age of Nationalism*. New York: Harpers.

Kramer, G. (1983) 'The Ecological Fallacy Revisited: Aggregate-versus-Individual Level Findings on Economics and Elections and Sociotropic Voting', *American Political Science Review*, 77: 92–111.

Kravis, I., A. Heston and R. Summers (1975) *A System of International comparisons of Gross Product and Purchasing Power*. Baltimore, MD: Johns Hopkins University Press.

Kuechler, M. (1986) 'The Utility of Surveys for Cross-national Research'. Paper presented to the XIth World Congress of the International Sociological Association, New Delhi.

Lerner, F. (1958) *The Passing of Traditional Society*. Glencoe, IL: Free Press.

Levy, M. (1952) *The Structure of Society*. Princeton, NJ: Princeton University Press.

Lipset, S. (1960) *Political Man: The Social Basis of Politics*. Garden City, NY: Doubleday.

Lipset, S. and S. Rokkan (eds) (1967) *Party Systems and Voter Alignments: Cross National Perspectives*. New York: Free Press.

Lydall, H. (1989) *Yugoslavia in Crises*. New York: Oxford University Press.

McClelland, D. and D. Winter (1969) *Motivating Economic Achievement*. New York: Free Press.

Meadows, D., J. Randers and W. Behrens (1974) *The Limits to Growth*. New York: Signet Books.

Migdal, J. (1988) *Strong Societies and Weak States: State–Society Relations in the Third World*. Princeton, NJ: Princeton University Press.

Mill, J. (1843; 1961) *A System of Logic, Ratiocinative and Inductive*. London: Longman.

Naroll, R. (1976) 'Galton's Problem and HRAF', *Behavioral Science*, 11: 123–48.

Ragin, G. (1987) *The Comparative Method*. Berkeley, CA: University of California Press.

Reed, S. (1983) 'Patterns of Diffusion in Japan and America', *Comparative Political Studies*. 16: 215–34.

Rokkan, S. with A. Campbell, P. Torsvik and H. Valen (1970) *Citizens, Elections and Parties: Approaches to the Comparative Study of Development*. New York: McKay.

Rostow, W. (1960) *The Stages of Economic Growth*. Cambridge: Cambridge University Press.

Singer, J. and M. Small (1972) *The Wages of War: 1816–1865*. New York: Wiley.

Skocpol, T. (1979) *State and Social Revolution*. Cambridge: Cambridge University Press.

Skocpol, T. (ed.) (1984) *Vision and Method in Historical Sociology*. New York: Cambridge University Press.

Smelser, N. (1976) *Comparative Methods in the Social Sciences*. Englewood Cliffs, NJ: Prentice-Hall.

Smith, P. (1969) *Politics and Beef in Argentina*. New York: Columbia University Press.

Taylor, C. and M. Hudson (1976) *World Handbook of Political and Social Indicators*. 2nd end, New Haven, CT: Yale University Press.

Teune, H. (1973) 'Public Policy: Macro Perspectives', in G. Zaltman (ed.), *Processes and Phenomena of Social Change*. New York: Wiley.

Teune, H. (1981) 'Concepts of Evidence in Systems Analysis: Testing Macro Systems Theories', *Quantity and Quality*, 15: 55–70.

Teune, H. (1984a) 'Integration', in G. Sartori (ed.), *Social Science Concepts: A Systematic Analysis*. Beverly Hills, CA: Sage Publications.

Teune, H. (1984b) 'The Study of Eastern Europe and the Development of Macro Political Theory', in R. Linden and B. Rockman (eds), *Elite Studies and Communist Politics*. Pittsburgh, PA: University of Pittsburgh Press.

Teune, H. (1988a) 'Growth and Pathologies of Giant Cities', in M. Dogan and J. Kasarda (eds), *The Metropolis Era*, vol. 1. Newbury Park, CA: Sage Publications.

Teune, H. (1988b) *Growth*. Newbury Park, CA: Sage Publications.

Teune, H. (1988c) 'Human Nature as a Moral Foundation for International Studies', *Journal of International Studies*, 20 (Tokyo).

Teune, H. (1990) 'Current Issues in Social Ecology', in B. Hamm (ed.), *Progress in Social Ecology*. New Delhi: Mittal Publications.

Verba, S., N. Nie and Jae-on Kim (1971) *Modes of Democratic Participation*. Beverly Hills, CA: Sage Publications.

Wallerstein, I. (1974) *The Modern World System*. New York: Academic Press.

Ward, R. (ed.) (1964) *Studying Politics Abroad: Field Research in Developing Areas*. Boston, MA: Little, Brown.

Wilensky, H. (1975) *The Welfare State*. Berkeley, CA: University of California Press.

PART II

THEORETICAL REFLECTIONS ON COMPARATIVE RESEARCH

4

Socio-legal Concepts and their Comparison

Vincenzo Ferrari

Between Centralistic and Federalistic Comparisons

Sociology of law perennially faces a paradox. Even more than jurisprudence, it has developed on an international and intercultural level since its very beginnings. It can even be said that its *raison d'être* stems, very largely, from the need for comparing different 'legal cultures', as Lawrence Friedman (1975) calls them. However, the difficulties which are commonly encountered by comparative lawyers seem to become exceedingly acute for legal sociologists, for at least two reasons. First, sociology of law does not look at law in itself, but rather as a contextual variable affecting, and being affected by, a countless number of other variables, which in their turn intervene in the analysis. Second, and consequently, sociology of law, though compelled to adopt 'juristic' concepts, cannot interpret them, mechanically, according to those meanings which are prescribed within the context of the legal system, as dogmatically conceived. In other words, it cannot purport, from its own peculiar perspective, that such meanings be 'derivable' from one concept to another, according to a 'self-referential' logic, as Niklas Luhmann (1988) would put it. As a descriptive *and critical* science, sociology of law cannot ignore that the semiotic tools it handles are in fact highly variable and that all meanings are highly dependent upon decisions: about which – one should add – very little is known, except for their being affected by more or less symmetric power relationships among social actors. Briefly, sociology of law cannot indulge in giving its words a mythical status, thereby running into the danger of becoming 'wild', as realist and neo-positivist legal philosophers recurrently say about dogmatic jurisprudence (Ross, 1957; Jori, 1974).

Confronted with such difficulties, legal sociologists have been continuously trying to come to meta-theoretical clarifications for the sake of comparison. A significant example, which is useful when classifying actual comparative studies, is that of Adam Podgórecki (1974), who distinguishes between two kinds of comparison, which he defines, respectively, as 'a-prioric centralistic' and 'federalistic'. In the former 'some preconceived research conception is taken for granted. Referring to prior knowledge, various social systems are selected for comparative analyses, and detailed hypotheses to be tested in those systems are derived from the a-prioric general theories' (1974: 107). In the latter, 'independent studies on similar problems are undertaken in various countries, with due consideration for the specific systemic, economic, legal and political peculiarities of each of them' (ibid.). 'Federalistic' investigations, in their turn, are subsequently distinguished into two subcategories. They are 'diagnostic' if they confine themselves to 'disclose the diversity or similarity of certain characteristics such as, for example, family models, leisure habits, and types of functioning of the local authorities, in various societies'. On the other side they are 'theoretical' if their aim is, 'besides fact finding, to verify definite relationships'. In some way, 'diagnostic-federalistic' studies can be taken as not going beyond the surface of the problems. They may indicate 'that in given social systems there are monogamous families or that nuclear family units prevail, while in another society there are more polygamous or patriarchal families', but they reveal nothing about relationships among variables affecting such phenomena. In their turn, 'a-prioric-centralistic' and also 'theoretical-federalistic' studies, though precisely addressed to examine such relationships among variables, impinge on to the most severe of all problems: that of the 'homogeneous' or 'non-homogeneous' character of the variables under scrutiny and of the systems within which these interact (1974: 108–9).

Needless to say, a number of questions could be raised about this classification. 'A-prioric-centralistic' and 'theoretical-federalistic' comparative studies, for example, look quite similar, though Podgórecki seems to suggest that theory should be pre-existing in the former and rather be induced from verified hypotheses in the latter. Indeed, theory can ultimately deal, in both types, mainly with systems and variables being more or less 'homogeneous'. Again, it can be questioned whether it might ever be possible, even in 'theoretical-federalistic' comparisons, to draw 'theoretical' hypotheses not referring to prior knowledge, though open to further modification and reorientation.

Such questions can, however, be put aside in this context. Actually, the purpose of using this classification is exactly that of showing how comparative studies in sociology of law, perhaps for a measure of natural scholarly prudence, have increasingly been addressed towards the 'diagnostic-federalistic' model rather than towards the 'theoretical' models, be they 'a-prioric-centralistic' or 'federalistic'. To be more precise, one could say that the more general and abstract the concepts, the more 'federalistic' and 'diagnostic' the comparison which employs or implies them.

Phenomena which can be circumscribed and defined in a *relatively* easy way can give rise to good research projects which may even be defined as 'centralistic', since they adopt the same basic notions and gather empirical evidence on variables which are considered as 'homogeneous' through making a priori reference to a theory. One example is the recent investigation on 'litigation rates', the relative homogeneity of which was secured by the systems compared, all in Western Europe, being juridically, politically and economically similar (Blankenburg, 1989).

Once social phenomena increase in complexity and become less definable through higher range theorizing, the tendency toward federalism, of the diagnostic type, becomes more pronounced. In the strict socio-legal field, for example, we find projects like that on 'informal justice' (Abel, 1982) or that on the legal profession (Abel and Lewis, 1988), which gave rise to research of a typically 'localistic' approach. Not only contexts, but also basic concepts appeared so difficult to reduce to elementary common characteristics, that researchers of different nationalities felt obliged to proceed separately, whereas the central project organizers, in their comprehensive reports, had to confine themselves to a purely qualitative kind of comparison, although relying on (locally gathered) empirical evidence.

Similar experiences are found within anthropology of law. For example, the studies conducted in the framework of the Berkeley Village Law Project, addressed as they were to studying the disputing process in different societies, actually adopted common concepts and methods: suffice it to mention the notion of dispute, seen as an empirical unit capable of revealing the 'legal' phenomenon, and the 'village approach', whereby disputes were studied through a direct ethnographic observation of little communities. Notwithstanding this common orientation, the single studies developed autonomously and monographically: this being a consequence (one might say) not only of the basically ethnographic method, but also of the more or less explicit intention of the scholars not to venture into the field of theoretical pre-definitions, including that of law (Nader and Todd, 1979). It must be stressed that here we are talking about a study which was especially influential in stimulating intercultural reflection: a research which is indeed on the threshold between centralism and theoretical federalism.

Studies conceived to cross that threshold, though they may be stimulated by brilliant theorizing (see, for example, Gulliver, 1979) seem to face virtually insurmountable obstacles of a methodological kind. The so called 'LEG project', launched in 1976 by the Institute of Sociology of Law for Europe, can serve as an example. The project's aim was certainly ambitious and at least implicitly 'central-istic': studying the disputing process in a variety of 'local legal systems', according to theoretical hypotheses derived from such scholars as Eugen Ehrlich or Leon Petrazycki, who examined those norm sets which are 'spontaneously', or 'intuitively', produced by primary social groups or communities.[1] The 'system' approach, however, was immediately questioned and put aside by reasons, as usual, of homogeneity of the contexts examined. The project was thus reconceptualized under the label of 'local use of law'. But the idea of localism (common, it should be stressed, to that adopted by Nader and Todd) also seemed inapplicable to countries in which the various 'localities' showed a high degree of integration within their respective overall national societies. A new title was then found, 'Law and Dispute Treatment', expressing the researchers' common interest towards 'alternative' types of justice, while still allowing them to adopt very different approaches. Two 'cluster groups' were formed at this stage, one addressed to studying intuitive law in pre-modern small communities, the other focusing on specific 'life areas', typically modern, like that of consumer protection. By no means, however, was the rush toward extreme federalism exhausted. The first volume on the inquiry appeared in 1983 with a number of rigorously monographic pilot studies and was explicitly addressed by the editors, in a provocative introduction, to question the explanatory power of the concept of 'dispute', the last mark of the project's original unity. This concept was defined as 'empirical' and *therefore* 'idealistic', by no means fitting in with 'qualitatively' different contexts, like 'capitalist' or 'transitional' societies (Cain and Kulcsár, 1983). It should be stressed that behind this definition was precisely the claim that a (Marxist) theory, 'pre-existing' as in the case of 'centralistic' comparative studies, ought to be adopted. However, the effect of this claim, for a renewed paradox, was such that the 'federalistic' character of the inquiry was highly accentuated, also for the multiplicity of theories that the various researchers came to adopt or to imply at the end of the project.

Problems of 'Vertical' and 'Horizontal' Comparison

Does the discussion above imply that some kind of untheoretical or multitheoretical federalism must be the inevitable outcome of a comparative inquiry in sociology of law?

It may well be so. As stated before, making comparisons is even more difficult in sociology of law than in jurisprudence, because the countless variables which characterize the social context within which law operates add innumerable problems to those which commonly puzzle comparative lawyers. Indeed, the way to comparison seems to be barred from two sides, which can be defined, very roughly, but in some way classically (Friedman, 1975), as 'vertical' and 'horizontal'. 'Vertical' comparison, as it is meant here, concerns social contexts showing a very different level of economic and technological development (Felstiner, 1974). 'Horizontal' comparison, in its turn, is concerned with social contexts sharing a relatively similar level of economic and technological development, but largely differing in their development, their production organization, their political regime and other relevant characteristics.

Let us examine some of the problems which arise with regard to both kinds of comparison, in the specific domain of sociology of law. As far as 'vertical' comparison is concerned (and this kind of comparison, it should be stressed, is also conceivable *within* a single political entity – for example, between the 'official' state law and the 'intuitive' or 'folk' law of a particular community), it is notoriously hard to find an agreement, though on stipulative bases, on the very notion of 'law'. In highly developed societies, even in the idea of lay people, law seems to coincide with prescriptions enacted authoritatively by a governing body. Abiding or deviant behaviour seems to reflect complex attitudes *towards* the law, since people, who are distinctively separate from the ruling elite, look at law as a separate thing, a matter of like and dislike, of agreement and disagreement. Claims are addressed to the political authority and, in turn, the latter's decisions are expressed in the legitimizing form of law, whether already existing or just projected or promised. Law appears, in any case, to be a matter of bargaining (Tomeo, 1981; Febbrajo, 1988a, 1988b) and is a highly abstract and symbolic medium. On the other side, in simpler, developing or anyway 'closed' traditional societies (or better communities, to go back to the classical Toenniesian concept), law seems to coincide with custom, with factual regularity in social behaviour. Political authorities, whatever their characters and the origins of their power, are looked at as depositaries and interpreters of that *factum* which is felt as binding. Deviance is often perceived as a sort of unnatural anomaly: therefore, if law is again conceived as a rule, or a pattern of behaviour, abstraction and symbolism seem to get rarefied. It is now, rather, a scholarly task to construct symbols which may express that *factum* within the 'developed' society which only communicates through abstractions.

Communication in itself is another difficult problem in 'vertical' comparisons. A scholar is part of the developed society under study, even though he or she may not share its language or culture. His or her work is addressed to recording symbols which were produced and crystallized by human interaction, prior to his or her intervention. Such symbols are later translated into the language of the scholar's own discipline.[2] In simpler or developing societies, the role of the scholar is basically different. As already remembered, the scholar must construct linguistic symbols which may reflect the 'internal' vision of the studied reality, as it is transmitted to her or him by native people, and *then* translate them into a technical-scientific lexicon. Two steps are to be taken and the scholar has to face the difficult task of *choosing* a linguistic code. It may make no sense to 'translate' into technical legal terms a 'juridical reality' which does not express itself in written form.[3] At the same time it is very difficult to elaborate a specific code which may technically express concepts claiming a scientific status. In fact, all descriptions of so-called 'primitive' societies reflect this multiplicity of levels of perception-communication. The lack of a sophisticated level of social and critical self-representation may obviously lead to serious misunderstandings (incidentally, it should not be excluded that the idea itself that power and law are less closely connected in those contexts might well be one of them), although it may even facilitate the scholar's task in some cases.

Turning to 'horizontal' comparison, the obstacles do not seem any less severe. Again, the concept of law is the basic source of problems. Legal systems are manifold and reflect highly different cultures, traditions, kinds of power organization, doctrinal styles of study and interpretation (Losano, 1988). Custom can be considered as a significant example of such diversity. Customary law, which is the most representative symbol of 'primitive' societies, sneaks into developed societies in ways which never cease to astonish experienced researchers.[4] It can be argued that its impact is reflected differently by different kinds of political power structures and, obviously, by the different characters assumed by any single legal system. Whereas in statutory law it is relatively easy to admit the idea of renewal, on the basis of legislative acts (Kulcsár, 1987; Pocar, 1988), it is well known that in common law systems the question is intriguing: how to reconcile the idea of legal change, if brought about through judicial activity, with the *stare decisis* principle?

The problems which concern other variables, directly or indirectly influencing law, are no less worrying. The most relevant case, already referred to above, is that of social conflict, a category which appears to be closely linked with law, from whatever ideological position one might look at the matter.[5] Especially in the Marxist tradition, conflict is seen as basically different, in qualitative terms, if recurring in societies showing a different mode of production. As Cain and Kulcsár argue, in 'capitalist' societies conflict is assumed to be essentially of a class nature, collective, structural and not removable unless the whole economic order is changed. By contrast, in societies 'in transition toward socialism', conflict is purported to be essentially individual, contingent and removable within the system, which *per se* is addressed to its final suppression. Such arguments (which stem from an a priori and unquestionable theoretical choice – that the 'mode of production' is the primary notion, enjoying an absolute explanatory power) (Cain and Kulcsár, 1983: 19) suggest that no comparison can be carried through between capitalist and socialist countries, although both types of countries showed very similar conditions only a few decades ago.

We do not need to insist any further, at this point, on describing the difficulties which are commonly encountered along the way of socio-legal comparison. It should be clear that such difficulties so often concern even the primary notions which any comparison should stem from: law, state, power, economic organization, normative sources, conflict and other concepts of the same scope. Since such general concepts seem to change their meaning according to the different theories within which they are employed, it seems, therefore, particularly difficult to imagine that scholars may come to those semantic agreements which only allow wide and rigorous comparison.

Difficulties stemming from the obstacles mentioned should not be underestimated. However, comparative studies within sociology of law ought to meet the challenges. This is all the more important because jurisprudence itself, which deals with the same topic – namely, law – seems to have taken the road of centralistic unity, in at least two ways. On the one hand, law itself tends to become uniform. Modern legal systems become increasingly similar despite traditional differences, being shaped by lawgivers whose background and purposes are, in turn, increasingly comparable all around the world. Social actors – employers and unions, judges and arbitration courts – are even more influential in this respect, since they tend nowadays to behave according to very uniform patterns, and actually 'create' uniform law (Friedman, 1975). On the other hand, comparative lawyers, engaged in making their analytical tools more and more sophisticated, seem to be increasingly convinced that general concepts, traditionally looked at as semantically too ambiguous to be comparable, have in fact much more in common than it was ever supposed. In Max Rheinstein's words:

it is an impressive experience to realize how little the private systems of the world differ from one another. Wide divergencies exist in public law, between private enterprise countries and socialist countries. In the latter, the field of private law is narrower than in the former, but insofar as private law exists, it is of striking similarity, irrespective of whether the country is one of free enterprise or of socialist planning, whether it is democratic or authoritarian. (Rheinstein, 1972: 6)

The picture remains virtually unchanged when we leave the field of private law. The concept of 'access to justice' (Cappelletti, 1982), though general, has become a true meeting point between comparative lawyers of different cultures (Cappelletti et al., 1978–79): and here we have, also, a significant bridge notion between law and the social sciences.

Is it possible to imagine that, through increased sophistication in methods, sociology of law may discover that each of its own general concepts can also be brought to a common semantic core, so that theoretical comparability might be allowed?

William M. Evan, a protagonist in the recent revival of sociology of law, takes Rheinstein's opinion as a starting point to express his optimism about 'the potentialities for a possibly fruitful intersection of interests between comparative law and the sociology of law'. He proposes to define comparable general concepts through the construction of indicators expressing middle-range empirical uniformities and hypotheses. According to Evan, a content analysis of laws existing in various countries can allow us to construct common indicators through which concepts expressing the traditional sectors of law could be compared empirically. He refers to and tries to define 'private law', 'corporation law', 'labour law', 'inheritance law', 'tax law', 'family law' and 'criminal law' (Evan, 1984: 52 ff.). For example, what is called 'property law' in various systems becomes comparable through indicators which may express 'the degree to which propertied classes are favored over propertyless classes' (for example, in landlord–tenant or landowner–peasant relationships) and the 'degree of protection of private ownership of property vs. public ownership of property'. Comparison in 'labour law', in its turn, should be based on indicators expressing 'the degree to which workers' rights are institutionalized to unionize, to bargain collectively, to protect themselves against arbitrary and capricious treatment by management, and to strike'; the 'degree to which unions are made responsible to their members'; the 'degree of protection of management's control over corporate decisions' (Evan, 1984: 53).

Without going into a critical scrutiny of these theses, suffice it to say that Evan's proposals seem fruitful since they suggest fulfilling the apparently modest duty to make linguistic expressions compatible, and then comparable, through the use of formulations which may be translated into unambiguous symbols. Obviously, it would be easy to observe that the most general concepts – 'private', 'public' and, first and foremost, 'law' – must still be defined. Hence, agreements on definitions of these concepts must be found as well, before proceeding further on the way of comparison.

For an Analytical Reconstruction of 'Law' as a Socio-legal Concept

Agreements on how to define concepts, in the social sciences, can only be reached through the help of the analytical method, this being a precondition for both empirical use and comparison. The basic problem is to disclose those misunderstandings which stem from terminological ambiguity and, subsequently, to build up a common and unambiguous lexicon, which might be used by scholars for drawing middle-range, testable hypotheses. It should be added that clearness in terminology is all the more necessary once we accept that the choice of theoretical concepts comes prior to drawing such hypotheses. No one, in today's epistemology, would deny theoretical concepts showing a degree of arbitrariness. Indeed, they are but 'instruments of human activity, found out and shaped according to needs' (Scarpelli, 1985: 41), in view of knowing a 'reality' which includes men themselves and is also a consequence of their own representations, but does not coincide with either thing.

The concept of law is no exception to this. Law has given rise to so many definitions throughout centuries of philosophical thinking, that an agreement on what should be meant by this word has recurrently appeared a hopeless venture to many scholars. On the other hand, this concept is so frequently recurrent in scientific discourse that defining it becomes a stringent necessity and, one should stress, not only for the sake of intercultural comparison. Indeed the concept is also central in all kind of analyses within one single culture.

The question may prove, in some ways, simpler than it is generally supposed to be, since it shows a basically terminological nature (Williams, 1956). If we admit that 'the justification for a concept of law does not reside in its existence outside the human mind, but in its value as an analytic, heuristic device' (Pospísil, 1971: 19), it does not seem impossible to *agree* on a concept, then on a definition of law, which might be sociologically acceptable. The problem, in this perspective, is twofold. On the one hand, as already remembered, it is a question of choosing, to some extent even artificially, among current lexical meanings; on the other hand, there is the need for not departing too much from the most common and socially practised use of the word. The outcome of this procedure is an 'explanatory' definition of the concept, as it has been termed (Jori, 1983).

General theory of law offers the best starting point for this venture, even if we search for a sociological definition of law, on two conditions: that, first, no unconditioned commitment is made to any single school's one-sided view, as Treves has repeatedly warned (1947, 1961, 1988), and that, second, the accepted definition might be adapted to empirical hypotheses concerned with law in action; that is, as a variable amongst variables.

A number of the characteristics commonly recognized as 'essential' to law by jurists, although from diverse viewpoints, might seem to fit in with this goal (Ferrari, 1989). Law may be taken to be 'normative', which means, sociologically, that it consists of symbolized models of (purportedly) 'due' behaviour (Wróblewski, 1988), communicated as messages (Jackson, 1985) in social interaction. Such messages may be described as 'heteronomous' in the Kantian tradition (Ross, 1968), since they are the consequence of social actors trying to limit their action's scope reciprocally. They may be considered, further, as 'institutional', since they belong to a socially recognized system pretending to be all-embracing (Kelsen, 1960; Bobbio, 1960), and also 'hypothetical', in that they are functionally conceived to induce people to act on impulse of a threat (Kelsen, 1934, 1960) or of a promise (Aubert, 1983, 1984; Bobbio, 1977). Finally, they are potentially subject to the judgement of 'third parties' called on to decide, through specific decision-making processes, or, if we prefer, 'secondary rules' (Hart, 1961; Ross, 1958), whether action was such that threatened or promised reaction ought to follow (Carbonnier, 1978).

This definition should not appear too syncretistic. By no means does it try to suggest what the 'essence' of law is. Rather, it is only intended to be a 'heuristic device', as Pospísil says. It is more explanatory than, strictly speaking, stipulative, but it stresses, at the same time, that some major doctrinal contrasts between law theorists might probably be overruled, at least from an 'external' and sociological viewpoint, precisely because these contrasts seem to concern more the words used in definitions than the concepts defined. Reference can be made, first, to the opposition between 'normativism' (seeing law as a set of norms), and 'institutionalism' (seeing it as social organization); second, to the contrast between, again, 'normativism', as above defined, and 'legal realism', according to which law is not norm, but rather fact; third, the opposition between formalism, which sees law as coinciding with formal expressions entailing general precepts, and 'anti-formalism', which describes it as a product of largely free and discretionary activity of authorities who proclaim it on a concrete level.

In fact, sociologically speaking, we may agree on law 'being' all these things. Law 'is' norm *and* fact and the norm itself 'is' a fact; it 'is' a set of precepts *and* a symbol of the social organization and values to which they are referred; it 'is' a product of *both* general and special normative activity, partially or sometimes (perceived as) free, and partially or sometimes (perceived as) binding. These terms are therefore not, by necessity, reciprocally incompatible. Rather, as Williams (1956) said, they can be translated into detailed hypotheses which a scholar should be able to test empirically. One can ask, for example, the following questions. What is the status of norms that exist only on paper, but remain unimplemented or forgotten in practice? To what extent is there a coincidence between the kind of 'legal consciousness' which prevails amongst a social group and its representation in official laws and legal texts? To what extent do concrete judges feel to be bound by law? To what extent are they conscious of their own freedom to choose between contrasting interpretations? To what extent do they conceal their own values behind a formal homage to law? Which rhetorical arguments do they use for that purpose?

With regard to this definition of law, doubts can obviously be cast about its fitting in with any conceivable human society – this being, apparently, a condition for the concept's value in comparative studies.

The most serious problems, in this respect, are linked to the concept of 'norm', or 'rule', especially if we think of a norm as an expression of heteronomy and, no less, if law is taken as basically connected with some eventual 'judicial' activity. The former idea might seem to imply that a large number of more or less mechanically repeated customary behaviours should be excluded from the field of law, while the latter might be taken as suggesting that law should be reduced, quite restrictively, to the structures and functions of a 'judicial system'. In fact, such problems do not seem insuperable in the light of recent theorizing in both theory of law and sociology of law.

The doubts which could be raised about the assertion that law has a 'normative' and 'heteronomous' character might be dispelled once we describe a rule, quite simply, as a message conveying a model of uniform and constant behaviour. This is a view which is suggested to sociologists by an interactionist approach, ready to recognize the importance, in human communication, of symbolic means of 'persuasion', as they are analysed by the *Nouvelle rhétorique* theorists (Perelman and Olbrechts-Tyteca, 1958). Such models are actually recognizable in all societies, although sometimes they might be socially *communicated* as bare facts (in the sense of 'this is what has always been done', so common, according to legal anthropologists, within 'primitive' societies). But even in these cases, there is no reason to deny their 'juridical' nature. Rather, this kind of description, which sees law as mere factual regularity of behaviour, only reveals, generally, that the concerned people's mentality does not even admit hypothetically the idea of such models being infringed. But the fact that a *model* is communicated implies the idea of its being 'binding' to a certain extent: and this brings us back again to the most common concept of law.

Doubts arising with regard to legal rules being eventually submissible to judgement might perhaps be dispelled once it is recognized that what really matters is not the stereotype of a judge as we are accustomed to conceive of it (tradition teaches, for instance, that a judge is a third party not involved in the conflict, whereas biased judges, essentially sentencing for their own sake, seem to be exceedingly frequent), but rather the activity – that is, the judgement itself. The idea that a legal rule is hypothetical – that is, expressed in the classical Kelsenian form 'if . . . then' – implies the idea of a doubt followed by a decision (did the condition occur? if so, which consequence ought to, and might, follow?). It does not matter, in other words, who judges and how. What matters is, rather, that there *may be* a judgement, that there may be someone who raises a doubt and actually decides upon it, that there is a gap between action and reaction, also chronologically. This wide conception, which is obviously intended to exclude immediate, impulsive reactions (as in the case of mob lynching) from the field of 'legal' behaviour, again, seems to be applicable to a wide range of societies, 'vertically' or 'horizontally' comparable.

Not only one, but three general socio-legal concepts might, at this point, have been brought back to the sphere of comparability: the law, the norm (or rule) and the judgement. The terminological and conceptual analysis has apparently extended their semantic area, but it is easy to understand that the plurality of specific elements that have been added to certain terms (let us again think of 'law') turns into a true restriction. A phenomenon, in short, is more circumscribed whilst it is seen as occurring in a wider set of social contexts than we may usually admit.

Counterarguments

What has been said so far, though suggesting on the one hand that we can proceed in the way of comparable general concepts, might on the other hand impinge on a charge which is highly feared by analysts: that the concepts proposed are so all-embracing that they conceal any relevant difference and, with it, the 'reality' itself which should be disclosed.

Another charge might point to an alleged 'high range' nature of the concepts proposed for an analytical reconstruction, which was explicitly conceived and proposed in view of using them to build up empirically testable 'middle-range' hypotheses. Such an argument would indicate that there is a fundamental discrepancy between the proposals described and an approach which shows a Mertonian profile.

Last but not least, a third kind of criticism, often put forward by 'globalist' or 'holistic' theorists, might anyway remain: that the adoption of such general concepts, though well-defined for the sake of empirical hypotheses, conceals the 'qualitative' character of the distinction between phenomena.

It would obviously be pretentious to counter such kinds of criticism with sound arguments in a short space. The following statements will, therefore, appear to some extent apodictic.

A tentative answer to the first criticism might be that the adoption of general formulations, analytically defined, by no means prevents the researcher from drawing up distinctions *within* concepts, so that more limited fragments of reality can be recognized and classified: this being in itself of analytical value. Indeed, this is being done continuously, also with reference to concepts like the ones which have been discussed. Suffice it to mention, in the field of legal theory, the contributions of Bobbio (1958) or Conte (1983) on norms and, on a more purely socio-legal level, those of Eckhoff (1966), Abel (1974), Kurczewski (1983) and Ost (1983) on judges and judgements. Needless to say, other basic concepts could be produced as examples, from the legal system to sanctions, from the functions of law to legitimation. A scientist's task is precisely that of distinguishing between phenomena, although they might belong to the same class. So, the fact that general concepts, accurately defined for a heuristic purpose, be drawn up, is simply a way to facilitate communication. Once that has been stated, it can easily be admitted that law is differently shaped in autocratic and in democratic societies, in *laissez-faire* and in collective economic systems. These are major variables to be taken into account in comparisons. But the fact that phenomena may be referred back to common categories, although it may sometimes be misleading (categories are not given, as is often argued, but should be themselves falsifiable and modifiable), brings with it other advantages, beyond easier communication. First, it teaches us to mistrust radical theoretical oppositions, which are, so often, artificially constructed (Maggi, 1977). There are many intermediate forms between market and collective economy. Between democracy and autocracy, there exist many intermediate kinds of regimes, which easily blend, and even turn, into one another. In fact, extreme concepts are but ideal types, while belief in their being 'real' is, by definition, a pure form of idealism. Second, unitary concepts help recognize the endeavours which are made to persuade people that substantial changes have occurred in correspondence with changes in terminology. Quite paradoxically, there are 'names' which actually induce unmasking nominalism.

On the second question, concerning the more or less 'high range' of our discourse, a sharp distinction must be drawn between the range of concepts and the range of the hypotheses put forward for empirical testing and, consequently, of the theories which are derived from them. What Robert Merton refused was the high range of the latter, not of the former. His criticism was especially addressed against 'the all-inclusive speculations comprising a master conceptual scheme from which it is hoped to derive a very large number of empirically observed uniformities of social behavior' (Merton, 1951: 5). What makes such speculations unscientific is essentially the countless number of variables, most of them undefined or ideologically biased, which they are expected to encompass. On the other hand, it was not Merton's proposal to challenge the concepts *per se*, though general. The author himself used general concepts, like role, status, or anomie, in his endeavours to construct theories of the middle range. It is actually doubtful that there might be any scientific assertion, in sociology, not implying the use of at least one general concept, like that of law which we have been considering. Conflict, power, mode of production, integration, institution, structure, function: the list has no end.

The answer will be all the more apodictic in dealing, finally, with the old dilemma of 'quality' versus 'quantity'; that is, the third criticism likely to be addressed to this plea for an analytical construction of comparable general concepts. Rather than provide an answer, one can raise questions, again, about the meaning of the words used. Is it not true that 'quality' and 'quantity' are, again, but mere ideal types? Is it not true that 'quantification' is but a method by which better precision is sought in the description of 'qualitative' variations and distinctions? Does any 'quantitative' change not corresponding to a 'qualitative' change actually exist? Is the label of 'quality' not often used to conceal the fact that, despite efforts, phenomena are not defined with enough precision? Briefly, although it must be admitted that 'quantity' without 'quality' often depicts things as too flat, is it not true that unmeasurable 'quality' is, so often, mere wishful thinking?

Conclusion

The aim of this chapter was to reflect about comparison in sociology of law and, especially, to examine some of the problems connected with a comparative adoption of general concepts which are typical of this discipline. The author's main contention was that no theoretical comparison is possible, in the social science, unless reference is made to concepts entailing a general status, and that the only chance to make such concepts truly comparable consists of submitting them, first of all, to an analytical scrutiny.

Certainly, the analytical method is not a panacea. It should not lead us to forget concrete questions lying behind definitions, nor does it permit us to solve fundamental problems once for all. This may be immediately demonstrated by using the example of law, a concept which was chosen, symbolically and somewhat provocatively, because of its absolute centrality: it is obvious that other definitions might be opposed, with sound arguments, to the one which is proposed here. However, the analytical method, as repeatedly stressed by neo-positivistic philosophy, helps avoid the danger of yielding to metaphysics, for it shows that concepts are not given, but rather chosen, and that disagreements often concern expressions rather than ideas. Briefly, it shows that there is a gap between substance and words.

Such confusion, which is especially easy in the field of comparisons, is a concrete threat for the social sciences, whether they are leaning towards extreme empiricism or towards extreme conceptualism.

Notes

This chapter is dedicated to the late Professor Giovanni Tarello. I wish to thank Mr Pete Kercher for revising the original English text.

1. The proposal for this project was put forward by Jacek Kurczewski in an initial paper entitled 'Local Legal Systems as a Research Object' (European Coordination Centre of Research and Documentation in the Social Sciences, Vienna, 1976).

2. Specific problems are obviously raised in sociology of law, since scholars are here confronted with a special, somewhat artificial, lexicon, constructed by jurists for use in their own discourse. On the linguistics of law and legal science (and on law as a 'language' in itself), the literature is very rich in both theory and sociology of law. For the former viewpoint see, among many other works, the essays collected by Scarpelli (1976); for the latter, see the controversy on law's being more or less 'self-referential', as Niklas Luhmann says, cf. Teubner (1987, 1988).

3. A renowned Italian example of this kind of 'translation', certainly intended to be somewhat provocative *vis-à-vis* a hyperstatalist legal culture, was offered by a

Sardinian scholar, Antonio Pigliaru, who worded in sophisticated legal lexicon the unwritten rules of the so-called 'vendetta barbaricina', the traditional legal order practised in Barbagia (Pigliaru, 1968). Let one example suffice: 'la vendetta deve essere eseguita solo allorché si è conseguita oltre ogni dubbio possibile la certezza circa l'esistenza della responsabilità a titolo di dolo da parte dell'agente' ('vengeance shall be carried out only after having established the certainty beyond all reasonable doubt that the agent is responsible for the fact in the presence of *mens rea*') (1968: 116).

4. It is impressive, for instance, how various examples of common exploitation of land, alternative to private ownership, have survived in Italy, despite economic change and a number of endeavours made by law-givers, starting very early in the last century, to abolish or, at least, severely limit them. Common rights of various kinds have not been abolished, against the formal provisions of an *ad hoc* Act adopted in 1924, in about one-fifth of the Sardinian territory (Ferrari, 1983; Masia, 1989). Six 'partecipanze agrarie', authentic legal sub-systems of hundreds or even thousands of partners cyclically exploiting pieces of communal land, still legally exist in Emilia Romagna as they did centuries ago (Bassanelli, 1979). The South Tyrolean *Hof*, an individually owned farm using the neighbouring woods in common with other farms, is still legally and obligatorily inherited by the first-born despite the system of *partage forcé* which has been enforced in continental Europe in the last two centuries (Frassoldati, 1963; Pospísil, 1971).

5. It is significant, although to a certain extent quite obvious, to note that *both* the theories of social integration (*à la* Parsons) *and* the theories of conflict (from Marx to Gumplowicz, from Weber to Dahrendorf) stress the relationship between conflict and law.

References

Abel, Richard L. (1974) 'A Comparative Theory of Dispute Institutions in Society', *Law and Society Review*, 8: 217–347.

Abel, Richard L. (ed.) (1982) *The Politics of Informal Justice*, New York: Academic Press.

Abel, Richard L. and Philip S.C. Lewis (eds) (1988) *Lawyers in Society*, 2 vols, Berkeley–Los Angeles: University of California Press.

Aubert, Vilhelm (1983) *In Search of Law: Sociological Approaches to Law*. Oxford: Martin Robertson.

Aubert, Vilhelm (1984) 'Punishment, Reward and Human Rights', pp. 77–105 in U. Scarpelli and V. Tomeo (eds), *Società, norme e valori. Studi in onore di Renato Treves*. Milan: Giuffré.

Bassanelli, Luigi (1979) *Le partecipanze agrarie emiliane*. Milan: Angeli.

Blankenburg, Erhard (ed.) (1989) *Prozessflut? Indikatorenvergleich von Rechtskulturen auf dem europäischen Kontinent*. Cologne: Bundesanzeiger.

Bobbio, Norberto (1958) *Teoria della norma giuridica*. Turin: Giappichelli.

Bobbio, Norberto (1960) *Teoria dell'ordinamento giuridico*. Turin: Giappichelli.

Bobbio, Norberto (1977) *Dalla struttura alla funzione: nuovi studi di teoria del diritto*. Milan: Comunità.

Cain, Maureen and Kálmán Kulcsár (eds) (1983) *The Study of Disputes*. Budapest: Akadémiai Kiadó.

Cappelletti, Mauro (1982) 'Accesso alla giustizia come programma di riforma e come metodo di pensiero', *Rivista di diritto processuale*, 2: 233–45.

Cappelletti, Mauro, Brian Garth, John Weisner and Klaus F. Koch (1978–79) *Access to Justice*. 4 vols. Milan–Alphen aan der Rijn: Giuffré-Sijthoff and Noordhoff.

Carbonnier, Jean (1978) *Sociologie juridique*. Paris: A. Colin (first published 1972).

Conte, Amedeo G. (1983) 'Regola costitutiva, condizione, antinomia', pp. 21–39 in U. Scarpelli *La teoria generale del diritto: problemi e tendenze attuali. Studi dedicati a Norberto Bobbio*. Milan: Comunità.

Eckhoff, Torstein (1966) 'The Mediator, the Judge, and the Administrator in Conflict Resolution', *Acta Sociologica*: 148–72.

Evan, William M. (1984) 'Macrosociology and Sociology of Law', pp. 23–59 in U. Scarpelli and V. Tomeo (eds), *Società, norme e valori. Studi in onore di Renato Treves*. Milan: Giuffré.

Febbrajo, Alberto (1988a) 'From Hierarchical to Circular Model: Some Introductory Remarks', pp. 3–22 in *European Yearbook in the Sociology of Law*, 1. Milan: Giuffré.

Febbrajo, Alberto (1988b) 'Appunti socio-giuridici sul "gioco" della concertazione', *Sociologia del diritto*, XV (1): 7–19.

Felstiner, William L. (1974) 'Influences of Social Organization on Dispute Processing', *Law and Society Review*, 9 (1): 63–94.

Ferrari, Vincenzo (1983) 'Reazione e pratica sociale in tema di usi civici: osservazioni sociologico-giuridiche', *Sociologia del diritto*, X (1): 61–94.

Ferrari, Vincenzo (1989) *Funzioni del diritto: saggio critico-ricostruttivo*. Roma–Bari: Laterza (first published 1987).

Frassoldati, Carlo (1963) *Il maso chiuso e le comunità agrario-forestali dell'Alto Adige*. Milan: Giuffré.

Friedman, Lawrence M. (1975) *The Legal System: a Social Science Perspective*. New York: Russell Sage.

Gulliver, Philip H. (1979) *Disputes and Negotiations: a Cross-cultural Perspective*. New York: Academic Press.

Hart, Herbert L.A. (1961) *The Concept of Law*. Oxford: Clarendon Press.

Jackson, Bernard S. (1985) *Semiotics and Legal Theory*. London: Routledge & Kegan Paul.

Jori, Mario (1974) 'Il giurista selvaggio: un contributo alla metodologia della descrizione sociale', *Sociologia del diritto*, I (1): 85–108.

Jori, Mario (1983) 'Oggetto e metodo della scienza giuridica', pp. 177–229 in U. Scarpelli (ed.) *La teoria generale del diritto. Problemi e tendenze attuali. Studi dedicati a Norberto Bobbio*. Milan: Comunità.

Kelsen, Hans (1934) *Reine Rechtslehre: Einleitung in die rechtswissenschaftliche Problematik*. Vienna: Franz Deuticke Verlag.

Kelsen, Hans (1960) *Reine Rechtslehre*. Vienna: Franz Deuticke Verlag.

Kulcsár, Kálmán (1987) *Modernization and Law (Theses and Thoughts)*. Budapest: Academy of Sciences.

Kurczewski, Jacek (1983) 'Dispute and its Settlement', pp. 224–40 in M. Cain and K. Kulcsár (eds), *The Study of Disputes*. Budapest: Akadémiai Kiadó.

Losano, Mario G. (1988) *I grandi sistemi giuridici contemporanei: introduzione ai diritti europei ed extraeuropei*. Turin: Einaudi (first published 1978).

Luhmann, Niklas, (1988) 'The Sociological Observation of the Theory and the Practice of Law', pp. 23–42 in *European Yearbook in the Sociology of Law*, 1. Milan: Giuffré.

Maggi, Bruno (1977) *Organizzazione: teoria e metodo. Guida all'indagine sui problemi organizzativi*. Milan: ISEDI.

Masia, Michelina (1989) 'Il controllo dell'uso della terra', doctoral thesis, Università di Milano.

Merton, Robert K. (1951) *Social Theory and Social Structure*. Glencoe, IL: Free Press (first published 1949).

Nader, L. and H.F. Todd (1979) *The Disputing Process – Law in Ten Societies*. New York: Columbia University Press.

Ost, François (1983) 'Juge-pacificateur, juge-arbitre, juge-entraîneur: trois modèles de justice', in Ph. Gérard, François Ost and M. van de Kerchove (eds), *Fonction de juger et pouvoir judiciaire. Transformations et déplacements*. Bruxelles, Publications des Facultés Universitaires Saint-Louis.

Perelman, Chaïm and Lucie Olbrechts-Tyteca (1958) *Traité de l'argumentation*. Paris: Presses Universitaires de France.

Pigliaru, Antonio (1968) *Il banditismo in Sardegna: la vendetta barbaricina*. Milan: Giuffré (1st edn 1959, *La vendetta barbaricina come ordinamento giuridico*, Milan: Giuffré).

Pocar, Valerio (1988) *Norme giuridiche e norme sociali: lezioni di sociologia del diritto*. Milan: Unicopli.

Podgórecki, Adam (1974) *Law and Society*. London: Routledge & Kegan Paul.

Pospísil, Leopold (1971) *Anthropology of Law: A Comparative Theory*. New York: Harper & Row.

Rheinstein, Max (1972) *Marriage Stability: Divorce and the Law*. Chicago, IL: University of Chicago Press.

Ross, Alf (1957) 'Tû-tû', *Harvard Law Review*, 70: 812–25.

Ross, Alf (1958) *On Law and Justice*. London: Steven & Sons.

Ross, Alf (1968) *Directives and Norms*. London.

Scarpelli, Uberto (ed.) (1976) *Diritto e analisi del linguaggio*. Milan: Comunità.

Scarpelli, Uberto (ed.) (1983) *La teoria generale del diritto: problemi e tendenze attuali. Studi dedicati a Norberto Bobbio*. Milan: Comunità.

Scarpelli, Uberto (1985) *Contributo alla semantica del linguaggio normativo*. Re-edited by A. Pintore. Milan: Giuffré (first published 1959, Turin: Memorie dell'Accademia delle Scienze).

Scarpelli, Uberto and Vincenzo Tomeo (eds) (1984) *Società, norme e valori. Studi in onore di Renato Treves*. Milan: Giuffré.

Teubner, Gunther (1987) *Autopoietic Law: A New Approach to Legal Theory*. Berlin: de Gruyter.

Teubner, Gunther (1988) 'Hypercycle in Law and Organization: the Relationship Between Self-observation, Self-constitution and Autopoiesis', pp. 43–79 in *European Yearbook in the Sociology of Law*, 1. Milan: Giuffré.

Tomeo, Vincenzo (1981) *Il diritto come struttura del conflitto*. Milan: Angeli.

Treves, Renato (1947) *Diritto e cultura*. Turin: Giappichelli.

Treves, Renato (1961) *Lezioni di filosofia del diritto*. Milan: La Goliardica.

Treves, Renato (1988) *Sociologia del diritto: origini, tendenze, problemi*. Turin: Einaudi (first published 1987).

Williams, Glanville (1956) 'The Controversy Concerning the Word "Law"', pp. 134–56 in Peter Laslett (ed.), *Philosophy, Politics and Society*. Oxford: Blackwell.

Wróblewski, Jerzy (1988) 'Law and Socio-economic Change: Introductory Observations', *European Yearbook in the Sociology of Law*, 1. Milan: Giuffré, pp. 117–40.

5

Paradigm Crisis and Social Movements: A Latin American Perspective

Fernando Calderon and Alejandro Piscitelli

Trans-national and Trans-societal Research: An Overview

In the nineteenth century, pioneers in statistics, sociology and anthropology were ardent defenders of the comparative method. They made great efforts to create a nucleus of knowledge of international and intercultural validity, bearing in mind the variations in the functioning and development of human societies.

Over time, however, this goal proved difficult to reconcile with the growing demands in the social sciences to submit to more accuracy in scientific analysis. In order to reach this aim, universal comparisons were sacrificed and research was limited to collecting local facts – particularly so in anthropology and sociology – or to abstract non-empirical model building – particularly within economics. As a result, the social disciplines gained in methodological accuracy but had to abandon the systematic knowledge obtained through trans-cultural and trans-national comparisons. The aftermath of this development has been unnerving:

> since Galileo, the quantitative and anti-anthropocentric orientation stemming from the natural sciences, faced the human sciences with an ironclad dilemma: either they had to assume a weak scientific status to arrive at relevant results, or they had to assume a strong scientific status to attain results short in high points. (Guinzburg, 1983: 98)

The self-imposed limitation was evident in the first surges of comparative research. The works of Murdock (1940) on the Human Relations Area Files (HRAF), the comparative studies of the nation-states on their way to industrialization together with the works of Eisenstadt (1963), Bendix (1964) and Lipset (1963); the comparative studies of change and modernization in developing countries by McClelland (1961), Smith and Inkeles (1966) and Almond and Verba (1963), not to mention the works of Osgood (1967) with regard to the trans-cultural value of the semantic differential technique; or the contributions of the Whitings (1966) in putting together normalized calendars to register information on the different ways of educating children from different countries, are only some of the works which attempted to answer – more in an empirical than in a conceptual way – the main questions posed by trans-societal research.

Though many of these works have been influential as models for comparative research, there is little doubt that most of them were lacking both in breadth and scope. There was little indication of which variables were to be compared, what the units of analysis were or to which system level the variables belonged, which categories of hypotheses were to be compared, and which contextual dimensions such a type of analysis should include.

Besides, any real contribution to theory construction in the social sciences should also be related to the epistemological stand the researcher takes concerning the utility of research results and the transforming potential of the studies into social usefulness. Therefore, it depends very much on which epistemological ally a researcher decides to join, as this commitment co-determines attitudes toward diagnosing and making trans-national and trans-societal forecasts.

Research at the trans-national and trans-societal level spans a wide continuum of attitudes. At one extreme are found those researchers for whom all societies can be compared and at least appear as objects to be tested against unified and hypothetical-deductive patterns of universalistic explanations. At the other extreme are found those researchers who claim that each society is culturally and historically unique, and that there is no gain in apprehension by comparing it with other societies.

In the Latin American case the social sciences are undermined when only social knowledge at the regional level is being pursued. This kind of research goes along with the a priori validation of methodologies which are generated in the atmosphere of academic and Eurocentric studies (Strasser, 1977).

However, the comparative tradition of Latin American studies, which takes the region as a specific unit of analysis, has changed over time, in part as a result of theoretical modifications in the way the region has been studied. The starting point for this type of analysis is a double continuity and a double transformation between 'us' and 'the others': the Latin American region exists as an empirical object which differs from all other regions (Africa, Europe, the Latin American national states, and even the different regions within Latin America). This notwithstanding, the Latin American region also maintains a deep common historical identity. This situation implies a methodology which not only feeds on universal classifications but also needs to coin its own categories.

The double-sided relationship of both continuity and discontinuity in the region as compared to other parts of the world leads us to assume the existence of a complex, uncomfortable and enthralling relationship between the Latin American identity and the methodological levels of analysis focusing on it.

Paradigm Crisis and the Challenges of the Future

The new challenges for the social sciences within the Latin American region point to the shortcomings of a methodology which was traditionally understood in terms of a set of criteria and proceedings which allow social scientists to work on factual areas according to their own comprehension of a society. Making theoretical-methodological conceptions suitable to this task requires a radical change.

From the seventies onwards the social sciences have met this challenge and experienced a renewal which has brought about relatively important changes in the agenda of the Latin American social scientists. Some of the background for these changes have been, first, a strong feeling that the ideological traditions based on theoretical and practical orientations – particularly functionalism and Marxism – which for so long provided theoretical legitimacy for social theories, were now relatively exhausted; and second, an epistemological renewal, which started by questioning classical physics – and its dated epistemology through a reassessment of theoretical trans-disciplinary models – particularly second-order cybernetics, and self-reproduction and self-organizing theories (Morin, 1986; Gargani, 1983).

Functionalism and theories of modernization

Modernization and dependency theories, independently or concurrently, inadvertently helped uncover the difficulties, both of a conceptual and of a political nature, which the researcher faced when confronted by contradictory paradigms relating to the validation and legitimation of knowledge.

During the forties and fifties spokesmen for theories of development and modernization were certain that, in the 'peripheral' countries, the internal markets would by themselves be capable of developing their economies, something that in turn would force changes in income distribution. According to these theories policies should be directed towards development concentrated on the acquisition of a technological infrastructure that could promote the diversification of the productive structures. Implied in these policies was also the development and continuation of state interventions. To strengthen and to modernize the state was an important instrument for an efficient development policy, in particular given the fact there were already historical antecedents of national state developments in the Latin American region.

The theory of development transposed the transition problem from underdevelopment to development through the creation of an internal sector, which was supposed to be dynamic enough to obtain growth as well as transference of centres of decision. In the meantime sociologists were trying to explain the process of transition from traditional to modern societies.

Redfield and Hoselitz, as well as Parsons and Merton from a non-Latin American perspective, together with local analysts, amongst them Gino Germani (1971), founder of 'scientific sociology' in Argentina, proclaimed the thesis of structural dualism arguing that Latin American societies belonged to the traditional type and had to become modernized in order to survive. The scheme encapsulated in structural dualism was heavily criticized. Concepts such as traditional and modern (said the critics) were not broad enough to embrace the diverse characteristics of Latin America. The same critics said that the idea of structural dualism neither distinguished between the specific structural components defining the societies under scrutiny, nor revealed the conditions which accounted for the functioning of the societies. Last, but not least, the theory of modernization lacked (they said) a testable relationship between the levels of economic development and the corresponding social structures described in the theory. The theories were criticized also from a methodological standpoint because of their tautological, teleological and ahistorical character. Amongst other things it was argued that the evidence was based on erroneous extrapolation of existing data.

Other critics argued that modernization theories were pro-system and functional for the dominating system, and actually dismissed the possibilities of social change in the name of ready-made modernization. Seen from the critics' side, theories of modernization forced the patterns of political, social and economical systems in Western Europe and the United States upon the future of the underdeveloped societies, thereby making the process of development follow suit to the agenda of the 'central' countries. The feeling was that the major sociological paradigms had been uncritically exported from the great universities to Latin America.

Some facts and some fads about dependency theory
When the theory of dependency was introduced it was intended to debunk modernization theory by changing the focus of interest from traditional/modern polarity to the subordination of the Latin American

countries to the world-wide capitalist system, and by assessing the current approaches to specific political, economical and social realities in Latin America.

The role of dependency theory became important within the region due to epistemological sensitivity towards the drawbacks of the theory of modernization and the will to break with the structuralist agenda. In its classical version the theory of dependency rejected the simplified descriptions provided by the theories of modernization. The rejection was combined with vague philosophical qualms and with a certain lack of critical spirit:

> nowadays, we know that it is not possible to start with a sociology built up from statistical data which is inadequate, or else with an overview of events tied together by a plot masterminded by uncontrolled ideological schemes. These include descriptions of social realities provided by experts which on a final analysis appear as the comparison of countries which were created following historical patterns sustained by the international system of power. (Castells and Cortes, 1972: 14)

The founders of dependency theory called attention to local analysis based on conceptions of science – fostered once more by the ideological apparatuses of the developed countries rather than by the concrete societies in which the researchers themselves lived. This seemed far more important than founding specific national sociologies.

The theorists of dependency claimed to uncover the evolutionary core embedded in the sociology of modernization and showed how it exhibited an approach to Latin American problems based on an ethnocentric extrapolation of the historical development of the modern capitalist countries. Their analysis demonstrated that any kind of data is socially constructed. Thus dependency theory provided a powerful anti-empirical and anti-functional basis to epistemological criticism, thereby anticipating a trend that would re-emerge only ten years later in the developed countries.

Dependency theorists such as Gunder Frank (development of underdevelopment) (1966); Cardoso and Faletto (dependent situation) (1969); Quijano (dependency and marginality) (1968); Dos Santos (dependent condition) (1972); Marini (sub-imperialism and subordinate capital accumulation formation) (1969) – adumbrated new paradigms out of which emerged theoretical instruments based on the historical and political problems weaving the web of Latin American societies. From the concrete analysis were also developed and applied new methods and techniques adequate to the goals of the research.[1]

The first critical comments against the theory of dependency came from various Marxist authors, and the criticism grew to pervade the entire academic field. Much of the influence came from European Marxism – particularly during the sixties – giving way to structural explanations and emphasis on the importance of economic classes, in order to understand social processes and the behaviour of social actors. In the meantime, other kind of theories were in the making, as, for example, a theory of social movements which attempted to bridge dependency and modernization theories.

Theorists of dependency had shown that dependency structures had a double structure, which consisted on the one hand of a modern industrialized and urban sector, and on the other hand of a rural or semi-rural, marginal sector lagging far behind. With this dualism in mind new hypotheses were formed. Here dependency relations were linked to the benefits and services provided by the capitalist society, in such a way that surplus production and the dispossession of the masses which capitalism entails were not endorsed at the same time.

For the same reason social movements were conceived in the theory of dependency as 'reflections' of the economic form, of the state organization or even of the party action itself. The state was seen as a producing society, whilst the bourgeoisie appeared as an unwanted actor in the film and the proletariat played the role of the unquestionable redeemer of the lot. This type of approach gave way to the re-emergence of eschatologic and teleologic explanations.

Behind these apparent weaknesses lurked an even more dangerous menace; dependency theory implied a reductionist structuralism that inhibited the analysis of concrete social practices. Whereas on the one hand the theorists of dependency were saying that social subjects were class subjects, they did not on the other hand analyse the contradictory relationship between social movements, the state, dominating groups and imperialism. 'In theory, the analysis of dependency did not substitute the theory of modernization, but only limited it by modifying its sense in a precise direction' (Micieli and Calderon, 1986: 12).

A wide variety of theories that attempted to portray the specificity of the Latin American region, using similar or different concepts, can be placed under the same structuralist umbrella: irrespective of the differences within these theories they all converge on the point that the structure of a society is different from the network of social relations which creates it. In so doing, the notion of totality appears as one of the stepping stones of the analysis. The logical precedence of the whole over the parts, the lack of a historical approach, and the elimination of the contingent and the aleatory are important common traits shared by these intellectual constructions.

The need to assess and include within the framework of the

analysis a re-evaluation of each of those missing elements in the structuralist theories gave way to the current methodological and theoretical innovations that enabled research to focus on new actors and processes in Latin America. The built-in limitations of structuralist theories could not account for the evolution of these processes triggered by the economic and political crisis in most of the Latin American countries, nor were they able to characterize the social agents provided by the same theories.

The acknowledgement of these limitations forced a heated debate focused on 'forgotten' facts, as well as theoretical schemes that had been dismissed previously as outdated. Sometimes this renewal followed discussions which had started in the central countries, and sometimes it anticipated them. On the whole, this process gained momentum in the late seventies. At the time of writing it is in full flood, and is bringing forward a redefinition of part of the practices of the social sciences in Latin America.

From Methodological Problems to Concrete Analysis in the Region

The changes in the political, social, economic and cultural arena in Latin America entailed deep transformations in the social sciences, not only in the theory formation, but also in the way research itself was approached. A renewed look at the social processes provided new questions and forced a redefinition of the ways in which research was carried out. As a consequence, the empirical field was delimited, new concepts were produced and the reliability of data was once more assessed, processed and analysed.

The acknowledgement of the emergence of unsolved methodological problems and the scant diffusion of research done in this area showed the gap that existed in the region between theory construction and its methodological use. The picture was further complicated by the fact that epistemological and ideological options placed constraints on the methodological development, because every methodological step was permeated by underlying claims that went beyond theory itself and impinged on the relationship between the subjects and the objects of knowledge.

Current Latin American researchers confront conflicting demands. On the one hand, they must make use of the main paradigms and the methodological strategies available to produce quality research. On the other hand, they have to relate to the specific processes proper to the region: the general defeat of popular movements and of the leftist parties; the relative weakening of labour movements, with the exception of Brazil, the deindustrialization and endemic crisis and the limited and sometimes aborted processes of attempted democratization. Under guises rarely experienced in the central countries, Latin America is witnessing a reappraisal of civil society as an ordinary *Lebensraum*, and the importance of micro-politics in everyday life as well as the pluralism in people's behaviour is vindicated. At the same time Latin America experiences the counterpart of those highly acclaimed civil virtues: namely factionalism, violence and terrorism.

To pretend that a radical shift in theoretical approaches is well under way would be far from true. None the less, it is clear that the limitations of functionalist and structuralist theories have triggered a type of analysis that focuses on the complexities of Latin American social life, incorporating in their descriptions and explanations political, social and cultural as well as spatial and temporal dimensions passed over by previous research programmes.

These global changes in the Latin American social sciences have enriched the understanding of the historical processes that give room for a multiplicity of social micro-stages. Instead of perceiving society as a monolithic and rigid structure – once the economic mono-determination was duly questioned – the time became ripe for an insight into social relationships as a much more varied and complex phenomenon.

Given these conditions, what is the state of the art in comparative research in the region? Any survey shows that the global trends seen elsewhere are non-existent and that a multiplicity of approaches, which sometimes compete and sometimes converge, are emerging. At least five major kinds of approaches and influences on current research can be detected.

First, theories of social movements, as developed by Alain Touraine, have had an impact on theoretical and critical thinking more than at a methodological and empirical level. Some fieldwork has been done in the region which has tried to adapt (syncretize) the sociological intervention approach first developed by Touraine. A good example of this kind of research is being done by Eugenio Tironi in Santiago, Chile.

Second, class analysis – which seems particularly relevant in Central America – has been elaborated, broaching significant differences and nuances. It may not be surprising that its relevance as an analytical tool has increased in Central America – and decreased in the South Basin and in the Andean region where new regimes of conditioned political stability have emerged.

Third, at the community level, new practices have emerged which have influenced the social scientists. Ideas of reciprocity, cooperation and solidarity seem to have amplified. In the urban areas are found

communal dining rooms, mothers' committees, consumer cooperatives and other kinds of communitarian traditions, and in the rural
areas peasant movements: these represent only a few examples of
the increasing variety of social forms.

Fourth, the transformation in the Catholic church, after Puebla,
represents another important trend, pointing towards the return to
a popular church as shown by the active presence of the church-
based communities in new conceptualizations. Communitarianism
has had a strong influence on large groups of social researchers
promoting analysis in terms of participant observation and action
research, involving the researcher in the actor's goals. Here observing and acting blend into the research project, while popular
consciousness, a reassessment of practical knowledge and a return
to communitarianism connect to form alternative theories of new
development on a small scale, as seen in the work by Max Van
Neff.

Fifth, a more recent research trend is based on the plurality of
the behaviour of the actors, in the refusal to totalize social processes,
giving importance to new social movements (for example, those
initiated by women, ecologists or homosexuals), based on pluralism,
identity and autonomy, as shown in the studies by Campero,
Zermenio, Arditti, Dos Santos and their colleagues (Calderon,
1986).

Social movements as impervious to structural reductionism
The processes of democratization within the region have led to a
rethinking and reconsideration of the relations between society and
its institutional structures. In Latin America the institutional framework has been influenced not only by changes in the political
systems, but also by social movements of various types with
demands which have at times involved profound institutional changes
as well. The political events in which these 'extra-political' actors
have appeared are so numerous that one may well ask if the
increasing action on the local level is not paving the way for a new
social order.

These actors can be viewed in at least two ways, as (1) speaking
in terms of institutional experimentation and consciously pursuing
changes within institutions; or as (2) performing simple institutional
adjustment under conditions of crisis or under change of government,
as required by political systems in order to keep the system going.

To understand these questions better we need much more detailed
information on the course of social movements. When, for example,
do social movements overcome the demands of social citizenship as
well as secular demands of political participation, and under what

conditions do they penetrate an institutional system which they might socialize, thereby incorporating values from the most different components of society?

Some of the important characteristics of social movements are the following. Every social movement develops a participation scheme which is a result of its own objectives and the experiences it has had in organizing itself and in the struggles it has gone through. The patterns, levels and types of participation in such movements define to a certain extent the strength of its goals. A central problem here is the tension between the pyramidal or restricted character of participation within the group, and the ideology of democratic and extended participation – the dilemma of politics, in short, where the everyday life experience within the movements appears to be of special interest for further research.

A social movement also has its own 'tempo', which only in part is defined through its action. Even though every movement has its own history and continuity, the timing of its collapse will define its quality. The combination of 'diachronic times', together with synchronism of the movement, are fundamental to comparative studies. Multiple behaviours and meanings in the development of social movements could be the roots of a new social order, building up a new pattern of organization from a certain (consensual) focus on society as a whole.

Social movements further develop in multiple and heterogeneous ways within a geographical space, according to the uneven development of consciousness of certain issues and the organizational and economic aspects of a certain region. A national liberation movement, for example, may have different characteristics or even different significations in diverse geographical areas. Social movements do not have predetermined teleological goals, but redefine them within every struggle encountered.

The way in which theories of social movements have labelled and generalized the different kind of movements, from peasant movements to labour movements, and have emphasized generic historicism, is as wrong as it would be to overemphasize detailed local descriptions. Analysis of participating structures, temporality and regional space within the movement are key elements in the movements to be studied.

These generic comments are a basis for a research project of the different social movements that have emerged in Latin America during crises (Calderon, 1986; Calderon and Dos Santos, 1986). In the study it was highly relevant that the surveys were constructed in order:

1 to locate the social movements with regards to the current crisis and specify the characteristics of the movement;
2 to reveal the role that the movements play or continue to play in the generation and/or development of the crisis;
3 to understand why the social movements question the status quo, and focus particularly on the areas of conflict which might exceed national ideologies, as well as political parties;
4 identify how social movements characterize themselves and their everyday life, the ways òf participation in decision-making and the structure of the internal participation patterns inside each social movement; and
5 analyse how social movements relate to other social forces and equivalent social movements as well as to political parties, their conception of the nation and the perceived ties between the movement and the nation.

The analytical interrelation of these aspects allows for a more global understanding of social movements. Making them subjects of sociological analysis enables us to reinstate dimensions of comparative analysis throughout the region that were not available while using other analytical approaches either generated inside part of the region or exported from other countries. In the different studies already finished are also presented concrete accounts of the different actions that members of social movements may undertake in order to face a current crisis.

Obviously, it is necessary to have in mind a description of the particular crisis in each concrete case: for example, on an urban level, characteristics such as the widening gap between the productive system and the simple reproduction of the labour force, increase in unemployment, decrease in income, undernourishment, and the specific urban organization enter into the description. The level of analysis must correspond to each particular social movement, relative to a specific country, and located within a specific crisis. In some cases it might be suitable to highlight the organizational levels of different sectors, in some cases focusing on struggles, and in others on their influence (if any) as regards global relations of power.

One critical question in the analysis of civil society is the extent to which these new social subjects exist as a result of the use of categories not available in the dominant paradigms and unfamiliar to the main currents of thought in the developed societies,[2] or if, on the contrary, they have already been swallowed by the labelling clichés of these societies.

The representationalist and empiricist biases present in the social scientist make it easy to forget that social class is an analytical tool which makes possible a description of social structure in terms of a theoretical model. But more often than not, social class will not be seen in the empirical realities with which research is concerned. Whenever we address social reality looking for the social agents of change, we do not see ready-made classes acting organically as such. What we face, on the contrary, is the behaviour of a multiplicity of social actors grouped around a multiplicity of social movements with different degrees in their capacity to cope with the existing social system.

Some European observers have taken due consideration of the metamorphosis of the social actors in the Latin American region – and have acknowledged they are irreducible to class categorization. Such is the case of Melucci's theory (1976), in which structural factors overrule the impact of history and in which changes are dependent on social structures and endogenously triggered. Bajoit (1984) states in his turn that even if all actors take part in class relationships, there are other forms of relationship that carry more weight than class consciousness itself. For Touraine (1982) 'there is not such a thing as a class without consciousness. The idea that there may exist a class in itself and that the political or syndicate apparatuses are the ones that give consciousness to the class must be totally refused.'

One question to be addressed – which is loaded with methodological consequences – is whether in spite of the richness of these 'foreign' analyses there is something present in the social movements of the region impervious to the analytical categories provided by the European analysts. In spite of their caution, most of these authors still fall prey to the teleological and rationalistic biases, in which a certain inevitable and desirable fate awaits these social movements, thereby throwing away too easily the will and direction of the changes that the Latin American societies prescribe themselves.

In fact, it is all too easy to construct a pyramid of social movements at whose top are placed only those movements that address directly the need to fight in order to get the means of production, social control and power in their hands, and at whose base remain all those social movements that have on their agenda to change cultural institutions, the distribution of services or new ways of dealing with social relationships.

There is no such thing as a 'Latin American historical action system' in which a new action system is emerging from a simple and progressive rationalization of the main traits of collective social action. In a moment of world-wide paradigmatic crisis, methodology and theory are being revised daily to an extent that sometimes is not as visible in the centre countries as it is at the periphery.

The lack of a theoretical foundation and the crisis of epistemological beliefs, sometimes believed to be eternal, can be squarely met by the development of new styles of thought and research. Both the pecularities of the social formation of Latin America and the traditional and historical capacity towards the elaboration of syncretic thought systems, make the region stand out as an extraordinary social laboratory in which new uses of methodology are a must. The emerging programme of research on social movements is one of several arenas in which these theoretical and methodological innovations are now being tested.

The time is not yet ripe to provide final assessments as to the soundness of the methodology involved. None the less, there are already indications that the Latin American researchers are leading the way in the theory of social movements – as they did before, while coining the local versions of the theory of modernization and dependency theory – to reframe theory and methodology in order to cope with the changing realities the region is facing, and will continue to face in the coming years. In fact, the main questions posed by the theory of social movements, such as how must we deal with causality, syncretism, temporality and data, are all wide open.

Discussion

Although the notion of syncretism has not been tackled with the rigour it deserves, the concept is one of the stepping stones of this presentation, although the full impact must wait until further research is conducted. Syncretism is here defined as the always adaptive and transforming character of sociological approaches and concepts generated in places outside the region where the research is actually carried out.

In the same way that it is incorrect to see the theory of dependency as a mere translation of the theory of imperialism, it is unwise to read the diffusion of functionalism in the region as a mere acritical cultural propagation. Germani did not copy Parsons – he transformed him. The same was done by Cardoso and Faletto with the works of Marx and Weber. There has always been a very creative move in the local use and reassessment of the sociological categories generated in the central countries.

By syncretism we point exactly to this movement: the creative metamorphosis of the old forms into new ones, the universal level transposed to the local level, the ahistorical turned into the concrete. Some day the ecology of ideas (Bateson, 1974) will put the role played by syncretism in the coinage of local theories in its due place (Geertz, 1983).

What current research shows is that there is a better chance that social scientists will be able to provide new answers by pursuing further the paths opened by the theory of social movements – as far as the behaviour of new social actors is concerned – rather than by treading in the paths of other approaches that, in spite of their relative successes, were not able to change to the rhythm of the times.

Notes

1. A review of this type of research was published by OECD (1988).

2. The epistemological standpoint underlying some of the social movements literature remains equidistant both from empiricism and formalism, from structuralism and phenomenology, from naturalism and anti-naturalism, from representationalism and solipsism. It partially endorses the tenets of constructivism (Dumouchel and Dupuy, 1983; Watzlawick, 1984; Bocchi and Cerutti, 1986) with methodological and theoretical underpinnings explored elsewhere (Piscitelli, 1987, 1989).

References

Alger, C. (1988) 'Los nexos locales-mundiales: su percepción, análisis y enfoque', *Revista Internacional de Ciencias Sociales*, 117: 339–58.

Almond, G.A. and S. Verba (1963) *The Civic Culture*. Princeton, NJ: Princeton University Press.

Bajoit, G. (1984) 'Esquisse d'un instrument d'analyse pour les mouvements populaires'. Mimeo, Université de Louvain.

Bateson, G. (1974) *Steps in the Ecology of Mind*. New York: Ballantine.

Bendix, R. (1964) *Nation-building and Citizenship*. New York: Wiley.

Bocchi, G. and M. Cerutti (eds) (1986) *La sfida della complessita*. Milan: Feltrinelli.

Calderon, F. (1986) 'Los movimientos sociales ante la crisis', in F. Calderon (ed.), *Los movimientos sociales ante la crisis*. Buenos Aires: CLACSO.

Calderon, F. and M. Dos Santos (1986) 'Movimientos sociales y democracia: los conflictos por la constitucion de un nuevo orden', in *Los conflictos por la constitucion de un nuevo orden*. Buenos Aires: CLACSO.

Calderon, F., J. Blanes and G. Flores (1982) 'Formaciones y movimientos regionales en Bolivia'. Mimeo, La Paz: Ceres.

Cardoso, F.H. (1972) '"Teoria de la dependencia" o análisis concreto de situaciones de dependencia', in H.H. Godoy and L.I. Ramallo (eds), *Teoria, metodologia y politica del desarrollo de America Latina*. Buenos Aires: FLACSO.

Cardoso, F.H. and E. Faletto (1969) *Dependencia y desarrollo en America Latina*. Mexico: Siglo XXI.

Castells, M. and F. Cortes (1972) *Analisis causal y tecnicas estadisticas en la investigacion sociologica*. Santiago: FLACSO.

Dos Santos, T. (1972) *Socialismo o fascismo. El nuevo carácter de la dependencia y el dilema latinoamericano*. Santiago: Prensa Latinoamericana.

Dumouchel, P. and J.P. Dupuy (eds) (1983) *L'auto-organisation: du physique au politique*. Paris: Seuil.

Eisenstadt, S.N. (1963)*The Political System of Empires*. New York: Free Press.
Friberg, M. and B. Hettne (1988) 'Movilizacion local y political del sistema mundial', *Revista Internacional de Ciencias Sociales*, 117: 359–78.
Gargani, A. (ed.) (1983) *Crisis de la razon: nuevos modelos en la relacion entre saber y actividad humana*. Mexico: Siglo XXI.
Geertz, C. (1983) *Local Knowledge*. New York: Basic Books.
Germani, G. (1971) *Politica y sociedad en una epoca en transicion*. Buenos Aires: Paldos.
Guinzburg, C. (1983) 'Il paradigma dei segni', in A. Gargani, *Crisis della ragioni*. Turin: Einaudi.
Gunder Frank, A. (1966) 'El desarrollo del subdesarrollo', *Desarrollo*, 1 (1).
Lipset, S.M. (1963) *The First New Nation: the United States in Historical and Comparative Perspective*. New York: Basic Books.
McClelland, D. (1961) *The Achieving Society*. Princeton, NJ: Van Nostrand.
Marini, R. (1969) *Subdesarrollo y revolución*. Mexico: Siglo XXI.
Melucci, A. (1976) 'L'azione ribelle. Formazione e struttura dei movimenti sociali', in A. Melucci, *Movimenti di rivolta*. Milan: Etas Libri.
Merton, R.K. (1959) *The Social System*. Glencoe, IL: Free Press.
Micieli, C. and F. Calderon (1986) 'El encantamiento de las estructuras: las ciencias sociales en la decada de 1960', *David and Goliath*, xvi, (50): 10–13, Buenos Aires.
Morin, E. (1986) *La Méthode. T.3 La connaissance de la connaissance*. Paris: Seuil.
Murdock, G.P. (1940) 'The cross-cultural survey', *American Sociological Review*, 5 (3): 361–70.
OECD (1988) *Répertoire des activités de recherche en matière de développement en Amérique Latine*. Paris.
Osgood, C. (1967) 'On the strategy of cross-national research into subjective culture'. *Information sur les sciences sociales*, 6 (1): 6–37.
Parsons, T. (1959) *Social Theory and Social Structure*. Glencoe, IL: Free Press.
Piscitelli, A. (1987) 'Estado, poder y dominación. Programas de investigación en conflicto'. Mimeo, Buenos Aires.
Piscitelli, A. (1989) 'Programa duro en sociologia del conocimiento y contra-revolucion micro-sociologica. Un estudio en ecología de las ideas'. Mimeo, Buenos Aires.
Quijano, A. (1968) *Dependencia, cambio social y urbanizacion en Latinoamerica*. ILPES.
Rokkan, S. (1981) 'Investigacion trans-cultural, trans-societal y trans-nacional', in J. Havert (ed.), *Corrientes de la investigacion en las ciencias sociales, 1 Aspectos Interdisciplinarios*. Madrid: Tecnos.
Smith, D.H. and A. Inkeles (1966) 'The Om scale: a comparative social psychological measure of individual modernity', *Sociometry*, 26 (4): 353–77.
Strasser, C. (1977) *La razon cientifica en politica y sociologia*. Buenos Aires: Amorrortu.
Touraine, A. et al. (1982) *Mouvements sociaux d'aujourd'hui, acteurs et analystes*. Paris: Les éditions ouvrières.
Watzlawick, P. (ed.) (1984) *The Invented Reality*. New York: Norton.
Weffort, F.C. (1972) 'Notas sobre "teoria de la dependencia": teoria de clase o ideologia nacional', in H.H. Godoy and L.I. Ramallo (eds) *Teoria, metodologia y politica del desarrollo de America Latina*. Buenos Aires: FLACSO.
Whiting, J.W.M. et al. (1966) *Field Guide for the Study of Socialization*. New York: Wiley.

6

Theory Formation in Social Research: A Plea for Pluralism

Johan Galtung

Intellectual Style and the Social Science Enterprise

Two intellectual styles seem to dominate social science activity, here referred to as the *story-tellers* and the *pyramid-builders*. The former correspond roughly to what in another context I have referred to as the Saxonic/Nipponic style and the latter to the Teutonic/Gallic style (Galtung, 1988: ch. 1.2). They do not exclude each other.

The story-teller is a collectionist, and the major tool would be a (big) stack of index cards. Whether he mines social reality for findings or the library for quotations the procedure is the same: one card, one finding/quote. On top of the card is entered, meticulously, the location of the finding; where in the data, where in the library. When the stack has an appropriate size, or the algorithm generating the stack produces no qualitatively new entries – the data have been squeezed to the bitter end; the algorithm of pursuing footnote references leads to no new books or articles – the cards are placed face up on a big table and used as stepping stones for telling a reasonably coherent story. The quotations and or the data are woven together in a verbal tale. If the cards contain quotations they are, in the end, alphabetized according to the last name of the first author. That list is called a 'bibliography' and the correspondence between quotation and name is called a 'reference'; placed in a foot- or end-note. If the cards contain 'data' from social rather than library reality, the top of the card would give some reference to how the data were collected/processed. The sum total of these card headings are often collected in a chapter, called 'Methodology', with one section for data-collection and one for data-processing.

Mining reality for data and mining the library for quotations converge in the interview, only that the author of the quotation is intercepted before he commits his thoughts to the written or printed page. In addition, the author is usually anonymous, being too important or too unimportant. The known authors to whom quotations are attributed are of the middle range, although the heavy over-representation of the 'competent others', the author's colleagues, may make them unknown to the rest of the world. What this actually means is that the step from careful journalism to story-telling social science is a short one, making the latter 'journalism with footnotes', and making journalism 'social science without footnotes'. The differences should be appreciated, but they are not overwhelming. Moreover, is this type of comment a slur on journalists, social scientists, both or neither?

The basic point to be made, however, is located elsewhere. Story-telling, using library quotations, is sometimes confused with 'theory' because no new data are produced. Many people seem to believe in some kind of data–theory, empirical study–theoretical study dichotomy, oblivious of the possibilities of both–and and neither–nor. Theory is not the negation of data. Theory formation is a particular style of intellectual activity; today practically speaking absent from, for instance, US social science activity which has story-telling as its major style (except for purely methodological exercises). In a sense it is not so strange: if a college student takes forty courses and writes at least one mid-term and one final paper, altogether eighty efforts to tell stories, the pattern should set after some time. A student who has been through German and French high schools and universities is shaped differently; writing long, complex essays on abstract subjects, like 'The Relation between Freedom and Equality'.

This is where the pyramid-building enters as the second approach. The approach is not index-card-intensive, but brain-intensive; the basic tool is thought. In a different idiom, this calls for *meditation*, not *mediation* (through the reading of systematic data or the reading of others who may or may not have read systematic data). In its pure form theory is neither data, nor quotes; it is all symbolic form, cast in a natural or artificial language. However it is done, the enterprise has one dominant characteristic: asymmetry, like the asymmetry between general perspective and specific insights, between premises and conclusions, between hub and rim, between centre and periphery, between core and edge, between axioms and theorems-derivatives.[1]

Imagine that all statements in the two styles are written on cards, one for each statement. Then the basic difference is this: in the first style the order of presentation is more flexible; in the second case more rigid. In the second case the statements can be divided relatively unambiguously in two groups: perspective-premises-hub-centre-core-axioms in one, and insights-conclusions-rim-periphery-edge-theorems, and so on in the other. The statements have a non-flat topography; there is a flow, a gradient. The second group 'flows' from the first, possibly a better expression than 'follows'. Of course, the story-teller may also try to make the reader believe that he or she is following some logical scheme whereas in fact they have only chosen one order of presentation among many. Or they may be using the simplest ordering device of them all, a highly pre-logical one, chronology. The pyramid-builder does not have that freedom. The game is logical, however this is interpreted. There are rules of the game, there is intellectual discipline to be exercised. Words like 'inference' and 'deduction' come to mind, depending on whether one is climbing up or down the pyramid. This is not the style of disconnected TV flashes that may serve as the stepping stones for the story-telling of the newscast.[2] As dominant symbolic input we would expect the mass media to influence the general intellectual style in favour of story-telling, and to disfavour theory. Consequently, the whole theoretical exercise may be a waning, even dying one, and the theoretician a highly endangered species.

What do we Demand of a Good Theory?

The classical assumption is linked to the dichotomy between the real and the ideal worlds, with real = ideal + noise or real = essential + accidental. The ideal world, then, is seen as contradiction-free with everything flowing from first principles. A theory was the effort to capture that ideal world, abstracting away the empirical noise, all the accidental elements of the real world. The (mathematized) axiomatic system with the axioms embedding and embodying the ideal world expressed as first principles – themselves non-contradictory, mutually independent (necessary) and complete (sufficient), in the sense that the truth value of any correctly derived theorem can be decided – became the archetypical theory. The rule of simplicity combined elegance with the assumption that the Creator did not play dice, but had a non-contradictory plan.

This crystallized into the hypothetical–deductive or inductive–deductive methodology usually taken over (blindly) from the natural sciences; with a low number of axioms, n, from which a high number, N, of theorems can be inferred. The explanatory power could be operationalized as $E = 1 - n/N$, being zero if the axioms only account for themselves; converging asymptotically to 1 the more theorems can be inferred. Ideally the theorems should differ qualitatively, spanning a vast spectrum of different arenas of human behaviour, such as intra- and inter-personal, social and regional (civilizational) conflict or micro-, meso- and macro-physics.

Second, there is the link to the story-tellers with their weakly organized statements: all theorems that can be derived from the axioms should be confirmed by quotations or data; all confirmed data or quotations, and only those, should be derivable from the axioms. In short: logically valid = empirically confirmed (and vice versa).

So far so good. The problem is that this textbook prescription no longer makes any sense the moment we assume that the creation continues with humans, in conflict, as (co-)creators. Under that assumption a theory constructed according to the rules above becomes a strait-jacket, reflecting the past only. To see the essence of the real world as non-contradictory and basically unchangeable, mirrored in a non-contradictory deductive system is far from trivial. It is a very dramatic assumption about reality. And it is not sufficient to bring in time as a parameter, making the jump, described by Cassirer, from *Substanzbegriff* to *Funktionsbegriff*. Dynamic theory also serves as an iron cage for a non-transcending reality; and may well become a self-fulfilling prophecy, like Smithism (Adam Smith) and Marxism (Karl Marx). By enacting the theory people try to bring about the conditions for the theory to be confirmed in its consequences. Recent events in Eastern Europe tell us much about the limits to theory confirmation in social reality, at least to the theory of the benefits to be derived from central planning (as opposed to market mechanisms) – although 'central planning' is not a core concept in Marxism. But markets are central to Smithism, and events, or rather the constant situation in the periphery of the capitalist system tell us even more about the limits to theory confirmation in social reality. In either case the disconfirmation shows up as deficit in basic needs, the needs for (a minimum of) freedom in the first case and for (a minimum of) well-being in the second. But social disconfirmation has to be socially voiced, not only by social scientists observing but by the victims. And the victims of the market demand plan, and the victims of plan demand market – the contacts between them being weak. The voice of the social scientist is also weak, hardly heard in the struggle.

A good theory, then, should be able to reflect on the conditions for its own disconfirmation; not only disconfirmation in the scientific, but also in the political sense. In other words, it should include a meta-theory reflecting on the social function of that theory as ideology. This reflection will by necessity have to be recursive, calling for a meta-meta-theory reflecting on the social function of the meta-theory as ideology. And so on and so forth, but three levels may do as a starter. The scientist is not the sole judge.

This all has to do with the tremendous complexity of social reality, including the capacity of social reality for transcendence to a reality unforeseen and unforeseeable. *Natura non facit saltus*;

maybe, but social systems certainly do. And this should lead to a simple, but rather basic consideration in connection with theory formation. A good theory should be seen as one perspective among others rather than as a catch-all explanation. Not the form of the theory so much as our attitude to the theory is what matters. There is nothing wrong with a theory formed according to the two classical rules above *provided one does not believe in the theory*. The problem is not located in the shape of the pyramid, pointed or not, steep or not; the problem lies in the number of pyramids.

The tremendous advantage of theory formation is that it can yield unexpected insights, as opposed to weaving together already known ones. A good theory organizes a great variety of existing insights and produces new ones. This is where true *intellectual quality* is located, not in story-telling. The disadvantage lies in the double danger of believing that all these insights have empirical counterparts; *and* in not seeing the empirical reality not accounted for by the theory. The discourse underlying the theory may not accommodate such facts comfortably; alternative discourses may be subjugated. But even with openings in the discourse of the theory the deviant fact may be overlooked or disregarded simply to save a theory that has absorbed so much intellectual investment. In other words: the step from theory to theology is a short one, again leaving open whether this is a slur on one, both or neither.

This presents us with a nice dilemma. On the one hand we want to benefit from the advantage of a well-crafted theory as the great organizer of known and unknown insights. On the other hand we do not want to mistake the theory for reality. We want the theory to be our tool, not vice versa. How does one square that circle?

Easy. A multi-pyramidal intellectual landscape would make us squeeze a theory till it is dry; then start with a new theory, and so on; being eclectic to the very end. That way we should combine the unexpected insight without running into dogmatism. In other words, we would be poly- rather than monotheistic. In fact, the quite strong tendency in intellectual circles against a sin called 'eclecticism' probably comes from the monotheism so deeply embedded in Judaeo-Christian civilization. If you have made a theory then you are supposed to believe in it till the (empirical) evidence to the contrary becomes overwhelming. At that point you may convert to another theory and even issue statements like 'I no longer believe in plan; now I believe in the market' (or vice versa). Believing in both (Japanese economics); neither (green economics); or a little of either (social democracy) would be poly-, pan- and atheism.

An image: each theory sheds strong light on some area shrouded in darkness. Several theories aiming at the same area should provide for more light and interesting interferences. But they may also brighten up neighbouring areas with some overlaps or – of course – non-contiguous areas of ignorance. In any case, as so often pointed out, the greater the area of light, the greater the surrounding area of darkness.

However, there are other problems around. Each theory has to abstract from reality; the story-teller is better at catching empirical richness, giving a thick description. The theory emits sharp light, even a laser beam. But what we see may be a moon landscape, a moonscape, with no contours, no shadows. The style of the story-teller gives us those contours, with no intellectual quality but a lot of mini-lights in a lush rain forest. The story-teller provides some light everywhere, some kind of epistemological pantheism, to stick to that image. Again, I would certainly opt for both, both for the rich, down-to-earth description and for the sharp, pointed theories; in plural. A very ecumenical, or maybe I should say Hindu?, epistemological position.

A good theory, then, would be like a family or combination of a number of classical theories, squeezing each one of them as far as possible for their intellectual content, neither believing, nor disbelieving completely in any one of them. More particularly, there would be no assumption to the effect that the perspective established by one set of contradiction-free axioms can ever mirror a contradictory reality. A family of perspectives comes closer.

To do this requires a certain artisanal intellectual competence, with such elementary skills as care with definitions, ability to construct fruitful typologies, understanding of what inference means, knowing how to anchor the theory on the empirical end; yet tempering all of this with theoretical pluralism, epistemological eclecticism, a spirit of tolerance. Why? Or, rather why not? Because belief in theoretical singularism is tantamount to believing that a symbolic construct flowing from one set of non-contradictory, independent and complete statements can ever have a richness capable of reflecting anything like 'social reality'. That this belief is bordering on the crazy becomes very clear the moment we identify the idea of a singular theory as the product of a singular theoretician (a Smith, a Marx), provided there is a certain consistency to the theory production of one single theory producer (not the case with Smith, nor with Marx).

How could one person fathom the social universe? Even a super-person (Smith?, Marx?)? Or a school of them? Add one more person to the school, would that not add at least one perspective? Could it not rather be that the cult of a singular theoretician is another part of our collective subconscious, tied to the idea of the single prophet (Abraham, Moses, Jesus, Mohammed) to whom Deep Reality is revealed, for Him (it seems generally to be a man) to communicate to ordinary people? Have we not recreated the scientific genius in the image of the religious genius, the prophet, the founder of the religion ('God said, let Newton be, and all was light')? Maybe it is time to shed such ideas?

Moreover, a good theory should never leave us with the idea that the world is made once and for all. A good theory will always have some empty boxes for the reality not yet there, for potential as opposed to empirical reality. In fact, the theory should serve as a bridge from the empirical to the potential. And why should we be more neutral about the potential than we are about the empirical, about which we never fail to pass value judgements? A good theory does not have to but could well be formulated in value-explicit terms permitting us to contrast the empirical and the potential in terms of values and interests, indicating trajectories from the empirical to the potential. Why should a good theory not be action-indicative as in architecture or engineering?

A good theory, hence, will never rest content merely accounting for the *empirical*. Bringing values in explicitly, not brushing them under the carpet, the *critical* perspective on the empirical will be another aspect of theory construction. And a third will be the *constructive* aspect, envisaging an alternative reality as well as a trajectory for its realization. These three aspects of science support one another, also appealing to the total person doing this kind of work. But the realities may be contradictory.

The Micro–Macro Linkage

Let us now use some of this approach on the old problem of the macro–micro linkage.[3] This is not only an attractive problem in general epistemology; for those of us in an interdisciplinary field (peace studies, development studies, environment studies, women's studies, black studies and so on) the problem is existential, at the very core of our efforts to come to grips with social reality.

Most authors seem to see micro–macro in a *diachronic mode*, with *causality* operating from one 'level' to the other. The approach is *reductionist* if the causality is always seen as originating from the same 'level'. Thus, it is hardly unfair to see the two giants in the exercise of the Teutonic, re- and deductionist intellectual style, Marx and Freud as exemplars. To Marx the social formation, and to Freud the personal formation are constitutive for the rest of human/social reality. If peace-development-ecological balance-gender equality-race equality are desired, then the basic intervention has to be done at the social level for Marx and the personal level for Freud. From causes generated at these levels effects will flow, even generously, to all other levels. Thus, Marx emphasized the causal flow from macro to micro in spelling out how the social formation makes an impact on the personal formation (the theory of alienation), Freud sees a flow from micro to macro in his theories of civilization in general and war in particular (the death drive). Marxism-Leninism also spells out a link to the even more macro in seeing international war and peace as generated by intra-social formations. Thus, both of them are potentially total theories.

Obviously this goes beyond the high explanatory power of the classical 'good' theory, measured above as $E = 1 - n/N$. These are theories of political power, $P = 1 - 1/N$, promising effects at all N levels as a consequence of the intervention on only one of them (also counting that one). Not political economy but economic politics, and with a very high dividend: do this one job, and there will be a windfall at all levels! Were Marx and Freud, or their followers, basically inspired by stock-exchange logic?

Of course, nobody in his or her right mind would throw out the causal flow approach to the micro–macro problem. Two-way causal flows, for instance, lead to interesting problems of relative strength. Whether a (strong) personality (Gorbachev?) can make more of an impact on society than a strong society (Stalinist?) on the personality, or vice versa, is a good problem. Possibly, the answer is found not so much in the strength of one of them as in the weakness of the other. After all, Gorbachev has been dealing with a Stalinist formation in crisis and disintegration; and the Stalinist formation systematically eliminated strong personalities standing in the way, depriving the others of such basic sources of inner strength as religion and alternative ideologies. Nor would anybody rule out of court one-way causal flows. Thus, peace research will not easily give up the causal flow from the Military-Bureaucratic-Corporate-Intelli-gentsia (MBCI) complex (harmonizing strategic planning, bureau-cratic power, profit motives and intellectual careerism) to arms races, provocative deployment, even wars. Whoever wants to reduce the latter will have to come to grips with the former. But one such flow is not the same as reductionist assumptions.

An alternative to a *diachronic* approach based on *causality* would be a *synchronic* approach based on *isomorphism*.[4] I then assume a human ability, indeed propensity, to endow all spaces with a structure, preferring the term 'space' to 'level', precisely in order to avoid the reductionism inherent in the idea of 'lower' and 'higher' levels. Thus, there is *nature space* (including humans, not to be confused with such anthropocentrisms as '(non-human) environment' and 'resources'), furnished with biota and abiota. There is *personal space*, the inner space of self and other, furnished with body, mind (cognitions, emotions, volitions) and spirit. There is *social space* with persons in interaction, sometimes being self-sufficient so that the certificate of 'society' can be issued. And there is *world space*, with societies and regions in interaction, which had better be self-sufficient – sustainable, which at present it is not – being the only world we have.

We would be hard pressed to find human beings who do not somehow recognize patterns in these spaces with a minimum of architecture, some structure, beyond seeing them merely as sets of totally unrelated elements. Thus, some elements will be seen as near one another (occupying a neighbourhood), others as more distant. Some will be seen as interacting, others as not; some as ranked, others as not, some as continuous with each other, others as not.

In short, I assume a common but poorly articulated language available to humankind couched in geometrical/topological terms. The primitive terms are not such mathematical starters as elements and relations and sets of elements and sets of relations (among them); together constituting structures. The primitive terms in the geometry of the common person would be above/at the same level/below, the singleton and the couple, the triangle and the quadrangle, the pyramid, the circle and the star. Translation from the formal to the vernacular offers no particular problem. Thus, it is often useful to put the answers given by 'respondents' to complex questions (for example, 'how do we best get peace in the world?', 'what do we mean by a developed society?') on a sheet of paper or a blackboard, asking the respondent to order, organize them. After a short while arrows are inserted for causal relations, neighbourhoods are formed by circling them. Structures, even very rich structures, emerge. No prior training seems to be needed. People are born scientists.

Let us assume a drive toward homomorphism, even isomorphism. This may come about in two ways. People may have fairly firm views on the structure of one of the spaces and project that structure on to the other. A good example would be a (social) Darwinist structure, attributed to nature and spreading from there to the other spaces (in the mind of the beholder), even to personal space – for instance, as the spirit firmly victorious in the giant fight with mind and body. The archetype would be the pyramid. But then a predilection for pyramids might have been the starting point; projecting the pyramid on any space. In the same vein the circle or wheel could have been the starting point, carrying visions of equidistance, with all elements relating equally to one another (although, equipped with a centre, the wheel can also be seen as the projection of a pyramid, or rather a cone, on two-dimensional space). In either case the result is the same: *homomorphism*.

Take the *homomorphism* between the Big Bang theory of the creation of the universe, and the Western self-image as being the source or cradle of modernity and development according to the formulas 'Western History = Universal History' and 'Westernization = Modernization = Development'. In both cases we are dealing with a centre–periphery structure with tremendous centrifugal force emanating explosively from the centre. The former can be seen as the legitimation of the latter; nature is like that. The latter can be seen as providing a setting within which the Big Bang theory comes naturally, as a projection of Western military, political, economic and cultural imperialism on the universe, with a single centre and one-way causation as major structural components. Or, both of them can be seen as the projection of a predilection for a star-shaped, centre–periphery structure that somehow got engraved on the mind of the beholder, on anything – for instance, on the universe or on political geography and history (thus, it is easily seen what kind of road map that person would come up with given sufficient power). However, whether operating inductively, inductively–deductively or purely deductively, this is still causal reasoning from one space to the other, even when two-way traffic is assumed.

But the *homomorphism/heteromorphism hypotheses* remove some diachronic/causal bias since there is no longer any causal flow from one or some space(s) to other(s). The two hypotheses cut across the spaces, being about the set of spaces:

1 *The higher the homomorphism, the more stable the images*, and, which is not quite the same:
2 *The higher the heteromorphism, the less stable the images.*

In the first case the images (of nature, personal, social and world spaces) reinforce one another; in the second case they work against one another. But where, just where do these structural comparisons take place, leading to the conclusion of homo- or heteromorphism?

I assume two such places, not only one. The first is obvious: the individual (sub)conscious, with conclusions in terms of coherence/incoherence and a hypothesis of some kind of pleasure/displeasure forming the link to the 'drive' towards homomorphism. The second place would be the collective (sub)conscious. I take this to be nothing mystical in the sense of being non-falsifiable, but to be collectively shared individual (sub)consciousnesses. Social space, by definition with individuals interacting, is then a place where images are compared, *not only across individuals, but also across spaces.*

And just as some persons may be more important in defining the images than others, some space(s) may be more important than others. Take the pyramid and the circle for social space. (For more on this, see Galtung, 1988: ch. 1.1.) Obviously, we are talking here about conservative versus liberal, or right wing versus left wing ideology, emphasizing hierarchy and equality, respectively. The point made goes beyond that, however, way into outer and inner space. The membership criterion as 'one of us' is not only where the person stands on social Darwinism, but (hypothesis) also the stand on nature Darwinism (as different from theories of creation), on international relations, on how personalities are constituted.

Reader: But you have not escaped from causality, nor from reductionism. What you have done is merely to locate the ultimate cause inside the individual human mind with some ideas as to how the collective human mind is constituted. You then hypothesize perceived structural similarity or dissimilarity among images to be a major driving force. This may or may not be so. But I do not see this as purely diachronic, nor as non-causal.

Author: I agree, except for some rather major points.

First, maybe the ultimate root of social phenomena is inside the human mind, individual and/or collective, regardless of how we conceive of the micro–macro relationships. I do not think a revolution is like an earthquake, regardless of how much it is referred to as a 'social earthquake'. An earthquake works on us regardless of whether we have a theory or not; we may not even have the concept of an 'earthquake'. I doubt that the same is the case for a revolution. In other words, I do not assume automaticity for human/ social phenomena. This would also apply to Marx and Freud. The phenomena they referred to were basically altered by their ability to put their own concepts and theories regarding these phenomena into our minds. Theories change reality, and personal/social/world reality much more than nature reality, without making a 100–0 per cent division out of this distinction. Thus, secular earthquake theories deprived the gods of a major tool.

Second, if theories change reality, then we should be interested in the factors influencing theories. I am not denying that data and experience with empirical reality in general play their role. Thus, any effort to reduce or control the apparitions of militarism in world space, in the interaction between societies, will come to nothing if the structural basis in social space is not reduced or controlled. Given a triggering event, the MBCI-complex will be capable of reproducing inter-societal militarism. But empiricism is only one factor, homomorphism is another.

Reader: Doesn't this come dangerously close to solipsism – 'it is all in our minds' kind of loose talk?

Author: Not necessarily. I am not denying there is something 'out there', also in personal, social and world spaces. All I am saying is the rather trivial point that a theory, any theory, not only reflects but also constructs social reality. This also goes for how we approach the four spaces. We construct their relations according to causality and/or isomorphism. The causal approach relates them in time, through one- or two-way causal flows; with reductionism always placing one and the same space in front of the chain. The structural approach compares the spaces and maps them on a set with homomorphism and heteromorphism. I think we generally start, without much reflection, taking one of these approaches for granted, and it might be interesting to know what makes us choose one rather than the other.

Reader: Or both, maybe?

Author: Or both. They do not exclude each other. But there is a problem shared by them both: how much of our theory formation is reflection and how much is construction of reality? And if we partly construct reality by choosing theory, should we not prefer the theory that gives us the best reality? And how do we know which of two realities is better?

Reader: Are you seriously suggesting that by choosing not only theory but the form of a theory we also choose, in part, our world?

Author: Certainly. The choice is far from innocent. A diachronic, reductionist choice lends itself to all kinds of heavy single factor policies, setting one space right first, with the hope that the other spaces will follow suit. A synchronic approach may look forbidding, there is no place to start. But it lends itself to many small steps, equally divided among the spaces, changing pyramids into circles, for instance; including changing our perceptions of reality as pyramids into perceptions as circles. So the pragmatic implications are tremendous. Theory is politics.

Reader: But this means that any theory choice is actually a choice on behalf of humanity?

Author: You said it –

Is a Universal Social Science Possible?

By 'universal social science' we mean something like 'valid in space and time', meaning a social science transcending geography and history with all that implies of structural and cultural diversity. This would go beyond comparisons of societies with one another in space and over time. It would also include theories of how they interact synchronically and how they transform diachronically – a giant task, in other words, but modern social science is working at it with equally giant data banks. On the far end of the comparative social studies approach there is a goal justifying the game. The name of the game is comparative social research; the name of the goal is universal social science.

It is not difficult to understand what universal social science might look like. A distinction would be made between social laws and parameters for those laws. A given society would be classified according to a finite set of parameters. Those parameters would then be fed into the universal social science and out come the social laws for that type of society.

This is the general programme for *nomothetic* science. It does not matter whether the class of societies constituted by any choice of parameter values has 0, 1 or several members. Nomothetic is not about 'several' as opposed to only 'one'. The basic assumption in nomothetic science lies in the possibility of inferring much from little, assuming that the laws fill in the rest. To the contrary, *ideographic* science claims to work without those laws, inferring little from much in its description of the unit of analysis; a person, a society, a world. Where nomothetic science proceeds by deducing from general principles, ideographic science would focus on the internal dialectic of the unit of analysis, claiming that this dialectic is singular to that system and cannot be found elsewhere.

Put differently: nomothetic science proceeds from a limited number of properties of the system analysed, detached from their concrete relationship, in other words *atomistically* (and/or from parts of a system, detached from the rest). The description is thin; the rest lies in the correct deduction from the laws. *Erklären*. Ideographic science proceeds by a very high, in principle unlimited, number of properties in their concrete relationship, in other words *holistically* (and/or from a total, very encompassing system). The description is thick. There are no explicit outside laws to fall back upon. Consequently, the author probably relies upon 'common sense' or a high level of familiarity with the subject, *Einfühlung, verstehen*.

Although dramatically different, these should not be seen as antithetical, irreconcilable or mutually exclusive. The nomothetic researcher will fill in details (sometimes referred to as the 'qualitative stuff') neither found in the explicit description nor in the laws; the ideographic researcher will supply some 'laws' of his or her own that may not easily survive the light of day (meaning explicitness). Important is the general distinction between a scientific meta-language based on atomism-deductionism in the case of the nomothetic approach to holism-dialectics in the case of the holistic approach. This gives us two additional languages, atomism-dialectics which was highly important for the micro-physics of nuclear and quantum physics, taking a presumably indivisible whole as the seat of basic dialectics, and holism-deductionism, equally important for the macro-physics of the whole universe, particularly in cosmological theories.

Others might subdivide the languages of social research differently. But the conclusion may nevertheless be the same: the problem of a universal social science, making the project not only difficult or impossible but even meaningless, is not located in the differences between the personal, social and world; over space (only for two of them) and over time (for all three). After all, there is a lot of difference between all objects exposed to free fall (or its approximation in the atmosphere); nevertheless we have Newton's laws. The problem is located not in the differences among the units, but among the languages of research.

Obviously, for universal social science, as also for comparative social research, a nomothetic meta-language would have to be chosen, leading to the question of which one. Newton's language used space, time and force (and their derivatives) only – a very thin description indeed, leaving out, for instance, the colour, the shape and in general the aesthetic qualities of the 'falling objects'. A consensus on this discourse would hardly have been possible had the 'falling objects' participated in the dialogue.

It is worth pointing out that this is not the same as Kuhn's problem of changing paradigms. A given meta-language can accommodate any number of paradigms. If the meta-language is ideographic then it also becomes idiosyncratic, a reflection of what is inside the analyst projected on to the unit of analysis. If the meta-language is nomothetic the characteristics chosen also define the discourse. Given the unlimited set of characteristics from which to choose a finite, usually small, number of characteristics, any number of discourses or paradigms may emerge, permitting any number of Kuhnian transitions or revolutions from one to the other. Thus, shall we discuss 'development' as growth/saving/investment? Or structure and culture? Or sustainability? Or independence/dependence of their foreign economies? Or basic needs satisfaction?

But could we not do all of that? If the number of characteristics is limited the number of discourses is also limited, meaning that the task is arduous, but limited. But imagine that the number of characteristics is unlimited, partly because new analysts see new analytical dimensions, partly because the units themselves undergo transformations that have to be accounted for by bringing in new dimensions of analysis. In that case the task is not only a long-term one, but unlimited in time (which is not the same as infinite). Universal social science would then at best be approached asymptotically, through a process of convergence. But even so the assumption would be that no qualitatively new aspects of the units show up, in the consciousness of the analyst or 'out there'. And for that assumption to be valid it is not enough to assume that the units of analysis enter some kind of 'end of history' with no more structural transformation. We must also assume that there is no basic transformation in the subjects of analysis, the analysts and their images of what is going on. Again, this assumes homogeneity both in space and over time of the analysts; uniformly trained and incapable of undergoing personal transformations. Transformation neither of the objects of analysis nor of the subjects doing the analysis seems very close to any reasonable definition of death, of either or of both.

In addition, all of this assumes consensus about a nomothetic meta-language. Three other languages have been indicated; one ideographic, the other two in-between languages. By imposing the nomothetic meta-language, through universal training, as condition for certification of anybody as social analyst, we may clear the ground, even if the preceding paragraph indicates that there is still a far distance to go. The other three may be ruled out of court as pre-scientific, or something like that. References may be made to the success of the Newtonian discourse, nomothetic and highly parsimonious as such. But the objections are obvious. The major departures from Newtonian physics, the quantum theory of micro-physics and the relativity theory of macro-physics were framed in other languages that suddenly made both time and space highly problematic, discontinuous and contiguous. Moreover, the holistic/dialectical approach preserves all the richness of reality, including aesthetic and sacred aspects. Would the theory of fractals have been possible if people had continued simplifying coast-lines and so on to make them fit nomothetic meta-languages?[5]

Should one then impose a mix of these four languages, giving people training in all four with a weighting corresponding to their acceptability in the 'scientific community'? Where the imposition of one language alone would be clearly fascist, some kind of epistemological colonialism, this would smack of friendly fascism with its touch of tolerance – but only touch: the problem lies, of course, in the choice of dimensions to characterize meta-languages. Others would see it differently, making the diamond shine by cutting it at other angles, or by not cutting at all.

Consequently, we are left with the conclusion that the price to be paid for a unified social science is something like the entropy death on both sides of the observer–observed equation. Who is entitled to extract that price, or demand that cost, for such a minor benefit? The answer, 'it has been done in the natural sciences' should carry no weight, first, because the objects either do not voice their concerns or we do not understand their language and, second, because not only new paradigms but new meta-languages are emerging all the time framing new questions, not only new answers to old questions. Rather, we should learn to enjoy the pluralism inherent in our task, to understand better the human condition, both in its empirical manifestations and in its latent potentials. For that we have to be polyglot, not only in the languages of the societies we study but also in the languages we use to comprehend what we study. To cling to 'quantitative methods' or 'historical methods' as if either one is not only necessary but also sufficient is like trying to turn the vice of being monoglot (mother tongue, for example, English, only) into a virtue. If we can learn foreign languages and translate from one into the other so can we do with social science meta-languages, and with intellectual styles. Thus, the world has more to offer than the data-heavy Saxonic-Nipponic intellectual style and the theory-heavy Gallic-Teutonic style; for instance, Arab, Hindu and Sinic styles. The world is still rich. We still do not live in a world dominated by one country, one meta-language, and one intellectual style, beamed all over the universe.

Conclusion

In short, the whole scientific enterprise is an invitation to an ecumenical delight, combining the intellectually flat but lush landscape of the story-teller with the intellectual brilliance of the pyramid-builders, in plural. It is an invitation to try to come to grips with the totality of messages developed by the human/social sciences (again in plural), from the intra-personal micro to the inter-world macro (soon there will be such a thing), not assuming the priority of any one of them. And it is an invitation to explore the diversity of social science languages. Any effort to reduce this diversity is doomed to fail; underneath the repression resistance movements will form and sooner or later take over. There is a principle of variety at work here. Only by cultivating variety not only among social scientists but also within us can we be mentally prepared to reflect and construct variety around us. To believe that we, singly or combined, have enough variety to comprehend our surroundings fully is arrogance; to reduce spaces down to our own level is repression; to homogenize ourselves even further is collective suicide.[6]

Notes

This essay was first presented at the Theory Seminar, Department of Sociology, University of Hawaii, spring 1989. I am indebted to Deane Neubauer and Kiyoshi Ikeda for the initiative and to Peter Manicas and Joseph Seldin as co-presenters.

1. See Alexander (1988: ch. 2) for a review of the current revival of 'grand theory'.
2. US 18-year-olds are reputed to have been through 18,000 hours of TV, 15,000 hours of schooling and 340,000 commercials. None of these would train in reasoning from premises to conclusions.
3. For some examples of the micro–macro debate, see Alexander and Giesen (1987); Collins (1981: 984–1014); Collins (1988: 242–53).
4. Isomorphism stands for structural identity, homomorphism for the weaker, more useful similarity, the mapping being less than one to one.
5. The theory of fractals is partly based on the assumption that macro-spaces are mirrored in micro-spaces.
6. This isomorphism between single-multiple-flat theoretical landscapes and mono-theism-polytheism-pantheism can then serve as a nucleus of another theory, relating religious tenets of faith (millennia old) to philosophy of science (generations old).

References

Alexander, J.C. (1988) 'The New Theoretical Movement', in N.J. Smelser (ed.), *Handbook of Sociology*. New York: Sage.

Alexander, J.C. and B. Giesen (1987) 'From Reduction to Linkage: Their Long View of the Macro–Micro Debate', Introduction, *The Micro–Macro Link*, J.C. Alexander et al. (eds). Berkeley: University of California Press.

Collins, Randall (1981) 'On the Microfoundations of Macrosociology', *American Journal of Sociology*, 86 (5).

Collins, Randall (1988) 'The Micro Contribution to Macro Sociology', *Sociological Theory*, 6.

Galtung, Johan (1988) *Methodology and Development*. Copenhagen: Ejlers.

PART III

METHODOLOGICAL APPROACHES TO COMPARATIVE RESEARCH

7

Comparing Semi-corruption among Parliamentarians in Britain and Australia

Eva Etzioni-Halevy

Sociological analysis has a tendency to divide social reality into the legitimate and the illegitimate; the proper and the corrupt. By contrast, that which falls in the grey zone in between, semi-deviance, especially semi-corruption, is a slice of reality which has not received the attention it deserves. This chapter is concerned with one type of semi-corruption: that of members of parliament maintaining private, outside, pecuniary interests, and it compares this phenomenon across two nations: Britain and Australia. It first sets out the theoretical framework for the comparison. Next, some methodological problems of comparing semi-corruption across nations are highlighted. Finally, the comparison's main results are presented, and analysed in the light of these problems.

The Theoretical Framework

Semi-corruption is here viewed as the result of a deliberate choice made by a political elite to maintain a collusion with other elites, which leads to the over-representation of corporate interests – at the expense of unorganized interests – in the political arena, and thereby to the exacerbation of inequalities. This conceptualization is, of course, in contrast to the Marxist-structural position, in the framework of which one would have to argue that over-representation of corporate-capitalist interests, and the resulting inequalities, are inherent in the constraints of the capitalist system, and in the power wielded by capitalists in it. Here it is argued that such a perspective would be a simplistic, if not a reductionist, model of what actually happens. For, first, apart from the power of the capitalist elite, that of the trade-union elite has to be reckoned with as well. Second, while the capitalists wield economic power, the political-parliamentary elite has the power of determining the extent to which it will or will not allow such economic power to be translated into the political sphere.

Rejecting a Marxist-structural perspective, this analysis is presented in the framework of a democratic-elite or a demo-elite theoretical perspective. In the wake of Max Weber, Gaetano Mosca, Joseph Schumpeter and Raymond Aron, the central argument of this perspective (as presented at greater length elsewhere, 1989) is that in Western countries there is a relative autonomy of elites[1] from one another, and in particular of certain other elites from the governing political elite, that this limits the power of each elite, and that this is one of the most distinctive features of Western democracy.

Historically, this has come about through successive elites' struggles, leading, for instance, to the gradual development of the autonomy of parliamentary/party (particularly opposition) elites, and to that of trade unions and their elites from the government. These struggles have also manifested themselves as struggles for the development of the principles of democracy, including the principle of free elections, and of freedom of speech and association. Consequently, the relative autonomy of elites has become enshrined in and legitimized by, these principles, and has been institutionalized in certain democratic structures. Indeed – apart from whatever powers and freedoms they may grant to the public – this relative autonomy of elites is what the principles and structural arrange-ments of democracy are chiefly about. For instance, the principles of free elections and freedom of speech and association – as institutionalized in parliamentary structures, party systems and electoral arrangements – protect the relative autonomy of parlia-mentary/political party (particularly oppositional) elites. The principle of freedom of association – as institutionalized in relatively free trade unions – also protects the autonomy of the trade-union elite, as well as that of the elites of other associations and organizations.

However, relative autonomy never spells complete autonomy, and elite autonomy is variable as well as fragile: at times it is deficient, or breaks down. This is usually the result of deliberate elite decisions and actions, and where it is the case, this not only obviates the ability of elites to limit one another's power, and thus the principles of democracy, but thereby also creates a fertile soil for corruption or semi-corruption.

Semi-corruption, the Collusion of Elites and Inequality

Political corruption and semi-corruption are here defined as the exchange of resources accruing from public office for other resources, respectively in illegitimate or semi-legitimate ways. Corruption is thus illegitimate, that is, in transgression of laws and prevalent social norms. Not so semi-corruption, which generally is in line with some, but contrary to other, widely held norms and values. It may be recognized by the controversiality which surrounds its propriety, and the ambivalence with which it is regarded: it is usually condoned by some but condemned by others, and/or condoned and condemned by the same people.

Elites are here defined as persons, or groups of persons, who wield power on the basis of being the chief controllers of resources in society, with each elite specializing in the control of certain types of resources. Autonomy is here defined as having control of resources that are relatively immune from external (particularly government) control. In a democracy, elites have achieved a degree of such immunity in their control of resources. But some elites have also deliberately maintained a degree of dependence on other elites, which in turn facilitates the exchange of resources between them, even in illegitimate or semi-legitimate ways. Such a deliberate collusion of elites thus fertilizes the soil on which corruption or semi-corruption is likely to flourish. This works first and foremost for the mutual advantage of those directly involved in the exchange. But when it becomes a general pattern its effects are multiplied, and it works to the advantage of the (frequently corporate) elites involved as a whole – that is, in favour of those who already enjoy significant advantages.

The Argument in a Nutshell

In short, it is argued that the development of Western democracy has been intertwined with struggles for, and achievements in terms of, the relative autonomy of elites, that these achievements have been incomplete and occasionally deficient, that such deficiencies can be seen not as the result of structural constraints, but rather as the outcome of deliberate decisions made by elites, that when elites opt for such cosy, incestuously close relations amongst them, this is likely to give rise to political corruption or semi-corruption, as recognizable by the controversiality and ambivalence with which it is regarded. This, in turn, works to the advantage of the (frequently corporate) elites involved in the practice as over the general public, and thereby results in the exacerbation of (already existing) social, economic and political inequalities. Illustrative support for this argument comes from a comparative study of outside pecuniary interests of members of parliament in Britain and Australia.

Comparing Semi-corruption across Nations: Some Methodological Considerations

The appropriateness of a comparative study
The idea of studying this type of semi-corruption – involving the political-parliamentary elite – in at least two political systems (that is, in a comparative perspective) follows logically from, indeed is inherent in, the theoretical perspective here presented and in the argument emanating from it. For, unlike the Marxist-structural theory, which views socio-political inequalities in Western democracies as inherent in the capitalist system and thus frequently generalizes across all capitalist democracies, the demo-elite theory here presented emphasizes, besides the common denominator of democracies, some significant differences amongst them. By contending that, within the general framework of relative elite autonomy in Western democracy, elites may make different decisions with respect to the degree of their mutual autonomy versus dependence, this theoretical perspective in effect calls for a comparative study in order to examine this argument on the empirical level. By arguing that within the general framework of Western democracy, semi-corruption – and the inequalities exacerbated by it – are the result of such collusions, deliberately entered into by some elites more than by others, this theory makes a comparative study practically mandatory.

The selection of countries for comparison
Consequently, the basic assumption guiding this study has been that the significance of the phenomena under study – no less than their explanation – could best be brought out by exploring their manifestations in at least two political structures. The problem was, however, to locate the proper targets for comparison. For, obviously, to compare wholly identical phenomena would have been of little interest, and to compare totally dissimilar ones would have made little sense. The range of targets thus seemed to lie in between, requiring the study of political structures with a broad common denominator, on the basis of which contrasts could be highlighted and differentiating factors could be singled out.

In this context, the broadest common denominator would have to be the Western-democratic political structure, in the framework of which more subtle differences could be discerned. This common denominator, too, was evidently indicated by the demo-elite theoretical perspective, focusing on the relative autonomy of elites as a feature common and distinctive to Western democracies. While some non-Western countries now seem to be moving in the general direction of Western democracy, and while some initial indications of elite autonomy are visible in them, none the less the phenomenon of elite autonomy has not taken root there to a sufficient extent to enable us to view it as a denominator they have in common with more established Western democracies, on the background of which obviations of elite autonomy could be focused on. Hence the choice had to fall on well-established Western democracies.

Within those, moreover, the choice had to fall on countries with similar parliamentary systems or structures. Since the theoretical argument called for a study of some aspects of the roles and activities of political-parliamentary elites, the idea was that it was within similar parliamentary systems that the peculiarities in the manner in which the parliamentary elites defined their roles could best be compared and highlighted. The choice of countries with similar parliamentary structures was also indicated by the above theoretical argument; namely, that within Western democracies, differences in the degree of elite autonomy would be the result not of structural constraints, but of deliberate choices made by elites. To support this argument, it would have to be shown that within similar structural frameworks, and despite such similarities, elites still can make, and have made, different choices with respect to their own autonomy. And this could be shown only if the parliamentary structures of the countries compared indeed closely resembled each other.

In light of these considerations, an almost self-evident choice was a comparison of the phenomena under study in the British and Australian (federal) parliaments,[2] where these conditions applied: the Australian polity emerged from, and was modelled after the British (Westminster) system, and structural similarities were thus pervasive. Even here, the political-parliamentary structures were not identical: over the years, certain differences (such as the Australian federal structure) had emerged, as further illustrated below. But Britain and Australia were as similar in their political-parliamentary structures as two separate countries could be, and the choice of these countries for comparison thus seemed to be eminently suitable.

Britain and Australia also happened to be countries in which I had a special interest, and to which (because of language and other factors) I had especially easy access. The selection of the countries for comparison was thus also a pragmatic one, as it so often necessarily is. But the choice was certainly not merely pragmatic: I had equally as easy an access to other political structures (such as those of the United States and Israel) yet chose to confine myself to Britain and Australia, because of their structural similarities. No amount of soul-searching could tell me whether theoretical-methodological or pragmatic, objective or subjective factors were predominant in my choice, Thus, I can only hope that it has been guided by the former considerations more than by the latter ones.

This is important to me because, once the study was under way, the problem had to be faced whether the choice of countries for comparison had in fact been as felicitous as had initially been thought – as is explained below.

The problem of equivalence

Ever since Almond and Verba published their classical, but much criticized, study (1963) comparing the civic (that is, political) cultures of several nations, sociologists have been conscious of, and highly sensitive to, the problem of equivalence across systems (see, for example, the chapter by H. Teune in this volume). This, of course, is the problem of whether 'something' compared in different countries, or nations, is in fact the same, or equivalent in its significance, in the different settings; whether it holds an equivalent meaning for the people, actors or participants in the different countries, embedded as they are in different cultural contexts. The problem arises especially as the 'something' to be compared may be of different magnitude in the various settings, so that disparities in size or quantity may be translated not only into differences in quality, but into differences in meaning as well.

This problem is pertinent in all comparative studies, but its pertinence is even more evident when, as is the case in this study, not only people's actual patterns of action but also their norms and standards, their definitions of the situation and of their own roles, are to be compared. The problem is doubly prominent where the 'something' to be compared is as elusive as semi-corruption – the identification of which depends wholly on the meaning with which people endow their situations and their roles within it.

It is now widely recognized that this problem has no perfect solution, but that the search for its minimalization must lie in the comparison of countries in which the cultural contexts surrounding the 'something' to be compared are as similar as possible. Once again, this is so especially where corruption and even more so where semi-corruption are concerned. As has been pointed out in numerous studies (see, for instance, Heidenheimer et al., 1989) what may be defined as corrupt in a modern setting (such as nepotism) may be considered perfectly legitimate, if not obligatory, in a traditional one. Even within modern cultures, a mode of action that may be considered corrupt in one culture may be regarded with much more leniency in another one.

This is most emphatically so with respect to semi-corruption, which (as noted) is empirically recognizable purely on the basis of the controversiality which surrounds its propriety, and the ambivalence with which it is regarded by the participants. In principle, the possibility cannot be ruled out that the same pattern of action may be regarded as entirely proper in one modern setting, but with a degree of ambivalence in another one.

From this viewpoint, too, the choice of Britain and Australia for comparison had initially seemed an especially apt one: not only was the Australian political system modelled after the British one, but British rules of political propriety were adopted in Australia as well, as will be illustrated in the historical retrospect below. Not only are most Australians (still) of British origin, but this is even more so with respect to the Australian political-parliamentary elite.

Despite all this, and surprisingly, the problem of the equivalence of meanings loomed larger than had initially been expected. This soon became evident from the fact that, although in some respects the participants in the study in the two countries reacted similarly to the phenomenon under study, they reacted differently to the study itself: the British participants saw members' pecuniary interests as a legitimate topic of study; although some of them reacted with hostility to awkward (and for them, possibly, impertinent) questions, they never put into doubt the legitimacy of the study itself.

In contrast, some Australian participants saw members' outside pecuniary interests as unproblematic and, consequently, doubted whether the practice was even worthy of academic attention. As one respondent put it bluntly: 'Academics think up problems like this, but in the real world it doesn't exist.' It was never entirely clear whether Australian respondents belittled the study of members' pecuniary interests because the practice (being – as will be seen below – much less pervasive than in Britain) was truly innocuous in their country, or whether this belittling of the practice, and of the study pertaining to it, was part of the process of the practice's legitimation, a point which will be resumed below.

The level of comparison
Another problem that has to be faced by all comparative studies – including this one – is the level at which the comparison is to be performed. This, in other words, is the level at which the systems compared are to be sliced into, and the chunks, or slices, which are to be compared. This, as Teune (in this volume) points out, also involves the problem of the macro- versus micro-comparison: if the systems under comparison are to be sliced into at the macro-level, the level of the whole, the number of observations required in order to reach reasonably valid conclusions may exceed what is feasible in a single study. If, on the other hand, the systems are sliced into

at a lower level of generality, closer to the micro-level, then the problem arises of whether the micro in fact represents the macro, or whether observing something narrower within a broader system in fact tells us anything significant about the system as a whole.

Furthermore, some systems may well have a greater connectedness and uniformity than other systems. Hence the problem – particularly for a comparative analysis – is whether there are not some imperceptible differences in this respect between the settings to be compared: whether it may not be the case that in one setting the micro does, in fact, adequately represent the macro, while in another setting it does not, and how one is to tell the difference between the two.

From this point of view, the comparison of the activities of elites within political structures, or of political elites, is an especially appropriate one. For with respect to elites, the distinction between the micro and the macro melts away: elites are relatively small groups of persons, whose activities may be studied directly. They thus present a limited setting, open to analysis at the micro-level. Yet what they decide to do and actually do, has implications for the political system as a whole; indeed, it *is* a major part of the political system as a whole, and thus is clearly at the level of macro-analysis. Thus the problem that what may be merely micro in one setting may represent the macro in another setting, which may have greatly complicated the comparison between them, disappears where the study of elites is concerned.

The Comparative Study

The theoretical issues and methodological considerations reviewed obviously have had direct implications for the design of the study. Thus, the theoretical argument pertains to elites, and because elites are at the core of the political structure, where macro and micro merge into each other, there exist a variety of documents pertaining to both their past and present activities. Capitalizing on this, the gathering of information has been based, in the first instance, on the analysis of documents. Here, the fact that the political-parliamentary structures to be compared were so similar assumed special importance, for it meant that the documents generated by these structures were similar as well. Thus, both the British and Australian parliaments, apart from laying down certain pertinent laws and regulations, had also set up committees on members' interests, which generated reports and parliamentary debates, and these were all analysed in this study. Also, both parliaments had resolved to make it incumbent on members to declare outside pecuniary interests in registers of members' interests, the summary, comparison and analysis of which is at the core of this study.

Counteracting this advantage is the problem that members of elites are generally aware of their own importance, as well as exceedingly busy people. Hence they are difficult to access. They are generally not open to survey analysis, and need to be located and approached personally, their trust has to be gained, and at times they have to be coaxed into participating in a study. Making the initial contact for an interview, be it person-to-person or by presenting questions in writing, is therefore time- and energy-consuming. Since the study of elites is so labour-intensive, and since elites in two countries were included, and especially as the two countries are geographically so distant from each other, it was difficult to reach large proportions of the elites concerned in each of the countries compared.

However, since the quantitative information sought was available in documents, the information that remained to be obtained from interviews was such that it could easily be supplied by a small number of key informants. Furthermore, as the major issue explored, that of semi-corruption, could be empirically recognized by controversiality and ambivalence, it was sufficient to find out whether some participants had views on the legitimacy of the phenomenon under study which directly contradicted those of other participants, and whether some respondents had self-contradictory views about it, and whether this was true in both countries involved; it was not necessary to establish whether all respondents had such contradictory or self-contradictory views. In this respect, too, then, small numbers of respondents sufficed for the purpose of this study.

Thus, instead of being based on interviews with all, or with a representative sample of members of parliament, this study relied on interviews with key informants and participants, mostly, but not only, members of parliament involved with the committees on members' interests, or members who had participated in recent parliamentary debates on the topic. Twenty interviews were conducted, ten in Britain, and ten in Australia. In Britain, all interviews were conducted in face-to-face meetings; in Australia, three were conducted in face-to-face situations and, at the request of the respondents, three were conducted through lengthy telephone conversations and four consisted of respondents answering questions in writing.

The results of this study are now presented, in an attempt to bring out their interrelationships with the theoretical and methodological considerations and issues which guided it.

A Brief Comparative Retrospect

Presentation of the study's results with respect to the situation at present must be preceded by a (necessarily all too brief) historical retrospect. This retrospect is designed, first, to bring illustrative support for the theoretical argument that the development of Western democracies was intertwined with struggles for the relative autonomy of elites – including parliamentary/party/oppositional elites. It is also designed to bring out the similarity (though not identity) of political/parliamentary structures between the two countries under study – on the basis of which they were selected for comparison. It is on the basis of these similarities that the different decisions made by the two parliamentary elites with respect to their relations with the economic elites will then be highlighted.

In Britain there were protracted struggles of the parliamentary elite for power *vis-à-vis*, and immunity from the interference of, the Crown or the government. For this purpose it endeavoured to achieve a variety of parliamentary privileges, foremost amongst them, freedom of speech, given statutory recognition in 1689 (Williams, 1985: 36). At that time parliament also gained the ability to assert its own power over the king through impeachment. In this manner the monarchy was weakened and the responsibility of government to parliament gradually emerged. At the beginning of the nineteenth century a prime minister could still resist ouster by the House of Commons, but towards the middle of the century loss of confidence of the House led to immediate resignation.

The growth of the power of parliament, however, would have had little significance without the development in it of an elite that formed a clear, independent opposition to the government. And such an opposition could not appear without the development of political parties, whose power was based on election by a widening electorate. This, too, happened gradually: parliamentary groups named Tories and Whigs had existed since the end of the seventeenth century, but they were not clearly demarcated, and the government could usually ensure a majority for itself in parliament through a system of patronage. As long as this system lasted, the government could not be said to face a clearly demarcated opposition.

Members of the House, while benefiting from patronage, gradually came to recognize it as an impediment to parliamentary and oppositional independence. This led to successive parliamentary resolutions and legislation intended to debar those holding offices from the Crown, and thus subservient to it, from membership of the House (Doig, 1984: 43). In conjunction with other reforms, this led to the weakening of the patronage system, which was gradually eliminated during the latter part of the nineteenth century. Also at this time, with the widening of the electorate, political parties began to outbid one another for popular support. It is at this time, then, that a party/oppositional elite depending for its power on electoral success – and thus relatively independent from the government – emerged.

Concomitantly there was also some push for the increased autonomy of the parliamentary elite from the economic elite, but it was belated and only partial. Thus, since the Tudor period and until the beginning of the twentieth century, British members of parliament were not paid for their services, or reimbursed for their expenses. Since electoral expenses were exorbitant, only the wealthy (that is, people who were members of the economic elite) or those who had wealthy sponsors (that is, were dependent on the economic elite) could become parliamentarians. These were frequently anxious to secure loans, contracts and a variety of other benefits from the public purse for their financial patrons (Williams, 1985: 20–2).

Only in 1912 was a parliamentary fee of £400 authorized. However, as this pay included coverage for parliamentary expenses, it was too low to provide members with the actual means of livelihood. Modest improvements in members' pay were won over time, but only in 1971 were pay increases and separate payment of allowances for parliamentary expenses introduced, which made it possible for members of parliament to subsist on their salaries (Williams, 1985: 23–31). Even today, it is considered by some that these do not amount to full-time pay, and that they must be supplemented through outside remuneration. Thus the ties between the parliamentary elite and possible outside employers, or members of the economic elite, have not been fully severed.

Part of the British parliamentary elite has also developed ties with the trade-union elite, which tried to ensure that its interests were represented in parliament by sponsoring particular members of parliament. This sponsorship, which generally covered electoral expenses, parliamentary salaries, office space and secretarial help, was important for Labour members, many of whom were of modest means (Muller, 1977).

In Australia. In the parliaments of the colonies (later states), as in Britain, government patronage declined, and clearly demarcated political parties developed only gradually, although both processes were contracted within the nineteenth century. By the time the federal parliament came into existence in 1901, these developments had been largely completed, but the parliamentary elite still made an effort to ensure that parliamentary independence from government was preserved in the future as well. This is evident, for instance, from the Australian Constitutional Provision (Section 44 (v)) – originating in similar British legislation – which precludes members from having a pecuniary interest in an agreement with the Commonwealth public service.

Although in most respects Australia followed Britain, its parliamentary elite opted for more distant relations with the economic elite. This may be explained partly by the fact that Australia preceded Britain by about a decade in the formation of a Labour Party, established in Australia in the 1890s. Since the Labour Party's political elite already existed when the federal parliament came into being, and because of the relatively egalitarian values also amongst the other parts of the Australian political elite, the decision was made right from the beginning that parliamentarians ought to receive full-time salaries (Solomon, 1978: 96), so that not only the wealthy or those sponsored by the wealthy could serve. Pay for parliamentarians in Australia therefore preceded such pay in Britain by twelve years.

In line with this, the conception was adopted right from the beginning that being a member of parliament was a full-time occupation, and this conception was deliberately institutionalized in the parliament's pattern of sitting. Although parliament sits only a limited number of days each year, sittings are spaced out so as to make additional employment difficult. Australian parliamentarians thus resembled their British counterparts in the degree of independence they managed to gain from government; but by institutionalizing full-time work for full-time pay – which made it both unnecessary and difficult for them to maintain outside employment, and/or union sponsorship – they deliberately surpassed their British counterparts in the degree of independence they gained from the economic and trade-union elites.

Comparing the situation today

The differences in the manner in which the parliamentary elites in Britain and Australia chose to arrange their relations with the economic elites in the past have had some implications for the situation today. In both countries there are various constitutional provisions, laws and parliamentary resolutions which prohibit members of parliament accepting payment for parliamentary services, but they are vague and not too restrictive. Parliamentarians (with the exception of ministers) are not required to divest themselves of their outside pecuniary interests, but must list them in registers open for inspection by the public.

Despite these similarities in rules and regulations, there are substantial differences between the two countries in what actually happens, as can be seen from their respective registers. These registers have some shortcomings. For instance, in both countries members are not required to register the magnitude of their interests: some may be major, others may be trifling. The registers still present the closest available approximation to what is actually going on, as is shown in Tables 7.1 and 7.2.

Table 7.1 *Classified entries in the Register of British Members' Interests, 1987*

Abbreviated heading in Register	Conservative MPs		Labour MPs		Alliance MPs		Others		Total	
	no.	%	no.	%	no.	%	no.	%	no.	%
1 Directorships	146	38.9	20	8.7	3	13.6	5	20.8	174	26.7
2 Employment or office[a]	174	46.4	36	15.7	15	22.3	6	25.0	221	34.0
3 Trade or profession[b]	155	41.6	54	23.1	7	31.8	9	37.5	225	34.6
4 Clients	16	4.2	1	0.4	9	40.9	0	0.0	26	4.0
5 Financial sponsorship[c]	5	1.3	148	64.6	0	0.0	1	4.1	154	23.6
6 Overseas visits	68	18.0	32	14.0	1	4.5	1	4.1	102	15.6
7 Payments from abroad	6	1.6	1	0.4	9	40.9	0	0.0	16	2.5
8 Land and property	60	16.0	2	0.9	1	4.5	3	12.5	66	10.2
9 Declarable shareholdings[d]	79	21.0	9	3.9	2	9.0	2	8.3	92	14.1
Number of MPs	375		229		22		24		650	

Tables 7.1 and 7.2 do not record the number of entries each member has made for each heading. As members made entries under more than one heading, the percentage columns do not add up to 100%. 'Directorships' refers to remunerated directorships only.

[a] 'Employment or office' refers mainly to paid consultantships for private companies, for lobby organizations or for pressure groups.

[b] 'Trade or profession' refers mainly to the pursuit of some profession such as journalism or law, or being an underwriter for Lloyds, though occasionally MPs have listed consultantships under this heading.

[c] 'Financial sponsorship' refers mainly to sponsorship by trade unions, although in some rare cases, pertaining to Conservative MPs, it refers to a gift or other type of sponsorship.

[d] Declarable shareholdings refers to 1% or more of a company's shareholdings.

Source: Compiled by the author from British Parliament, *Register of Members' Interests, 1987*

Table 7.2   *Classified entries in the Register of Australian Federal Members' Interests, 1986*

Abbreviated heading in Register	ALP MPs		Liberal MPs		NPA MPs		Total	
	no.	%	no.	%	no.	%	no.	%
Shareholdings[a]	23	28.7	28	62.2	18	90.0	69	47.6
Family and business trusts	6	7.5	13	28.9	8	40.0	27	18.6
Real estate[b]	18	22.5	15	33.3	13	65.0	46	31.7
Directorships	8	10.0	20	44.4	12	60.0	40	27.6
Partnerships[c]	6	7.5	14	31.1	12	60.0	32	22.0
Bonds and debentures	9	11.2	10	22.2	5	25.0	24	16.5
Other assets[d]	7	8.7	4	8.9	2	10.0	13	9.0
Other sources of income[e]	9	11.2	15	33.3	3	15.0	27	18.6
Gifts of more than A$250	2	2.5	0	0.0	0	0.0	2	1.4
Travel and hospitality[f]	11	13.7	4	8.9	3	15.0	18	12.4
Other interests	1	1.25	1	2.2	1	5.0	3	2.0
Number of MPs	80		45		20		145	

[a] Unlike in Britain, in Australia the registration of shareholdings is not limited to 1% of a company's shareholdings and above.
[b] For 'Real estate', only holdings other than the member's residence and holiday home have been included.
[c] 'Partnerships' refer most frequently to farming, but legal partnerships have been registered as well.
[d] 'Other assets' excludes household and personal effects, etc.
[e] Under 'Other sources of income' members have registered mainly income derived from sources mentioned in previous entries, though a minute number of members have registered writing, royalties or pursuit of another profession such as medicine or law.
[f] 'Travel and hospitality' includes only sponsored travel and hospitality.

Source: Compiled by the author from Australian Parliament, *Register of Members' Interests, 1986*

It can be seen that significant and similar percentages of parliamentarians in the two countries hold remunerated directorships of companies. In both countries, most directorships are those of private companies (in Australia, by the account of respondents, they are mostly small family companies – that is, family businesses such as farms that have been turned into companies for the purpose of minimizing taxation). Important differences, however, emerge in other respects: whereas in Australia members occasionally engage in an outside profession, these practices are far less widespread than they are in Britain. Even more prominently: in Britain, a significant proportion of particularly Conservative members hold paid consultantships for companies, for lobby groups or even for foreign governments, the word 'consultantship' being chiefly a euphemism for representing the employers' interests in parliament. By contrast, in the Australian federal parliament, such consultantships are largely absent.

Also, in Britain, Labour members typically enjoy sponsorship by trade unions, which frequently covers large parts of their electoral or constituency expenses. In Australia the custom of trade-union sponsorship of members of parliament is much less widespread, although it does occur occasionally. This fact would not be recorded in the Register of Members' Interests. Instead, all candidates for parliament make declarations on contributions for their electoral expenses, recorded in registers, the most recent one being the *Funding and Disclosure Returns of the 11 July 1987 Election*. Perusal of this document indicates that out of 868 candidates for both houses of parliament, only four declared contributions of A$1,000 or more from trade unions. According to respondents, most electoral contributions go to parties rather than to individuals, and although a donor may stipulate that a donation be directed to X's electorate (which would not be listed in the *Funding and Disclosure Returns*), the practice of members of parliament obtaining union sponsorship is not widespread in Australia.

In short, the differences in the outside pecuniary interests of parliamentarians in the two countries show that the two parliamentary elites have opted to continue the different patterns of relations with the economic elites which they have established in the past. This finding raises an important question which is directly related to the methodological issues discussed before: given these different dimensions of pecuniary interests in the two countries, could it be that quantity is translated into quality, and the phenomena under study are really not equivalent in the meanings they hold for the participants in the two countries?

As meanings are difficult to pin down, this question cannot be answered with any degree of certitude. Some indications, however, can be found by looking at the manner in which the participants themselves evaluated the practice. By looking at their evaluation of the practice's degree of propriety or impropriety, it should also be possible to tell whether – in line with the argument presented before – the practice may be regarded as semi-corruption, and whether this is the case in both countries under study.

Members' Outside Pecuniary Interests as Semi-corruption

Semi-corruption, as previously defined, may be recognized by the controversiality of its propriety and by the ambivalence with which it is met. Interestingly, despite the much smaller dimensions of the practice of outside pecuniary interests in Australia as compared to

Britain, both controversiality of, and ambivalence towards, the practice are clearly evident in Australia no less than in Britain. Thus, the controversiality of the practice is evident from the fact that in both Britain and Australia most respondents saw it as legitimate or proper, but some clearly regarded it as illegitimate or improper. The ambivalence of the practice was evident from hesitant, equivocal, self-contradictory statements as illustrated below.

Legitimation in Britain
Not surprisingly, Conservative members were more likely to legitimize private interests, while Labour members were more likely to justify union sponsorship, although this did not hold in all cases. Legitimation of both practices was generally based on the following lines of reasoning. British history and tradition: in the past, British parliamentarians were not paid, and then were paid only small amounts, and in line with this tradition, even at present were not paid 'full' salaries. Members' financial needs: because of this, members had to supplement their incomes. Further, they could not be required to sever their links with private companies because they might lose their seats, and by that time they might be too old to find new jobs. Keeping in touch with the community: members connected with private companies or unions were not 'cut off' from the 'real world', preserving a 'grassroots connection'. Members' honour: members were called 'honourable', and this had to be relied on. Declaring it makes it all right: anything that was open and above board could not be corrupt. There was no quid pro quo: retained or sponsored members were not bribed, or bought.

Legitimation in Australia
In Australia, too, members' financial needs, their integrity, the necessity of keeping in touch with the community, were invoked. In addition, it was held that if people were required to divest themselves of all outside interests, you would not get people willing to serve in parliament. It would not do much good either, for a connection with a company or a union might be maintained even if it was dormant. In both countries, however, not all participants found these lines of reasoning satisfactory.

Denigration and ambivalence in Britain
Some respondents denigrated the practice on the ground that it generated a conflict of interest: it interfered with members' undivided loyalty to their constituencies by creating loyalties to other interests. Other respondents showed ambivalence towards the practice as expressed, for instance, in the following self-contradictory statement:

'There could be a conflict of interest, but if interests are declared there is not much danger of that because others would be suspicious. But there is a danger. If too many members have consultancies it would put business interests first.'

Denigration and ambivalence in Australia
In Australia, negative attitudes towards the propriety of outside pecuniary interests were expressed, for instance, by respondents who warned that if the salaries of parliamentarians in Australia were to remain as low as they currently were, members would pick up more and more business interests and the situation would increasingly resemble that in Britain, or that – although members with certain interests in an issue were not allowed to vote on it in parliament – they would still be obliged to do so if otherwise the government would be defeated. Ambivalence towards the practice was expressed, for instance, in the following musings: 'How do you define conflict of interest? If someone makes money out of being a parliamentarian this is wrong . . . [but] if someone feels strongly about something, he won't sell out.'

It could be seen, then, that despite its different dimensions in Britain and Australia, in both countries the propriety of the practice was surrounded by controversiality and ambivalence. The data thus support the argument presented at the beginning; namely, that this type of collusion amongst elites may be seen as semi-corruption. The finding is also important from the viewpoint of some of the methodological considerations raised above: despite the misgivings that initially have been entertained about this, the findings showed that in this important respect the significance the practice held for participants in both countries was quite similar. This, despite the fact that (as noted), in Australia several respondents tended to argue that the practice was not a problem there, hence not a worthy topic of academic study, while this attitude was not shared by British respondents.

What Members Supply in Return

While in some respects members' outside pecuniary interests held a similar meaning for the participants in the two countries, the different magnitude of the phenomenon in the two settings was still problematic for the comparative dimension of this study. Since, in contrast to Britain, the phenomenon of members being retained by companies or unions to represent their interests in parliament was not widespread in Australia, the question that arises in Britain – namely, what corporations, organizations and trade unions may expect to obtain in return for the resources they spend on retaining parliamentarians – simply does not arise in Australia. In this respect, then, there is nothing to compare, and the analysis of this issue must be confined to Britain only.

This issue is not a simple one, for companies or unions would tend to retain members who would be in sympathy with their general aims, and so would be promoting them in any case. None the less, it has been reported by respondents that there is much that parliamentarians can do, and have been doing specifically in favour of their companies or unions, in the following ways:

- *Providing information and advice*, including information on the government's way of thinking about matters that are of concern to retainers, thus providing them with an 'early warning system', which was 'worth a lot' to them.
- *Providing access* to the House, to a minister, or to the civil service, for instance, by arranging a visit, which otherwise might be more difficult to obtain. This does not ensure a favourable policy outcome but ensures that the clients' views are taken account of when policies are made.
- *Lobbying*, for instance, in the party room, in a committee, or in parliament itself. Although members cannot vote independently (except on matters of conscience), and although they cannot vote on issues in which they have an interest, they can have a major effect on legislation in its preliminary stage, at which point retained MPs could express, and lobby for, the views of their retainers. Or else, lobbying could take place by having 'a quiet word with the minister' on behalf of a retainer. The member would then have to declare his or her interest. Also, the minister would know that he or she is being watched by the civil service, and by the Public Accounts Committee. Despite all this, the possibility that a minister might be influenced by members' submissions on behalf of their clients could not be ruled out.
- *Lending status and respectability*, particularly to businesses; for instance, by participating in meetings with their clients. This would help enhance the firms' status which, in turn, would help them impress, reassure or mollify clients, and thereby increase or maintain profits.

In general, there is nothing unlawful in the various benefits that parliamentarians can and do confer on their retainers. Yet thereby those retainers gain representation for their interests which is denied to other citizens.

Conclusion

This chapter has analysed the outside pecuniary interests of members
of parliament in Britain as compared to Australia in the framework
of a demo-elite perspective. This perspective centres on the argument
that one of the most significant developments in Western democracy
has been the struggle for, and the achievement in terms of, the
relative autonomy of elites. These achievements have then been
institutionalized in democratic principles and structures. Yet, at
times, elites in democracies have deliberately opted for close
relations with other elites, thus partly obviating this autonomy, and
when this is the case, it fertilizes the soil for corruption or semi-
corruption, which in turn increases social inequalities.

Logically, the empirical examination of this theoretical argument
calls for a comparative study, and one which includes Western
democracies that are as structurally similar as possible. For, only
when at least two democratic countries are compared, and only
when their structural features are held constant, can it be shown
that possible differences between them in elite dependence are
indeed the result of deliberate and different decisions made by elites
as to their closeness to, versus distance from, other elites. The
countries chosen for comparison, Britain and Australia, seemed to
meet these criteria, as several (though not all) structural features
of their polities have been quite similar.

The results of the study showed that in its main thrust the
theoretical argument was supported in that, in spite of these
structural similarities, the British parliamentary elite has opted for
much closer relations with the economic elite than has its Australian
counterpart. However, because of these differences in elite choices,
the comparison also entailed some difficulties: it turned out that the
practice under study, that of parliamentarians maintaining outside
pecuniary interests, was considered as worthy of study by the
participants interviewed in Britain, but was considered as unproblematic and hence as unworthy of academic attention in Australia.

This difference in the manner in which the participants in the two
countries regarded this study raised some misgivings as to whether
the practice around which the study was focused did indeed hold
equivalent meanings across the two socio-political and cultural
systems. Reassurance on this point came from the fact that in both
countries the propriety of the practice was controversial, and there
was a significant degree of ambivalence towards it. This similarity
also led to the conclusion that – by the previously presented
definition of controversiality and ambivalence towards its propriety

– the practice was semi-corrupt in both of the settings concerned. Why a practice, the legitimacy of which was clearly controversial, and which aroused a degree of ambivalence and thus was semi-corrupt even in Australia, and certainly was not unproblematic there, should be *pronounced* to be unproblematic and hence unworthy of study, still remains a puzzle.

The different dimensions of the practice of outside pecuniary interests in the British as compared to the Australian parliament meant, however, that there was a certain phenomenon which existed only in the former, and where, therefore, no comparisons could be made. And this, indeed, was the final conclusion of this study: while both British and Australian members of parliament have outside pecuniary interests, only British parliamentarians have become mediators between corporate (private corporations' and trade unions') interests and the political arena (parliament and government). When all such mediating acts are combined, they may be seen to have a formidable impact on how information and views are fed into government decisions, and on how this works in the interests of corporations and trade unions and, in fact, in the interests of all concerned except those of the unorganized public. In this manner the interests of the capitalist/corporate sector are over-represented, and those of the public are under-represented in the political arena, and inequalities between them are exacerbated.

Notes

I am grateful to Professor Else Øyen of the University of Bergen, and to Dr Michael Shalev of the Hebrew University, Jerusalem, for their most helpful comments.

1. These concepts are defined later.
2. Only the House of Commons in Britain and the House of Representatives in Australia have been included in the study.

References

Almond, Gabriel and Sidney Verba (1963) *The Civic Culture*. Boston: Little, Brown.
Australian Parliament (1986) *Register of Members' Interests as at 8 August 1986*. Canberra: Government Printer.
Australian Electoral Commission (1987) *Funding and Disclosure Returns of the 11 July 1987 Election*. Microfilm.
British Parliament (1987) *Register of Members' Interests on the 8th December 1987*. London: Her Majesty's Stationery Office.
Doig, Alan (1984) *Corruption and Misconduct in Contemporary British Politics*. Harmondsworth, Middx: Penguin Books.
Etzioni-Halevy, Eva (1989) *Fragile Democracy*. New Brunswick, NJ: Transaction Books.
Heidenheimer, Arnold J., Michael Johnston and Victor T. Levine (eds) (1989)

Political Corruption: A Handbook. New Brunswick, NJ: Transaction Books (rev. edn).

Muller, William D. (1977) *The Kept Men?* Hassocks, Sussex: Harvester Press.

Solomon, David (1978) *Inside the Australian Parliament.* Sydney: George Allen & Unwin.

Teune, Henry (1990) 'Comparing Countries: Lessons Learned' (in this volume).

Williams, Sandra (1985) *Conflict of Interests.* Aldershot, Hants: Gower.

8

A Comparative Content Analysis of Biographies

Ralph H. Turner

Valid content analysis of documents such as biographies, autobiographies, letters and recorded conversations depends upon the assumption that words or phrases have uniform meanings for relevant audiences. When investigators are not from the same culture and subculture as the creators and users of the documents, it is imperative that they find some way to validate their interpretations. In comparative research involving documents from different countries the problem is magnified. Formally identical words or phrases may have different connotations in different countries. Furthermore, the investigator will usually understand the meanings from one culture better than the meanings from the other. In this chapter I report a fairly simple procedure which was used in comparing corporation biographies from Britain and the United States, taking into account the different connotations of some terms in the two countries and the difference in class background between the investigators and the intended audience for the biographies. The procedure, using national validation panels, is an adaptation from well-known procedures in social psychology. It has not, however, been widely used in content analysis (Berelson, 1952; Carney, 1979; Holsti, 1969; Krippendorff, 1980). Although the documents were all in English, a similar procedure could easily be employed for documents in different languages.

The Substantive Issue

Putatively open class societies differ not only in what they count as success but also in the career patterns they favour and support as routes to success. It has been suggested that British society tends to favour success through *sponsorship*, while American society leans toward success through competition in an open *contest* (Turner, 1960). The difference is lodged in the respective cultures, affecting the way people think about upward mobility and shaping the educational system and strategies for social control. Several hypotheses concerning British–American differences have been deduced from this broad distinction and previously subjected to partial empirical test (Turner, 1966).[1]

In the current investigation we sought to compare public biographies of executives for evidence of sponsorship or contest careers. We should not assume that public biographies are faithful accounts which tell the reader the extent to which their subjects 'succeeded' through sponsorship or contest. Instead, we assume that public biographies are 'slanted' for audience credibility, stressing sponsorship in a culture where that mode of ascent is best understood, and stressing contest features in a culture where they are best understood.

The Publicity-release Biographies

We first looked in mass circulation magazines for biographies of successful men and women. Several decades ago, in American magazine biographies, Leo Lowenthal (1943) had already noted declining attention to people from the serious world and the world of production, and increasing attention to people in the leisure spheres of entertainment and sports. Nevertheless, 'success' biographies are still a common feature in American magazines, although our investigation suggested a tendency for the once-popular rags-to-riches sagas to be replaced by moderate-riches-to-great-wealth stories. But a careful search revealed that, except in magazines dealing exclusively with entertainment and sports, 'success' biographies were notably absent from British periodicals.[2] Since corporations commonly prepare information about their top executives for public distribution in the form of publicity releases, we then decided to compare biographical materials released by large British and American corporations. The orienting question was whether the difference between sponsorship and contest cultures would be reflected in the way these materials were presented.

Requests were sent to fifty-three leading American corporations and fifty-one British corporations[3]. All American corporations replied, and fifty-two sent a total of 621 biographies of executives raised in the United States. Thirty-seven British corporations replied, and twenty-six sent a total of 134 biographies of executives raised in Britain. All but four of the American companies sent materials that had evidently been designed for mass distribution as a way of representing the company to the outside world. Only fourteen of the twenty-six British companies sent comparable materials. The remainder sent typewritten originals that appeared to have been especially prepared to satisfy the request, or extracts from house publications or commercial magazines.

Biographies from both countries were generally brief and factual, lacking the flesh-and-blood character and fictionalization normally found in magazine and newspaper biographies. Elements of plot and personal characterization are only found in a few of the longer biographies. The American biographies were, in most instances, longer and richer in detail than the British biographies.

Biographies were first analysed under ten themes; namely, vital data, parentage, education, work history, public sphere activities, performance and related qualities, rewards for performance, personal qualities, leisure usage, and residence. No important differences were found between countries in the attention given to these various themes. We were then ready for the more significant examination of awards and of the verb-phrases used to describe career progress.

Awards

The nature of awards mentioned in materials designed to project a favourable impression of a successful individual should be an important clue to the culture of career advancement. One can assume that only those awards that indicate valued forms of recognition from agents who are important for validating success will be mentioned. A contest system calls for highly visible credentials requiring no special skill for assessment, because the credentials are presented to a mass audience. Credentials in a sponsorship system serve more to identify members of the elite to one another and, hence, may require some sophistication before proper discriminations can be made. The contest system is characteristic of a society with multiple elites, and hence we might expect awards to come from constituent segments of the society, including the business community. A sponsorship pattern arises in a society with an integrated and centralized elite structure, so we might expect to find awards granted by a central agent representing the entire elite hierarchy rather than specialized elites (Turner, 1960).

From the foregoing observations, two guiding hypotheses were formulated. First, in American biographies, the mass validation of status under a contest system will be reflected in greater concern with making the nature of awards understandable to the ordinary reader than in British biographies. Second, awards mentioned in American biographies will more often be conferred by constituent 'establishments' in contrast to awards conferred by the central establishment in British biographies.

Many of the biographies contained a standard section entitled 'Honours and Awards' and all entries so listed were recorded and tabulated. Other references to awards could often be found throughout the text, and these too were recorded. Especially in British biographies, honorific titles and honorary degrees sometimes appeared after the executive's name without comment. These were also counted as awards. References to membership in organizations designated only by Greek letters and honorary societies in general were omitted because of the practical difficulties in determining which were honorary and which were social fraternities or open professional associations. As well as we can judge, inclusion of this category would not have altered any of the findings. Each mention of an award served as a unit in the analysis that follows.

Table 8.1 *Types of awards in biographies (percentages)*

Conferring agent	Britain		USA	
Government	53		11	
Civil		39		2
Military		14		9
Foreign government	17		7	
Civil		10		6
Military		7		1
Business and industry	11		22	
Foreign industry	2		1	
College and university	13		42	
Honorary degrees		4		31
Academic and scholastic		9		5
Achievement and distinguished service		0		6
Foreign honorary degrees	2		1	
Other agents	2		16	
Sports organizations		0		3
Religious organizations		0		3
Humane organizations		0		1
Community service organizations		0		2
Patriotic organizations		0		2
Farm organizations, clubs		0		1
Masonic lodge, fraternities		0		2
Other		2		2
Total (per cent)	100		99	
Total number of awards	123		456	

The distribution of awards according to a set of categories developed from the data is presented in Table 8.1. The first hypothesis receives only partial confirmation. The awards mentioned in British biographies do identify the superior status of the recipients to the general reader in clear and unambiguous fashion, contrary to the hypothesis. However, the mention of awards in American biographies was much more frequently accompanied by a brief statement of the reasons for conferral than was the case in British biographies. In the abundant listing of civil titles in British biographies, only three included any mention of reasons for the award.

Evidence for the second hypothesis is clearer. If government as award-giver best represents the idea of a centralized elite structure, the difference between 53 per cent of awards from government in Britain and only 11 per cent in the United States affords strong support for the hypothesis. If military awards are omitted, the difference between 39 per cent in British biographies and only 2 per cent in American biographies is even more striking. British government awards are mostly royal awards. Outstanding executives were granted peerages or baronetcies, knighted, given titles such as Commander of the British Empire or Order of the British Empire, made Privy Councillor, and given other recognitions of the same kind.

Business and industry, as the most relevant constituent segment, grant a fair number of awards in both countries. However, in conformity with the hypothesis, such awards are twice as frequent in the United States. Colleges and universities account for the largest number of awards in the United States, in one of the greatest differences between the countries, though British biographies report more strictly academic awards than American biographies. We shall return for further consideration of school awards later.

The other important difference between countries is in the 14 per cent given for sports, religious activity, humane accomplishments, patriotic activity, community service, farm work, and Masonic lodge and fraternity achievements in the American biographies. No awards in any of these categories are listed in British biographies. Although polite sports achievements are often socially important and community service is a partial qualification for many of the royal awards already discussed, only recognition by the Crown merits mention. In the United States a wide variety of local and specialized organizations grant awards in recognition of contributions to the activities they foster, and these awards are considered relevant to the executive career and important and valid enough as indicators of career progress to be mentioned in corporation biographies.

The hypothesis that the source of British awards reflects the recognition of a centralized elite structure and that the source of American awards reflects recognition of a structure of multiple elites is confirmed. The hypothesis that British awards identify members of the elite to one another while American awards identify the successful to a broader audience must be modified. The awards, and especially the routine use of honorific titles, clearly tell every reader who has been accorded elite recognition. However, under the contest system it is assumed that the general reader wants to know what the successful person accomplished, while in a sponsorship system it is enough for the general reader to know that the person's success has been recognized by the highest authority.

Thirty-one per cent of American awards were honorary college and university degrees, and 6 per cent were non-degree awards given by American academic institutions for achievement and distinguished service, compared with only 4 per cent of British awards. As a serendipitous finding, this observation suggests a *pseudo-sponsorship* pattern in the United States. Honorary degrees have some of the same quality as civil government awards in Britain. They are granted by a putatively disinterested agency. They are non-specific in nature, implying major service to the community rather than specific and segmental accomplishments. However, unlike British civil awards, they come from centres of prestige with relatively modest power. The honorary degree and service award, especially from minor colleges, must be understood as an exchange of benefits. In return for awarding an honorary degree, the college expects direct financial contributions and aid in raising funds, and hopes to gain lustre from its association with an influential and successful person. The executive's gain is less tangible, but probably involves a form of recognition that seems more broadly based than business achievement and which conveys an image of humane and service achievements that the business community cannot confer. The American pattern suggests a response to strains in the contest system. With no way to attain consensual induction into a truly comprehensive elite in America, members of the business elite advertise these ostensibly broadly based awards that identify them with a pseudo-elite of humane and service accomplishments.

Analysis of Verb Expressions

In spite of the parsimonious nature of the publicity materials, we anticipated that subtle indications of sponsorship and contest patterns of ascent might be found in the way in which career advancements were described. The verbs and verbal phrases used to describe movements from one position to another were taken as the key indicators. We chose verbs because they are the principal cultural resource for action and change, and mobility is action and change. The general characterization of sponsorship and contest systems led to the formulation of two hypotheses. First, the implied or explicit source of the impetus to advancement should be different. In a contest system, individuals are more often expected to supply the impetus themselves, to take the initiative in advancing themselves.

Alternatively, they may be chosen and supported for advancement by their subordinates and their peers. In contrast, sponsorship means that the impetus comes from superiors, or alternatively from the more impersonal 'system'. Second, the implication of *upward* movement should be clearer and more prevalent in the contest system, as each move is seen as a victory or the accumulation of points. Similarly, contest biographies should make clear that each step upward is a reward for some identifiable accomplishment. The latter observation is similar to the finding about awards, which were more often accompanied by accounts of the achievements that led to the award in American biographies. The idea is carried one step further by suggesting that the same principle should also influence the choice of verbs and verb phrases used in referring to a job change.

The two hypotheses are as follows. Third, in referring to job changes, American biographies will more often use verbs and verb phrases that imply personal impetus for the change or selection by subordinates and peers, while British biographies will more often use verbs and verb phrases that imply impetus from above or from an impersonal system. Fourth, American biographies will more often use verbs and verb phrases that clearly imply upward movement and that imply that the change of position came about as a reward for accomplishment of some sort, as compared with British biographies.

Fifty-eight different verbs and verb phrases describing job change were identified in the biographies. Some examples are as follows: 'accepted the position of', 'was appointed', 'was called upon to', 'climbed to the position of', 'was elected', 'the job of . . . fell to him', 'was given the job of', 'moved forward to the position of', 'was posted to', 'was persuaded to join', 'was seconded to', 'was sent for', 'was stationed at', 'seized the chance to become', 'worked his way up'.

Although the investigator could have classified each of the verbs and verb phrases according to the variables in the four hypotheses, this procedure might lead to invalid results. It could not be assumed that all of these terms had the same connotations in Britain and the United States; it could not be assumed that an American investigator could correctly assign connotations to the British use of terms; and it could not be assumed that an investigator, steeped in an American academic subculture, could correctly assign connotations to terms as they were used even by Americans in a business and industrial subculture. The intended audience for these biographical materials was plainly not the general public – journalists would rewrite some of them for that purpose – nor academics, but managers and executives in business and industry. What were needed were plainly two panels of judges, chosen from British and American business and industry.

A questionnaire was prepared for distribution to the two panels of judges. The questionnaire listed the fifty-eight verbs and verb expressions and asked the judge to answer 'yes' or 'no' to each of six questions concerning each expression. The questions were as follows:

1　Does the word or phrase suggest to you that the impetus for change of position came from the individual's *own initiative*?
2　Does the word or phrase suggest to you that the change of position came about on the initiative of the individual's *superiors*?
3　Does the word or phrase suggest to you that the change of position came about on the initiative of the individual's *equals*: that is, people in the same type or level of job as the individual?
4　Does the word or phrase suggest to you that the change came about as a matter of *routine in the system* (for example, rotation, seniority and so on)?
5　Does the word or phrase suggest to you that the change was earned, as a *reward* for outstanding accomplishment in the prior position?
6　Does the word or phrase suggest to you that the change was a move to a *higher or better position*?

At the time the data were gathered, available resources were not sufficient to design and survey rigorous samples of British and American business and industrial officials. Consequently small convenience samples were used, counting on a fairly high degree of consensus to lend validity to the results. The investigator distributed questionnaires to business executives and business-connected professionals of his personal acquaintance in Los Angeles. A total of fourteen completed and returned the questionnaires in the stamped envelopes provided. Cooperation from a similar group of twenty-six business and professional persons in London and the Midlands was secured by a British consultant.[4] It should be noted in passing that several of the respondents complained about the length and difficulty of the questionnaire, and might not have completed it but for personal ties to the investigator or the consultant.

For analysis, an expression was assigned to one of the categories indicated in the questionnaire whenever there was 60 per cent agreement among judges from a given country. Expressions on which there was less than 60 per cent agreement were not used. In each country, each verb expression was assigned to the categories to which that country's panel of judges had assigned it. The categories corresponding to the first four questions (regarding the impetus for job change) were almost always perceived as mutually exclusive. Consequently we classified each expression in only one of the categories: superiors, equals, self or system. The other two questions were tabulated separately, indicating whether the job change came as a reward and whether it was a move to a higher position. The resulting tabulations are presented in Table 8.2.

Table 8.2 *Uses of verbs and verb phrases (percentages)*

	Britain	USA	Difference
Agent			
Superiors	56.4	52.3	+ 4.1
Equals (peers)	2.7	18.6	−15.9
Self	11.3	4.0	+ 7.3
System	29.4	24.0	+ 5.4
Not classified	0.2	1.1	− 0.9
Total (per cent)	100.0	100.0	0.0
Total number of references	622	2,533	
Reward			
Reward implied	2.5	14.0	−11.5
Reward not implied	93.5	48.3	+45.2
Not classified	4.0	37.7	−33.7
Total	100.0	100.0	0.0
Upward movement			
Upward movement implied	14.8	34.8	−20.0
Upward movement not implied	34.2	16.7	+17.5
Not classified	50.9	48.5	+ 2.4
Total	99.9	100.0	− 0.1

Verbs and verb phrases in each country's biographies are classified according to the judgements by that country's panel.

The hypothesis of greater impetus from equals in American biographies appears to be well supported by the data. The differences in the remaining categories of superiors, self and system are much smaller and in the opposite direction, and should therefore not be interpreted individually. However, the hypothesis of greater self-impetus in American biographies is clearly disconfirmed. Also, the difference in the 'equals' category is largely explained by the much more frequent use of the verb 'elected' in American biographies. While judges in both countries agreed that this term implied peer selection, election can refer to selection from above. Perhaps the term 'election' was favoured in American materials because of its democratic ring, to describe a process that was much less than democratic in operation.

The hypotheses that American biographies will more often employ verb expressions that imply upward movement and reward for some accomplishment are well supported in Table 8.2. Whereas judges were in satisfactory agreement concerning the locus of the impetus for job change, levels of agreement were much lower in case of implied reward and upward movement. British judges were in fair agreement over implied reward, but verb expressions that were ambiguous to American judges accounted for over one-third of the references in the American biographies. If we recalculate percentages, omitting the ambiguous references, we still find substantial difference between 2.6 per cent references implying reward in British biographies compared with 22.5 per cent in American biographies. Ambiguity is even greater for implications of upward movement, and equally great in both sets of biographies. With ambiguous references omitted, 30.2 per cent of references in British biographies and 67.6 per cent in American biographies are read as implying upward movement.

Two variables are mixed in the foregoing analysis: namely, the frequency with which the verb expressions appear in the two

Table 8.3 *Uses of verbs and verb phrases, as classified by each country's panel (percentages)*

	British classification			US classification		
	Brit. biog.	US biog.	Diff.	Brit. biog.	US biog.	Diff.
Agent						
Superiors	56.4	52.2	+ 4.2	56.0	52.3	+ 3.7
Equals (peers)	2.7	18.6	−15.9	2.7	18.6	−15.9
Self	11.3	8.6	+ 2.7	9.6	4.0	+ 5.6
System	29.4	20.4	+ 9.0	26.2	24.0	+ 2.2
Not classified	0.2	0.2	0.0	5.5	1.1	+ 4.4
Total	100.0	100.0	0.0	100.0	100.0	0.0
Reward						
Reward implied	2.5	6.3	− 3.8	6.4	14.0	− 7.6
Reward not implied	93.5	88.0	+ 5.5	66.8	48.3	+18.5
Not classified	4.0	5.7	− 1.7	26.8	37.7	−10.9
Total	100.0	100.0	0.0	100.0	100.0	0.0
Upward movement						
Upward movement implied	14.8	16.7	− 1.9	17.2	34.8	−17.6
Upward movement not implied	34.2	48.0	−13.8	13.5	16.7	− 3.2
Not classified	50.9	35.3	+15.6	69.3	48.5	+20.8
Total	99.9	100.0	− 0.1	100.0	100.0	0.0

Verbs and verb phrases in each country's biographies are classified first according to the British panel's judgements and second according to the American panel's judgements.

national collections of biographies, and the assessments of meaning made by the two panels of judges. The findings of national differences might signify either that corporation officials reflect their respective national cultures in the verbs and verbal phrases they use to describe executives' career progression, or that business and professional-class readers interpret several frequently used verbs and verbal phrases differently according to their respective cultures.

In Table 8.3 we have supplemented the tabulations from Table 8.2 so as to show what happens when comparisons are made using the same classification for both countries. In effect, we have eliminated all variability attributable to the different meanings that readers from Britain and the United States read into the same verbal expressions, so as to reveal only the differences attributable to British and American officials' choice of terms. The finding that American biographies more often imply that the impetus for job change comes from peers is unchanged, whether we use the British or American panels as the basis for classifying terms. However, findings of reward and upward movement are quite different. When British ratings are used, differences in the frequency with which the idea of reward is conveyed are trivial. When American ratings are used, the differences are still substantial and in the same direction, but much less than in the original comparison. The original finding of American emphasis on upward movement disappears entirely and is replaced with a finding of greater ambiguity in British biographies when either panel's classification is used exclusively. The striking difference between 16.7 per cent and 48.0 per cent of American references conveying no implication of upward movement when British and American ratings, respectively, are used, shows how strongly inclined Americans are to read meanings of personal advancement into terms that convey no such meaning to British readers. Conversely, the 34.2 per cent of British expressions that convey no impression of advancement would have been reduced to 13.5 per cent had we used only the classifications by American judges.

The findings from Table 8.3 do not contradict those from Table 8.2, but clarify them. The national differences gleaned from the two sets of biographies owe more to the differing connotations of the same terms in the two countries than to the use of different terms in the two sets of biographies. To a substantial degree, sponsorship and contest shape the meanings that British and American business and professional persons read into the terms conventionally used to describe job changes in the careers of corporation executives. Had we classified all the verbal expressions according to a single coding scheme, we should have failed to discover an important difference in the cultures of American and British business and industry.

Substantive Conclusions

Substantively we sought one further test of the thesis that British culture and social structure favour upward mobility through sponsorship while American culture and social structure favour mobility through competition in an open contest. The guiding hypothesis was that the dominant mobility ideology would find expression in biographies of successful people in the two countries. As an alternative to published biographies, press-release biographies of executives were solicited from leading private corporations in both countries.

Several hypotheses concerning the two sets of corporation biographies were confirmed. Awards mentioned in British biographies were more often conferred by a central, integrating super-elite, while American awards came from a variety of segmental elites. Concern with mass recognition was indicated in the more frequent explanation of the accomplishments leading to honorific awards in American than in British biographies. Unpredicted but illuminating a side effect of the contest system was the high incidence of honorary degrees and other non-academic awards from colleges and universities in the American biographies, in what we have called a 'pseudo-sponsorship arrangement'.

Looking for a still more subtle expression of sponsorship and contest cultures, we conducted a content analysis of the verbs and verb phrases used to refer to job changes in the two sets of corporation biographies. American biographies more often conveyed the idea that the impetus for job changes came from one's peers, rather than from superiors, the system or the executive him- or herself. Particularly striking were the national differences in the extent to which American biographies, more than British biographies, conveyed the implication that job change came as the reward for some accomplishment and that the job change was a move upward. However, the latter two findings were less the consequence of the respective biographers' choice of words and phrases than of the meanings that British and American panels of business and professional people read into the same words.

Not all the evidence was consistent. It was not true, as was hypothesized, that the British 'hid their light under a bushel'. Indeed, British awards were probably made even more evident to everyone than American awards, though the opposite was true of the accomplishments leading to the awards. It was also not true that American biographies more often used terms that implied a self-impetus towards success.

Although alternative constructions could explain some of the individual findings, such as the suggestion that American society is either more egalitarian or more status-conscious than British society, it seems unlikely that alternative theses would explain the complete pattern of findings as well as the model of sponsored and contest mobility. The negative findings call for some refinement of the orienting thesis.

Methodological Conclusions: Content Analysis in Comparative Research

Content analysis encompasses a wide variety of procedures, ranging from highly intuitive to rigorously quantitative methods, though many practitioners prefer to restrict the term to the latter. In all cases the aim is to make inferences about public opinion, belief, attitudes, values or preoccupations, or about the nature or dynamics of social structure or culture, from the content of some form of human communication. Newspapers, periodicals, books, radio, television, documents, myths, stories, essays, speeches, conversations, letters, diaries, interviews and answers to open-ended survey questions have been analysed.

There are difficulties and disadvantages in the use of content analysis. Content analysis is usually an indirect method of observation because inferences are being made from the analysed communication content to something else that is not observed. If we make inferences about national character from the stories that people enjoy, we must assume that we understand why the stories are enjoyed and what story elements are figure and ground, respectively, to readers and listeners. Sampling is always a problem, since it is difficult and often impossible to equate the universe of communications with the universe of objects to which inferences are being made. The more intuitive methods of content analysis foreclose reproducibility. The more rigorous methods require difficult decisions in dividing communication content into units for analysis and in classifying the units. Often the rigorous methods restrict attention to contextual effects on the meanings of words and phrases.

One important advantage of content analysis is that it is an 'unobtrusive method'. Except when it is applied to interview and questionnaire protocols, there is no interaction with the investigator or even with a research setting, which might distort what was said or written, while the communication is being created. Another advantage is that communications can be read so as to make inferences about objects that are not directly observable to the investigator. For example, content analysis was widely used during World War II to discern critical processes and trends in enemy nations, and has been used to understand cultures and social structures in time past. Furthermore, the more rigorous forms of content analysis lead to an improved reproducibility and falsifiability, in comparison with more informal knowledge. Finally, content analysis is particularly useful when the research object is to identify the meanings of particular cultural features or the relative salience of different themes because it deals with meanings and because it can be applied to collective as well as individual communication products.

Although content analysis is widely employed in single-country studies, it has been under-used in comparative research. The most obvious application is to mass communication studies and, more indirectly, to public opinion. The prototype is the research reported by Ithiel Pool (1970), using the nine newspapers most closely tied to political elites in France, Germany, Great Britain, United States and Russia from 1890 to 1950. Investigators analysed the incidence and approval or disapproval of 416 symbols expressive of the major ideological struggles of the period, interpreted as social indicators of historic trends in ruling political thought.

The most distinctive contributions of content analysis are to the comparative analysis of cultures and cultural dynamics, since culture can never be reduced to a simple aggregation of individual attitudes and behaviour. Cultural values find expression in socialization materials, such as the readers used by children in school. David McClelland (1961, 1975) analysed readers in several countries in his comparative studies of the incidence and meaning configurations of the achievement motive and the power motive. Nicholas Vakar (1956) traced changing national cultural styles by comparing a list of the most common nouns in *Pravda* editorials with the most common nouns in standard word lists of French, German, English and pre-Soviet Russian. He found words dealing with expressive aspects of self more common in pre-Soviet Russian than in English or German, but less common in Soviet usage than in English, German or French, while verbs implying domination or manipulation were most salient. In more complex analysis, Namenwirth (1987) detected both long- and short-term cycles of changing cultural emphasis on Talcott Parsons' four pattern variables in Britain and the United States over two to three centuries, but following different patterns in the two countries. Milton Rokeach's (1979) scheme of fundamental terminal and instrumental values, though generally measured by the questionnaires he devised, has been applied in content analysis of ideological texts to compare cultural orientations cross-nationally.

While the commonest applications of content analysis depend upon counts of words or phrases, using translations to establish cross-cultural equivalence, the more difficult identification of themes and plots is better suited for comparing national world views. The early study by MacGranahan and Wayne (1948) of forty-five German and American plays performed in 1927 set a pattern for this genre of content analysis. They found striking national differences contrasting the pragmatic, individualistic, optimistic American world view to the more idealistic, absolutist and pessimistic German view. The application to cross-cultural protocol of such rigorous procedures as those employed by Livia Polanyi (1985) in analysing stories told in informal conversations among friends should bring us closer to understanding the body of collectively accepted meanings that form the bases for normal discourse in difference societies.

Methodologically, the current research has demonstrated the usefulness of a source of data that, to the best of our knowledge, has not previously been used in cross-cultural research. Although they are terse and generally unadorned factual accounts, the biographies of executives that corporations prepare as publicity releases have been a productive source of data. So simple an item of information as the list of awards received by executives was shown to reflect the respective sponsorship and contest cultures in the two countries. More subtle cultural effects were revealed in the choice of verbs and verbal phrases employed in referring to job changes in the executives' careers.

Particularly important for cross-cultural research was the exploration of a technique for dealing with the culturally divergent meanings ascribed to the same terms in two different societies that employ the same formal language, and for dealing with subculture differences between the investigator and subjects. After all of the relevant terms had first been extracted from both sets of biographies, the complete list was presented to panels of business and professional persons in the two countries, asking them to answer six simple questions about the connotations of each term. The aggregated judgements from each panel then served as the basis for classifying the terms used in the respective country's biographies. In this way the meanings of each nation's biographies to the appropriate audience in that country were identified. This technique also made it possible to sort out the differences resulting from the biographers' choice of words from the differences resulting from the meanings that the respective national audiences read into the words. This was accomplished by reclassifying each nation's terms according to the judgements made by the other nation's panel.

In applying this familiar panel technique, we were unable to secure large or systematic enough samples to claim that the panels' judgements were definitive for their class and national cultures.

Hence the findings remain tentative rather than conclusive. In polling the panels of judges, it was essential to couch the instructions and questions in such basic terms that cultural differences would not distort the judgement process. Based on my own fairly intimate familiarity with both cultures, I believe this aim was achieved. However, the research strategy could be elaborated to include an independent test for the identity of meanings of the instructions and questions in the two countries. While the procedure was applied in this case to protocols that were all in the same formal language, the method could easily be adapted for use with protocols in different languages. It is my principal methodological conclusion that the validity of content analysis in comparative research can be greatly improved by incorporation of appropriate variations and elaborations of the panel technique that my research exemplifies.

Notes

These data were collected in 1964 under a grant from the National Science Foundation. William Russell Ellis carried out much of the analysis.

1. Among the investigators who have applied or tested the sponsorship-contest distinction in comparing careers in Britain and the United States are the following: Baker, 1982; Crane, 1969; Demerath, 1983; Hopper, 1968; Kerckhoff, 1974, 1975; Treiman and Terrell, 1975.

2. If we assume that success biographies serve an exemplary function, their absence in British society is consistent with a sponsorship orientation. People of real quality are supposed to be discovered rather than to push themselves forward, and the sponsoring individual or agency initiates the newly chosen and trains them for the responsibilities of position.

3. American corporations were selected from *Moody's Industrials, Moody's Railroads, Moody's Public Utilities, Standard and Poor's Value Line Investment Survey* and *Fortune Plant and Product Directory*. Since British railways and public utilities were publicly owned, we drew the list of British corporations exclusively from the section on foreign companies in *Moody's Industrials*.

4. Questionnaires were distributed and collected in Britain by Penelope Leach, under the supervision of Professor A.N. Oppenheim.

References

Baker, Therese L. (1982) 'Class, Family, Education, and the Process of Status Attainment: A Comparison of American and British Women College Graduates', *Sociological Quarterly*, 23: 17–31.

Berelson, Bernard (1952) *Content Analysis in Communication Research*. New York: Free Press.

Carney, Thomas F. (1979) *Content Analysis: A Technique for Systematic Inference from Communications*. Winnipeg: University of Manitoba Press.

Crane, Diana (1969) 'Social Class Origin and Academic Success: The Influence of

Two Stratification Systems on Academic Careers', *Sociology of Education*, 42: 1–18.

Demerath III, N.J. (1983) 'Past and Future in Anglo-American Stratification: A Note on Prospective vs. Retrospective Ideologies', *Sociology and Social Research*, 67: 363–73.

Holsti, Ole R. (1969) *Content Analysis for the Social Sciences and Humanities*. Reading, MA: Addison-Wesley.

Hopper, Earl I. (1968) 'A Typology for the Classification of Educational Systems', *Sociology*, 2: 29–46.

Kerckhoff, Alan C. (1974) 'Stratification Processes and Outcomes in England and the US', *American Sociological Review*, 39: 789–801.

Kerckhoff, Alan C. (1975) 'Patterns of Educational Attainment in Great Britain', *American Journal of Sociology*, 80: 1428–37.

Krippendorff, Klaus (1980) *Content Analysis: An Introduction to its Methodology*. Beverly Hills, CA: Sage Publications.

Lowenthal, Leo (1943) 'Biographies in Popular Magazines', pp. 507–48 in P. Lazarsfeld and F. Stanton (eds), *Radio Research, 1942–3*. New York: Duell, Sloan & Pearce.

McClelland, David C. (1961) *The Achieving Society*. New York: Irvington Publishers.

McClelland, David C. (1975) *Power: The Inner Experience*. New York: Irvington Publishers.

McGranahan, Donald, V. and Ivor Wayne (1948) 'German and American Traits as Reflected in Popular Drama', *Human Relations*, 1: 429–55.

Namenwirth, J. Zvi (1987) *Dynamics of Culture*. Boston: Allen & Unwin.

Polanyi, Livia (1985) *Telling the American Story: A Structural and Cultural Analysis of Conversational Storytelling*. Norwood, NJ: Ablex Publishers.

Pool, Ithiel de Sola (1970) *The Prestige Press: A Comparative Study of Political Symbols*. Cambridge, MA: MIT Press.

Rokeach, Milton (1979) *Understanding Human Values: Individual and Societal*. New York: Free Press.

Treiman, Donald J. and Kermit Terrell (1975) 'The Process of Status Attainment in the United States and Great Britain', *American Journal of Sociology*, 81: 563–83.

Turner, Ralph H. (1960) 'Sponsored and Contest Mobility and the School System', *American Sociological Review*, 25: 855–67.

Turner, Ralph H. (1966) 'Acceptance of Irregular Mobility in Britain and the United States', *Sociometry*, 29: 334–52.

Vakar, Nicholas (1956) 'The Mass Communication Index: Some Observations on Communist Russian Discourse', *Symposium*, 10: 42–59.

9

Oral History Approaches to an International Social Movement

Daniel Bertaux

Le coeur a ses raisons que la Raison ne connaît pas.
Blaise Pascal

From 1983 to 1987 I participated in the research and writing of a book about the student movements of the sixties in six countries of the North Atlantic rim (Fraser et al., 1988). The book was not meant to be an explicitly comparative study of these movements; our only ambition was to retrace their history, in the United States and in five Western European countries, *as lived by their own prevailing actors*. For this purpose we interviewed about 250 former activists: eighty in the United States, sixty in England and Ireland, fifty in Italy, thirty in West Germany and as many in France.

The interviews were conducted in the form of life stories. It was the right time to collect such interviews: former activists were far enough from the sixties, in time and in ideology, to be able to look at their former commitments from a distance; their personal experiences, however, were still fresh, and recalling them revived old emotions.

In each country a nation history of the sixties was written by weaving together life stories, historical events and contexts; the result being an oral history of the student movement in that country.[1] These nation-based histories were then fused into one by our narrator-in-chief, Ronald Fraser, a British writer who completed the research for England and Ireland, and then had the difficult task of merging the six parallel histories into *one* narrative. This form corresponded to the group's initial hypothesis, that the sixties student movements were not separate, national movements but manifestations, in various countries, of one and the same movement of the post-war generation.[2] Therefore the book is not divided into nation-specific chapters, but narrates a common history which begins in the fifties, when our characters were in high school, and then moves to the early sixties and the Civil Rights movement of American Southern blacks; to the Free Speech movement in

Berkeley and other US universities, to the first university occupations in Turin, Berlin and Paris, to May 1968 in France, October 1968 in Belfast, and so on.[3]

Moving back and forth from one country to another of the Western world, we developed a genuinely international view of the sixties student movement and all it triggered. Curiously enough, this wide-angle vision led us away from a strict cross-national, classically comparative perspective. We soon realized that, instead of dealing with six isolated national movements which would have ignored one another and whose particular form, repertoire of actions and process of unfolding could be related to the particular features of their society, its culture and political system, we were facing social movements which had obviously (if unwittingly) influenced one another. According to Galton's theorem, in such a situation the quasi-experimental design of comparative research does *not* apply (Naroll, 1965; Scheuch, 1989).

The existence of numerous reciprocal influences and feedback between processes in various countries is, however, a fact of life, in a world which is not only unified by instantaneous computer-driven movement of finance capital, but is becoming more aware of its various parts as the media spread around its surface, making of the evening news a kind of world public space.[4] The consequences of this new phenomenon on cross-national comparative research have been examined by Piotr Sztompka. His conclusion is that, while the traditional quasi-experimental design does not hold any more, other designs, more appropriate to the social sciences, could be profitably substituted for it (Sztompka, 1988). Indeed, looking back at our research with a comparative framework in mind, what strikes me most today is not the differences between the student movements of various countries, but to the contrary, their similarities.

At first sight, the differences were more apparent. One of the major ones was that in Germany, France and Italy, most radical students had Marxist references and used a Marxist rhetoric in the political debates of the sixties, while in the United States and England such references were much weaker. Indeed, in the United States, student leaders often expressed a submerged anti-communism; for instance, Mario Savio, leader of the Berkeley Free Speech movement, consciously wished to avoid mimicking the style of Leninist leadership: 'We were all very conscious of not wanting to behave the way that we were told Communists behaved. I did not know any Communist. But I knew we were talking about very manipulative people, who would control the masses. And that was clearly bad' (Savio as quoted in Fraser et al., 1988: 93).

There were also considerable differences between student movements from country to country – for example, in the influence of the counter-culture, drugs, and the women's liberation movement. There were as often differences within a country, from one city to another or from one university to the next. It may be added that age cohorts separated by only a few years found themselves in radically different conditions and participated very differently – in different loci of the movement, with different styles of action and even different ideals – to the movements (Bertaux and Linhart, 1988).

However, what struck us as soon as we exchanged the transcripts of our interviews and read them was the similarity across countries of the values, hopes and emotions of activists who *initiated* the movements. In short: behind the obvious differences in style, content, claims and forms of discourse, the *sensitivities* of this generation's activists were variants of one and the same *Weltanschauung* – one and the same common *subjectivity*.

To understand the political movements of the sixties this subjectivity must be taken seriously. Subjectivity is *not* the contrary of objectivity, and to take it as an object (or rather focus) of study will not make sociology any less scientific than it is or claims to be. Subjectivity is central to an understanding of action, and especially so in the case of social movements, where action is not just norm-abiding behaviour but innovative and risky. The word itself is useful: such concepts as 'attitudes' or 'values' denote only one fraction of the personality, while 'subjectivity' refers to the *subject* in its totality. As such it is a constant reminder that it is through *acts* that the psyche genuinely expresses its content; and that reciprocally, action involves and commits not one aspect of a personality only, but the *whole* of the person.[5]

One of the most striking similarities we found has to do with collective subjectivity and, beyond, with sociality itself: it concerns the drastic change in the fabric of social life that takes place when a new movement is just born. From Berkeley to Berlin and from Turin to Belfast and Paris, we heard similar accounts of this phenomenon, which is perhaps what our interviewees remember most vividly. For instance, Laura Derossi, from Turin, thus recalls the first occupation of her university (Christmas, 1967) and the atmosphere of the following weeks: '[It was] a period of invention, creativity, novelty, wonder, amazement, joy, amusement, change, of happy collective living. I have the memory of something like a festival, a play, in which we were deeply motivated, had a great certainty of our rights and needs, a great self-awareness' (in Italian it sounds even better). In the first part of this chapter I will propose a sociological interpretation of such a recurrent experience.

Another similarity we observed concerns the personal roots of radicalism. We found that practically all young men and women who started movements were moved by strong moral feelings – by idealism, rather than by a drive towards self-interest. No rational choice theory may, so it seems, explain why in the relatively affluent and obviously fast-developing Western societies of the sixties, young middle-class (usually lower middle-class) students could break open normal trajectories to become radicals and revolutionaries, dropping their studies and prospects of careers to devote all their energies to foster 'revolution'. This phenomenon is, of course, at the core of our book. In this chapter the focus is on a single case, but one which includes a process that may contain universal elements.

Both of these issues have been dealt with before (see, for example, Smelser, 1962); but since the advent of the 'rational choice' orientation which has become so pervasive nowadays in the sociology of social movements and elsewhere, they have receded into the background. I would like to bring them up front again, both because they seem central to a sociological understanding of social movements, those of the eighties (Hegedus, 1989) as well as those of the sixties; and because they are bound to remain out of reach of a rational choice approach.

Social Movements *in statu nascenti*

The first moments of the existence of a social movement, these moments when it pops out of nothingness, coalesces, sprouts and blooms in a matter of minutes that, in retrospect, will have more weight than whole decades, these moments where what seemed impossible the day before suddenly becomes real – and conversely, where the daily routines of deferential resignation suddenly become unreal – these moments which instantly register into the hearts of all participants, have been compared to the experience of falling in love (Alberoni, 1979). The birth of a social movement is its crucial moment: because the collective emotion that welds together the participants is still pure of any afterthoughts, because the movement itself is immune from alterations forced upon it by its enemies or by its own, media-distorted self-image; because the sudden (and collective) discovery that action *is* possible is a fantastic mind-opener which, for every person there, means that a number of futures that seemed closed forever open their doors all at once.

The drastic changes in the fabric of social relations that accompanies, or rather that *is* a social movement *in statu nascenti* (in nascent state) long ago attracted the attention of social thinkers. These are exceptional moments when sociality seems to undergo a mutation; people who conceived of themselves as random-running individual atoms that made up a lonely crowd suddenly aggregate in drops of liquid sociality, while the apparently indestructible, solid, massive, well-structured institutional giants which embodied authority begin to melt and dissolve into air.

Exceptional as these 'historical' moments are, they are also *necessary* moments of social life. Most of them appear, in retrospect, as *moments fondateurs*: one needs only to think about the number of countries that claim a revolution as their own act of (self)-birth. But one can go even further: as Alberoni recalls in *Movimento e istituzione*, all great social thinkers have recognized that there is not one but *two* 'stati dello sociale' (two states of sociality). Toennies's *Gemeinschaft* versus *Gesellschaft*, Marx's categories of reification and class consciousness, Weber's ideal types of bureaucratic order and charismatic power, Durkheim's *organisation sociale* versus *effervescence collective*; moments which belong to Apollo and moments which belong to Dionysus (Nietzsche); Bergson's 'les deux sources de la morale et de la religion' (one source being *l'élan vital*, passion, love, creation, and the other repetitive routines); Mannheim's distinction between Utopia and ideology – every ambitious thinker of sociality recognized this duality of states.

For our sociological purpose, perhaps the most relevant distinction is Jean-Paul Sartre's *série* versus *groupe en fusion* (Sartre, 1960). Sartre calls *série* the normal state of crowds; that is, series of atomized individuals, each one seen as isolated in his or her inner world as a Leibnizian monad, going his or her own way and not caring about the other's ways. The ego-centred individual is, after all, a familiar figure of utilitarianism, economic theory, or methodological individualism. What Sartre is pointing out, however, is that, whenever and wherever this figure is actually walking in the street, it has a silent companion: social control. Pervasive, omnipresent, it is social control that actually *makes* members of a society into ego-centred individuals. The public space, be it the factory floor, the office high-rise, or the street, is wholly under the control of the established power. Every individual, whatever she or he thinks of the manifest public discourse 'All is well' and its latent content 'Nothing can be changed', whether he or she accepts the rule of this power or rejects it, does so *secretly*, thus behaving as if accepting it. Therefore each one, looking at all the others who work, comply and keep quiet, thinks they are alone in secretly rejecting this social order. The lack of freedom of expression, which is structurally enforced not only by despotic regimes but also through more subtle agencies (such as plant managers) in democratic regimes, induces the serial state of sociality. This 'state' can be compared – for what the analogy is worth – to the gaseous state of physical matter. Every individual, confronted with his or her own isolation, feels powerless to change anything – which is the point. Civil society is weak; the necessary 'collectiveness' of any society is wholly appropriated by a central institution (the state, the party, the company, the university) whose own social fabric seems (to pursue the physical analogy one step further) close to the crystal state, as it is made up of sets of rationally designed, well-organized institutional relationships (Bertaux, 1977).

When, however, frustration mounts in each person individually (for example, in each production line worker because of a speeding-up of the line, in each hard-working family because of a steep rise in the price of staple food, in each patriotic heart because of one more act of provocation by the foreign rulers occupying the country), it takes only a small event to trigger an instantaneous and massive change of state, from *série* to *groupe en fusion*. As soon as each person in a serialized mass realizes that some others contest the established power, as he or she takes one step forward to openly express support, a chain reaction spreads through the atomized series and transforms it into a fluid group (Sartre's *groupe en fusion*) which instantly moves from the status of subordinated passive object to that of *subject* capable of action.

Sartre (1960) has tentatively described the whole cycle through which a *groupe en fusion* may transform itself into a network, then an organization, an institution, soon a new bureaucracy ruling a serialized mass . . . . What is relevant, however, for the movements of the sixties (and beyond) is the very first step this theory describes, the *statu nascenti* moment. Collecting individual testimonies in the form of life stories, we could not help but be struck by the similarities between the descriptions that were given to us of such moments, whatever the country, the city or the circumstances – and the powerful effect that experiencing such a rare moment had upon individual subjectivities.

Among all such descriptions (many are quoted in Fraser et al., 1988) the best are probably those of the birth of the Berkeley Free Speech movement; perhaps because, this event being the first of its kind, the novelty was complete. Quoting at length the account that was given to Bret Eynon by one of the participants will allow the reader to perceive the making of a collective subjectivity that not only accompanied the event, but actually *gave birth* to it, like the invisible phyllum does for mushrooms.

Birth of the Free Speech movement
In September 1964, the Dean of the University of California at Berkeley ordered that Civil Rights groups and political organizations

be denied use of a strip of land on the edge of the campus which they had been using to set up their tables to recruit members, collect funds and hand out their publications. The groups (spread over a wide political spectrum) tried to negotiate. In vain: they were much too weak to impress the Dean's assistants. On 1 October, a police car was sent to arrest a student who, in spite of the ruling, was still operating a table for the Congress of Racial Equality (CORE). The policemen pushed him into their car, as students were watching. The car was beginning to move when suddenly it was blocked by people sitting in its way. Recalls Michael Rossman:

> I was the first one to sit down in front of the car. [But] there are in fact about 200 other people, who [claim they were] the first person to sit down in front of the car, and everyone of them is telling the truth: because it was this act of spontaneous initiative, just everybody sitting down. It doesn't take a leader, right?[6]
>
> So we sit around the car for two or three hours and it is this open space. It's this first educational thing. We've captured a police car. Nobody's – there's never been a police car driven onto an American campus for a political reason and captured. So it's open space, blank space. It's Blank Space City.
>
> What do we do? We stand on the car. Mario's the first one up on the car – just because somebody needs to say something. . . . Not as a leader: 'Listen! These are the directions!' but 'we're here. They've got Jack in this car . . . We're here to keep them from taking him away. We don't know what we're going to do. Let's talk about it.'
>
> That's partially the content of the first speech, right? This is the nature of the leadership, which is, to give voice to the common good, you know, the common consciousness.
>
> So then ensues just dialogue. For 30 hours people stand up on the car, take off their shoes, stand up on the car and talk. . . .
>
> So, there's this conversation, which is if you will the first teach-in. Of course it's not the first teach-in because it's not the first time people have talked to each other in the open air on a variety of things, but in that sense, it's certainly the first teach-in of the New Left, the first one I know about, and again, it happens before the form itself becomes defined the following spring, gets named the following spring. . . .
>
> This is the first time I've really heard a democratic public discussion in America. I am 24, 25. I've been in high class democratic company. But it's like watching the mystery dramas come alive . . . And no one could say it, even though it was so simple to say it, because the words themselves had been abused, you know – 'democratic' – ah! it's like watching God walk on earth. You know: 'Ooooh! THAT'S the meaning that was inside those dry terms!'. Here it is, it stalks among us, and nothing is changed, and yet everything is changed . . .

In retrospect we know that this tiny little event, the coalescence of a first drop of fluid sociality on a Californian campus, did have some influence on the later course of world history. The disproportion seems huge between the microscopic scale of the scene and the giant academic institutions, not to say the US war machine, that were eventually going to be seriously disturbed by forces unleashed then and there. But what gave these forces their strength?

Even the hardest-liner of rational choice theory will have to admit the behaviour of these students had nothing to do with personal interest and the instrumentally rational pursuit of individual goals. They were taking a risk – at the very least, the risk of being kicked out of this paradisiacal campus – for something which could not be defined in material terms, not even in terms of personal interest. But it would certainly be a gross misunderstanding to call their action irrational. They were acting out of indignation, out of moral outrage: a typical *Wertrational* action. Ethical reason, the reason of the heart, was underlying their action.

There is, however, in this scene much more to learn if one focuses not upon individuals as such but upon the new social texture that was rapidly taking shape then and there. Each one of the participants was undergoing a new experience and, through it, was getting innerly transformed from one minute to the next; but what is even more important is that *their relations* had already and radically changed. It is *this* change, a change in sociality, that is the crucial point.

Rossman's very subjective description points straight towards what might be the key difference between the two states of sociality; it is a difference in the *patterns of communication*. The nature of a relation between persons is closely related to the kind of communicative relation that has been established between them. From Rossman's testimony emerges quite clearly the idea that new flows of communication were created on the spot; as a consequence people quickly stopped behaving as competitive individuals, but rather felt animated by a desire of solidarity, brotherhood, by the desire to exchange and share, the excitement of participating in something exceptional; that is, by stripping off their individualistic garment.[7]

Similar exceptional moments happened all over the Western world when universities were occupied, workers took over 'their' factories, when whole towns moved into the general strike, and streets and squares became as many forums. The sociological hypothesis one may derive from many convergent testimonies is that sudden shifts in sociality, from serial state to melting-group state, go together with *drastic 'flip flops'* (in French, *basculements*) *of the existing communication channels*.

In any developed *Gesellschaft* whose institutional texture is made up of functionally differentiated institutions, the built-in structure of communication channels is wholly *vertical*. This is the case even in Western democracies, and to a much greater extent than is usually recognized. In any organization, be it an enterprise, an administration, a school, a party, communication is initiated by the persons in charge (those whom the Anglo-Saxon culture calls 'managers', a term which has no equivalent elsewhere). In an enterprise or an administration, communication flows downwards under the form of decisions, orientations, goals to be reached, direct orders or demands for information. What flows upwards is restricted to information required by the management. Communication between peers is normatively restricted to business-connected communication. In a school or university, given the professor–student relationship, the flow of communication is even more verticalized and one-way only. But this vertical structure is also characteristic of the relations of institutions to people as customers; that is, in the sphere of consumption and leisure. In the media, the flow also goes from centre to periphery, from the radio and TV stations to a serialized audience of passive listeners or viewers. Political meetings are ceremonies of celebration, as are (admittedly in a very different way) church ceremonies. Non-controlled communication is strictly restricted to the private sphere of life; in the public sphere all is norm-constrained. Invisible barriers prevent people who have not been introduced to one another from talking in public places unless they have a 'technical' reason to do so, and this norm which rules interaction in public places is much stronger than the mere protection of privacy would require. It is in fact a political norm, which is the first to disappear when the spell of the serializing order vacillates.

While the vertical, top-down structure of communication channels lies at the very core of the 'normal' (that is, serializing) state of sociality, the horizontal living network of communication channels is the core characteristic of the fluid state of sociality. The *contents* through the new channels are less important than the *existence* of these channels themselves. When serialized and thus 'silenced' people break out of the state of serial sociality, the very first thing they do seems precisely to communicate their state of mind to others, who are suddenly becoming *significant* others. Communication here is expressive as much as informative; it is emotionally loaded, and value-loaded too. It would be all too easy, for an external observer, to label it irrational; but with such a narrow conception of rationality, only robots would stand the test.

The hypothesis that a massive and instantaneous 'flip-flop' of the channels of communication is both a universal characteristic of a social movement in nascent state *and* is in fact what brings the new movement to life, may help understand better a crucial phenomenon of social life that fascinated the founding fathers of sociology. Much of what they pointed out as core characteristics of this phenomenon (such as the central role of charisma, the sudden rise of a new 'collective' consciousness, the abolition of individualism in such moments of *effervescence collective*) can be reformulated using the vocabulary of communication. Curiously enough, instead of making their intuitions obsolete, this exercise brings forth their very actuality: for, more than ever, social movements are unfolding in a world that is permanently looking at itself.

Paths to Commitment

While from a sociological perspective the assumption would be that social movements produce activism – and make activists out of non-activists – rather than the reverse, it is nevertheless interesting, when one has collected accounts describing individual (subjective) pathways to commitment, to pause and wonder whether they bring any new insights.

We usually began the interview by saying, 'What we would like to know is, how did you ever become an activist?'. And we encouraged people to go back to their teenage years. While every single person had of course a particular story to tell, we were again struck by the similarities, not only within a given country but across countries as well.

Born in the early forties, the eventual core activists of the sixties student movements in the United States and Western Europe remembered their pre-adolescence years as rather dull ('the dead-locked fifties') in a world thoroughly dominated by the adult generation, adult standards, adult culture, adult issues and pervasive conformism. Quite often they felt uneasy in such a (serialized) world and somehow marginalized in their own *Lebenswelt* (life world). This feeling is shared by Americans and Western Europeans alike. What we do not know is how many youngsters of their generation felt this way during the fifties; however, there is evidence (for example, in the literature of the times), that it was a general mood, in which case future activists would have been different not for feeling the way they felt, but perhaps by feeling it more strongly than others; and also by looking confusedly for an escape, while others may have been more resigned.

Coming of age in the sixties, these youngsters quickly discovered where they belonged: not to the passive, conformist 'masses' (in fact, serialized populations) but to the active minorities. Wherever there was movement they were attracted to it as though by a magnet. It was an attraction that went far beyond rational calculations; they rationalized with political words motivations which at first were thoroughly moral. But even beyond their moral feelings their subconscious drive may have been to join people like themselves: at last they had found them.

It is out of a sense of justice, of identification for the oppressed, of indignation against what was being done to some of their fellow men that many of these young, white, educated men and women moved first into activism; not through a cold evaluation of 'the potential costs and benefits of various lines of action' (McAdam, McCarthy and Zald, 1988: 707). Depending on their location in time and space they identified with Algerian victims of colonialism, with Southern blacks in the United States or with Vietnamese peasants. It is crucial that in all cases the victims of oppression were not passive victims but active subjects resisting and fighting oppression. This had decisive political meaning. For instance, the testimonies that our American colleagues Ronald Grele and Bret Eynon collected in the United States for the book tend to show that without the Civil Rights movement of young black students from 1960 onwards, there would have been no student movement to speak of in the United States until, at least, the draft to Vietnam several years later (Fraser et al., 1988: chs. 2 and 3).

Speaking in the name of the rational choice theorists, McAdam, McCarthy and Zald, after having summarily discarded the 'psychological accounts of activism' and the 'attitudinal correlates of activism', assert that 'Many social movements theorists have posited the assumption that individuals are calculating actors who attempt, within the bounds of limited rationality, to judge the potential costs and benefits of various lines of action' (McAdam et al., 1988: 707). This interpretation of why people become activists makes very little sense when applied to the 200 or so activists we interviewed. Perhaps the 'rational choice' perspective works better when applied to followers and joiners; that is, people who decide to join a social movement *after* it has been well established, after it has gained some sort of right to exist and political legitimacy, thus minimizing the risks involved in participation; perhaps it applies better to, say, 'movements' of suburban dwellers protecting the value of their real-estate property against unwelcome newcomers. But when applied to social movements challenging state authority and facing its multiple and sometimes terrifying means of coercion, it does not seem to work very well; indeed, its explanatory power is much greater in accounting for passivity than activism. In such situations the rational choice, from a purely egoistic/individualistic point of view, is indeed to collaborate with the oppressors.

To initiate a struggle against a much stronger and better-organized opponent amounts to irrationality in the cynical eyes of this powerful opponent. It is not, however, irrational *as such*. It follows *another* kind of rationality than the narrowly egoistic rationality that rational choice theorists see as the core of human nature. This other kind of rationality is precisely the one Max Weber called *Wertrationalität*. What is specific of this kind of rationality, a 'reasons of the heart' rationality, is precisely that it is guided by moral values, not by a cost-benefit calculus. Ethics, not profit, is guiding its course. As a consequence, *the action is taken precisely without taking into consideration the possible personal costs (or personal benefits)*.[8] This is probably why, looking at it from the outside, it is so tempting to label it 'irrational'. But this is a judgement that is only valid within the very limited bounds of instrumental rationality, the kind of rationality that has led so many governments, armies and other kinds of uncontrolled powers to act far beyond the bounds of human decency. It was precisely this kind of rationality that our activists were trying to fight.

Without the first risky initiatives of a handful of committed persons no social movement could ever come into existence and there would be no opportunity for a 'rational choice' between joining it or not. This being said, it remains to unfold the *process* by which a lay person becomes a fully committed activist. It is, indeed, a long process, with accelerating events (such as moments like the birth of the Free Speech movement), slower phases of maturation, and a constant feedback of experience upon commitment (much enhanced by the initial harshness of repression, which, far from deterring already committed activists, may radicalize them since they are not acting to gain benefits, but on moral grounds).

The various forms that a process leading to commitment can take are still little known. One thing is sure, however: it is not a linear and reversible process. In the theory of so-called rational choice, activists should instantly withdraw if the risks they are running are drastically raised. In historical reality, however, it can be seen that many activists who became committed to a cause out of *moral choice* could *not* just quit when it suddenly appeared that their life itself was at stake. Instead, they faced the new situation and, more often than not, made the choice to go on. It is this logic that has been consistently followed by, for instance, activists of political groups fighting dictatorships: first they use legal means, but when their group is forbidden they go underground instead of disbanding (which would be the rational behaviour that both rulers and rational choice theorists would expect of them). Without this kind of courage there would have been no Resistance in France, or Holland, or Italy, or Germany, or Poland during World War II. Is it the task of sociology to qualify this kind of conduct as resulting from an irrational choice? Or is it rather to understand the dynamics of moral choices that lead to irreversible consequences, and are themselves irreversible?

Somewhere along the process of becoming committed to a cause, there seem to be one or several *turning points* beyond which it is impossible to go back. But why is it impossible? The following excerpt may help us answer this question. It is taken verbatim from Mario Savio's interview by Bret Eynon in 1984. Savio, whose role as one of the leaders of the Free Speech movement began on 5 October 1964, when he jumped on the police car blocked by Berkeley students (see above), had taken part the previous summer in a civil rights campaign in Mississippi organized by the Student Non-violent Coordinating Committee (SNCC). It was the third time that young black students had organized a summer campaign, but the first time white volunteers were invited to participate in it. Savio had already worked with CORE; he asked to participate in the 1964 campaign.

'I only hoped that I would be good enough, that they [the experienced black students] would accept me.' He knew the risks of confronting the violence of Southern racists with a non-violent attitude, and accepted them in advance.

There is one event which happened in Mississippi (pauses) which touched me the most deeply, and summed the experience up for me, and changed my life. It was an event like ones that many other people had. It was impossible to be in Mississippi that summer without something touching you. You would have to be a stone. So everybody must have something.

The way we did (voter registration) was we'd go around, usually in groups of two, to the different farmhouses. We'd introduce ourselves, as civil rights workers who are here for the summer. I'd introduce myself, and say, 'I've come to ask you to come and register to vote.' A lot of people weren't registered to vote. The person I'd usually ask to speak to – usually the man of the house; these were traditional families – I'd say that's what I was here for.

There's a kind of way they'd talk to me. You could miss some of the words. It's really a dialect. But he'd explain to me how he couldn't do that. 'If I register to vote, I'll lose my job. They'll kick me off this land. How am I going to keep my kids?' And so forth. I knew it was true. So I would say something like, 'I know that's true; I know there is that danger, at least. It may not happen, but there is that danger. Also, because I won't be here after the summer, so I'm not going to be facing that danger. You have to face it yourself.' Then I'd say – I don't know how I had the guts to say this, I swear – 'Did your father vote?'

'No.'

'Did *his* father vote?'

'No.'

'Do you want your children to vote?'

I don't know how I got the guts to say that. And very frequently, in response to that, the person would say 'Okay, where do I go?'

There was a feeling, you see, in the air, that this was the moment of change. It was happening. The winds of change were blowing. The person coming to your door was an emissary from the change. Even if he was white! So then we'd arrange for a time when we'd come and pick the people up.

. . . You'd have to go, say, to the courthouse. You were not allowed to help people fill out the forms. It was the sheriff's wife, I remember, who was in charge. The law said someone could come and stand, but the person would have to go forward himself. So I remember, on this particular day – there was another white worker with me, another one of the volunteers – we came with this farmer. We're talking about an old man; he may have been sixty or seventy. He had a hat, and he was a bit stooped. He came in, and we all went into the courthouse, the three of us, and then he walked forward to the desk. He took his hat off, and he stood there.

Then she started in on him: 'What do you want, boy?' He was a man of sixty or seventy. We were just standing there. 'What do you want, boy?'

'I want to reddish, ma'am.' It's part of the dialect. They said 'reddish'. They turned 'register' into a two syllable word, 'reddish'. You got used to it. 'I want to reddish, ma'am.' But in a very small voice.

'What's that you say, boy?'

'I want to reddish, ma'am.'

'What's reddish? What are you talking about, boy?' And on and on and on. He never gave up. She finally had to give him the form. But she made him eat shit for it. (Pauses, then in small voice) She humiliated him. She tried to. I was watching this. That man's courage changed my life.

Until then, I was still sort of an observer in a certain way. Less and less so, okay? But here's somebody, who because of something *I* had done, was maybe risking his family, facing that kind of humiliation. He must have been afraid. I know I was afraid. Yet he stood his ground.

We used to sing. There were the civil rights songs. We'd sing about how we'll never turn back, 'ain't gonna turn around'. That was the point at which it all came real for me. That is, I'd chosen sides for the rest of my life. It's a very simply event, and it doesn't, probably, mean anything to anybody else. But it meant a lot to me.

This piece of testimony can be read from many perspectives. For instance, at the psycho-biographical level, Savio is clearly describing a turning point in his life; probably the very moment when a life-long commitment took hold of him. But the scene can also be deciphered as the expression of a macro-social drama: each of the protagonists is embodying a whole social group, in the other's eyes and in his or her own (the Southern blacks, the Southern conservative whites, the Northern white liberals); and the interpersonal relations they establish between themselves are direct derivations of the social relationships (structural and political) that obtain between these groups. It is, however, not theatre, but real-life drama, and in that very moment the old farmer is endangering much of his precarious conditions of living. The risk he is taking, without expecting any reward for himself, and the courage it takes to act as he does are what make the interaction dramatic, and what moves Savio's inner self.

The excerpt itself offers rich potentialities for interpretation and theorization; for example, along the lines of sociological hermeneutics that are exemplified in Oevermann (1988), Strauss (1987), or Bertaux and Bertaux-Wiame (1988). However, it is not on the psychological level or the macro-sociological one, but on an intermediate one, the level of *interaction*, that I want to focus briefly; for it is precisely at *this* level that what is happening to Savio can best be understood, and that one can see how far away we are from a 'rational choice' process.

Savio, the Italian-American Catholic born in New York, had come to Mississippi to help blacks register. Down South, visiting families in the company of local black activists, he had been moved by the warm welcome of these families, their ways of sharing with him the little they had. He had been threatened by the local whites, and at some point came very close to taking a severe beating. Up to that point, however, he may have been always in the position of somebody *giving*: giving his time, his energy and skills, and taking willingly the risk to give much more (some of the activists had already been killed and all were aware it might happen to any of them).

Whatever he had received so far in exchange had been of tremendous value to him: comradeship, the possibility of acting meaningfully, discovery of another world, of other human beings. It was, however, he himself who gave value to all these gifts. They were not taken from anyone. But here was suddenly, perhaps for the first time during that summer, perhaps for the first time in years, a person who was *giving* him something that this person valued tremendously. The costs that not only the old man, but also younger members of his family might have to pay for the daring act of registering could be very high. The risk was huge; and still the man was taking it, not only for himself, for his children and grandchildren, not only for his people; but also, in a way, for Savio himself. And it is *this* gift that made of this moment a turning point in Savio's life.

During that very moment a pact was silently sealed. A pact between Mario and all those who dare to fight for freedom, which was at the same time a pact between him and 'his conscience', as one used to say. Pacts need witnesses who guarantee they will be enforced; here there is at least one, the other volunteer. He remains probably unaware of his role, but his silent presence is enough. The sealing of the pact is, of course, taking place beyond consciousness, but manifests itself through very strong emotions. None can doubt Savio was deeply moved; he still is when telling the story twenty years later, so strongly that this emotion passes on to the listener.

To be moved is also to be *moved*, to be transported elsewhere; motion follows emotion. Now we know why Mario Savio was the first to jump on the police car, two months later. But sociologically speaking, the crucial point is that the inner process that took place within his heart and led him to act as he did, can in no way be reduced to a psychological process (as the evaluation of risk can). *It took an interaction*, it took an exchange of real, human gifts to set this process in motion. *Wertrational* action cannot take place in a social void; because it is thoroughly moral it is also thoroughly social.

Discussion

In the classic paradigm of comparative research, the goals of cross-national or cross-cultural projects are ultimately theoretical. Comparisons 'allow variables to vary', to use a vocabulary which is heavily biased but has become universal. What in a given country, or culture, is taken for granted does not apply, does not exist, or exists differently in another one. The variation that is thus introduced helps greatly in determining what is linked to what, what is produced with which effect, and how powerful are the consequences of a society's main structural features whose considerable consequences, precisely because they are structural, invariant, are too easily forgotten. The core difficulty is of course that many of these structural features 'vary' together from one culture to the next and that their patterns of causation are structural too (that is, the effects of one are dependent upon its interaction with the others; for instance, a market economy is no sufficient condition for electoral democracy, and Protestantism is no necessary condition for the development of capitalism).

Because, for cross-national comparisons, it seemed necessary to use techniques that would embrace whole societies, there has been a clear tendency to rely either on the synthetic approach of the historian or on the representative approach of the survey. Very little attention has been paid so far to the use of such approaches as interviews with lay persons, life stories or similar 'microsocial', 'qualitative' techniques used on samples whose representative status is not clear. Although some of the best works of anthropology are based on such apparently 'soft' methods of observation (such as the cross-cultural works of Geertz or Lévi-Strauss), the suspicion remains that their quality is based more on the talent of the anthropologists than on the scientificity of their approach. Behind this suspicion, however, lies a wholly mistaken conception of what is science, what is scientific research, what is theory; a generalized confusion between two processes, the process of generating hypotheses, and the process of proving that they hold (in such or such context). The emphasis put on the second of these processes, and especially the deadly mistake of loading the burden of the proof on the shoulders of the *individual* researcher (while this burden should be carried by the whole scientific community) has led towards a sterilization of the sociological imagination – which is one crucial element in the process of theorization. The quality of imagination in the theorizing subject (who can be an individual, or far better, a pair or a small number of committed researchers) accounts for much of the quality of the theorization that will be generated and proposed to the critique of the sociological community.

Interviewing selected persons about their life experience is an approach that has tremendous potentialities for sociological research, but which will only show all its potentialities within a post-scientist epistemology; that is, an epistemology which cares more about the originality, depth, radicality of new hypotheses than about their provability (given Popper's accurate law that a non-falsifiable hypothesis falls outside the realm of scientific research).

It has already been shown that life stories can be used for a very wide variety of purposes: not only to study the subjective side of social life, but also to understand whole sets of socio-structural relationships such as processes of migration, patterns of social trajectories, the social structuration of life cycles or even the inner workings of given crafts and trades (Bertaux, 1981; Bertaux and Bertaux-Wiame, 1981; Bertaux and Kohli, 1984). Whenever they are used for probing subjectivities, life-story interviews prove able to probe deep; perhaps because it is much easier to lie about one's opinions, values and even behaviour than about one's own life.

It is this specific quality of life stories, the wealth and complexity of the descriptions they bring forth of personal experiences, that give them value for sociological research *and* that would make them useful for comparative purposes. But to extract the wealth of sociological meanings latent in life stories is no easy task. Most of them remain implicit in a person's lived experience; it takes a sociological eye – some lay persons do possess it – to look through a particular experience and understand what is universal in it; to perceive, beyond described actions and interactions, the implicit sets of rules and norms, the underlying situations, processes and contradictions that have both made actions and interactions possible and that have shaped them in specific ways. It takes some training to hear, behind the solo of a human voice, the music of society and culture in the background. This music is all the more audible if, in conducting the interview, in asking the very first question, in choosing, even earlier, the right persons for interviewing, one has worked with sociological issues and riddles in mind.

Working with life stories as well as with other types of 'ethno-graphic' data thus forces the sociologists to inject as much sociological thinking as they can into every step of their research, from fieldwork to analysis and writing. This is a key difference with survey research: surveys, even if they are done in the most mechanical way, always bring *some* information; some unexpected empirical findings, be it only percentages. Not so with life stories; as raw data they do not mean much more to the sociological community than ordinary interviews. It is only by the hard work of grounded theorization 'from the data up' that some of the sociological meanings that are hidden in them and *between* them (between, for example, life stories of a brother and a sister; of several school children coming from different social backgrounds; or of activists of the same cohort) may be brought to light as working hypotheses, to be examined by the sociological community.

The two hypotheses I have put forward here, although illustrated each with extracts of a single interview, have been elaborated through a complex process where many elements, including our own experiences, have played a part. The comparative dimension lies in the tensions between my own experience of May–June 1968 in Paris, and the accounts of lived experience that my colleagues collected in the United States, in Italy, in Germany – and in France – some fifteen years later; between the evaluations that each interviewee, and each interviewer, in each country, made at a distance of the achievements and failures, personal meanings and historical meaning of the movements they participated in.

Hence the comparative dimension, that a casual reader might miss at first reading, underlies this chapter. Through sketches of some of the processes through which a given person grew up to become an activist, through an attempt at bringing to life the collective emotions of a movement just being born, I have tried to describe the individual paths leading from moral commitment to activism and the collective path from serial state to the formation of a collective subject of action. Because both processes seem to transcend nations and cultures, I have focused upon similarities, not differences. Letting the variables vary, we found nevertheless – behind obvious differences in the forms of action, which are always context-dependent – striking commonalities; if this holds then it is a confirmation of Sztompska's hypothesis that, in a world whose divisions are melting, comparative research needs new approaches.

Notes

Ronald Grele has read an earlier version of this chapter and made many helpful suggestions for bettering both its form and contents. I must however assume alone full responsibility for the final version.

1. In spite of its awkwardness, the expression 'oral history' is on the verge of entering the dictionary. It is used to designate the research and writing about past events, former ways of life and so on – in short, all the topics of traditional historians – when the basic sources are not already existing written documents (archives) but 'oral sources'; that is, the testimonies of living people. See Fraser (1979), Grele (1985), Thompson (1988).

2. This hypothesis was first put forward in our group by Anne Marie Tröger.

3. Throughout the research we have regretted being unable to include at least Japan (where the student movement was extremely strong as early as the fifties), Czechoslovakia and Poland where much happened in 1968 due to students, or Mexico where the student movement was perhaps the strongest in all Latin America and the repression was surely the bloodiest. The sheer lack of research funds available for such a research topic explains why we were constrained to limit ourselves to the Western developed world.

4. It may be that the first time in history this happened was, precisely, the sixties, as has been convincingly argued by Ortoleva (1988) and Gitlin (1980).

5. The new reflection on subjectivity is particularly interesting when it is developed in the context of a philosophically humanist context, as in the works of Passerini (1987, 1988) and Portelli (1985). The concept of subjectivity allows for moving back and forth between the individual, micro-social, meso- and macro-social levels much more freely than concepts such as opinions, attitudes, values or even ideology.

6. What is quoted here is an un-rewritten excerpt of an interview done by Bret Eynon. Usually such pieces of oral discourse are carefully rewritten to fit in the norms of written discourse. Since this chapter is about subjectivity, it seems necessary to give the reader access to the verbatim quotations. I want to express my hearty thanks to Bret Eynon (New York Social History Project of the City University of New York) for letting me use his interviews extensively, as well as the interviewees themselves. The interviews are deposited in the collection of the Columbia University Oral History Research Office, at present directed by Ronald Grele, who has granted me permission to use them.

7. It should be added that the value of *community*, of belonging to a human group, was still a deeply treasured ideal of the American creed. In Europe, by contrast, the notion of community carried with it unpleasant overtones related to the early phases of the various European fascisms; it was connected, albeit implicitly, to anti-democratic philosophies.

8. I am indebted to Pawel Kuczynski, sociologist and activist of the Solidarnost movement, for making this point crystal clear to me. The moral sources of radical political commitment show up very clearly in a research project based on life-story

interviews with Solidarnost activists at the time of military rule in Poland (December 1981 to 1989); the contrast is striking with the thoroughly cynical attitude of the members of the ruling elite also interviewed at the same time (Misztal and Wasilewski, 1986).

References

Alberoni, Francesco (1977) *Movimento e istituzione*. Bologna: Il Mulino.

Alberoni, Francesco (1979) *Innamoramento e amore*. Milan: Garzanti.

Bergson, Henri [1932] (1970) 'Les deux sources de la morale et de la religion', in *Oeuvres*. Paris: Presses Universitaires de France.

Bertaux, Daniel (1977) *Destins personnels et structure de classe*. Paris: Presses Universitaires de France.

Bertaux, Daniel (ed.) (1981) *Biography and Society: The Life-History Approach in the Social Sciences*. London and Beverly Hills: Sage Publications.

Bertaux, Daniel and Isabelle Bertaux-Wiame (1981) 'Artisanal Bakery in France: How it Lives and why it Survives', pp. 155–81 in Frank Bechhofer and Brian Elliott (eds), *The Petite Bourgeoisie: Comparative Studies of the Uneasy Stratum*. London: Macmillan.

Bertaux, Daniel and Isabelle Bertaux-Wiame (1988) 'Le patrimoine et sa lignée: transmission et mobilité sociale sur cinq générations', *Life Stories/Récits de vie*, 4: 8–26.

Bertaux, Daniel and Danièle Linhart (1988) 'Mai 68 et la formation de générations politiques en France', *Le Mouvement social*, 143 (April–June): 75–89.

Bertaux, Daniel and Martin Kohli (1984) 'The Life Story Approach: A Continental View', *Annual Review of Sociology*, 10: 149–67.

Durkheim, Emile [1912] (1960) *Les formes élémentaires de la vie religieuse. Le système totémique en Australie*. Paris: Presses Universitaire de France.

Fraser, Ronald (1979) *Blood of Spain: An Oral History of the Spanish Civil War*. New York: Pantheon.

Fraser, Ronald, Daniel Bertaux, Bret Eynon, Ronald Grele, Béatrix Le Wita, Luisa Passerini, Jochen Staadt and AnneMarie Troeger (1988) *1968: A Student Generation in Revolt*. London: Chatto and Windus; Augmented edn (1988) New York: Pantheon.

Gitlin, Todd (1980) *The Whole World is Watching: Mass Media in the Making and Unmaking of the New Left*. Berkeley: University of California Press.

Grele, Ronald J. (ed.) (1985) *Envelopes of Sound: The Art of Oral History*. New York: Transaction Books, 2nd edn.

Habermas, Jürgen (1985) *Der philosophische Diskurs der Moderne. Zwölf Vorlesungen*. Frankfurt am Main: Suhrkamp.

Hegedus, Zsuzsa (1989) 'Social Movements and Social Change in Self-Creative Society: New Civil Initiatives in the International Arena', *International Sociology*, 4(1) (March): 19–86.

Klandermans, Bert and Dirk Oegema (1987) 'Potentials, Networks, Motivations and Barriers: Steps towards Participation in Social Movements', *American Sociological Review*, 51 (Aug.): 519–31.

Lapeyronnie, Didier (1988) 'Mouvements sociaux et action politique. Existe-t-il une théorie de la mobilisation des ressources?' *Revue Française de Sociologie*, XXIX–4: 593–619.

McAdam, Dough, John D. McCarthy and Mayer N. Zald (1988) 'Social Movements', ch. 21 in Neil J. Smelser (ed.), *Handbook of Sociology*. Newbury Park, CA: Sage Publications, pp. 695–737.

Mannheim, Karl (1929) *Ideologie und Utopie*. Bonn: F. Cohen.

Misztal, Bronislaw and Jacek Wasilewski (1986) 'Les vainqueurs et les vaincus: la Pologne après décembre 1981', *Life Stories/Récits de vie*, 2, pp. 21–33.

Naroll, R. (1965) 'Galton's Problem: The Logic of Cross-cultural Research', *Social Research*, 32: 428–51.

Oevermann, Ulrich (1988) 'Eine exemplarische Fall-rekonstruktion zum Typus versozialwissenschaftlichen Identitätsformation', in Hanns-Georg Brose and Bruno Hildebrand (eds), *Von Ende des Individuums zur Individualität ohne Ende*. Opladen: Leske & Budrich, pp. 243–86.

Ortoleva, Peppino (1988) *Saggio sui movimenti del 1968 in Europe e in America*. Rome: Editori Riuniti.

Passerini, Luisa (1987) *Fascism in Popular Memory: The Cultural Experience of the Turin Working Class*. Cambridge: Cambridge University Press.

Passerini, Luisa (1988) *Storia e soggetivita*. Firenze-Scandicci: La Nuova Italia.

Passerini, Luisa (1988) *Autoritratto di gruppo*. Florence: Giunti Barbera.

Portelli, Alessandro (1985) *Biografia di una citta: storia e raconto, Terni 1830–1985*. Turin: Giulio Einaudi. See review by Paul Thompson, pp. 51–5 in *Life Stories/Récits de vie*, 3, 1987.

Sartre, Jean-Paul (1960) *Questions de méthode*. Paris: Gallimard.

Scheuch, Erwin K. (1989) 'Theoretical Implications of Comparative Survey Research: Why the Wheel of Cross-cultural Methodology Keeps on Being Reinvented?', *International Sociology*, 4(2) (June): 147–67.

Smelser, Neil J. (1962) *Theory of Collective Behavior*. New York: Free Press.

Strauss, Anselm J. (1987) *Qualitative Analysis for Social Scientists*. Cambridge: Cambridge University Press.

Sztompka, Piotr (1988) 'Conceptual Frameworks in Comparative Inquiry: Divergent or Convergent?', *International Sociology*, 3(3) (Sept.): 207–18.

Thompson, Paul (1988) *The Voice of the Past: Oral History*. Oxford: Oxford University Press, 2nd edn.

Toennies, Ferdinand [1887] (1963) *Gemeinschaft und Gesellschaft. Grundbegriffe der reinen Soziologie*. Darmstadt: Wissenschaftliche Buchgesellschaft.

Touraine, Alain (1984) *Le retour de l'acteur. Essai de sociologie*. Paris: Fayard.

Weber, Max (1920) *Wirtschaft und Gesellschaft: Grundriss der verstehenden Soziologie*. Tübingen: Mohr.

10

Sampling and Cross-classification Analysis in International Social Research

Karl M. van Meter

The difficulty of studying hidden populations, such as drug users, with traditional sociological research methods reveals a distinction between ascending methodologies adapted to the study of small or local populations and descending methodologies adapted to general populations. Snowball or chain referral sampling and hierarchically ascending classification analysis, and its more advanced form of cross-classification analysis, together form a coherent and rigorous ascending methodology for studying hidden populations.

Snowball sampling begins through contacts with probable members of a hidden population. In the case of drug users, 'street ethnographers' or simply 'big city savvy' furnish the necessary knowledge to find these persons who will act as initial snowball nominees. Each nominee is interviewed using an established questionnaire and then asked to 'nominate' other drug users to be interviewed. In the case of the study presented below, the average number of persons 'nominated' by an interviewee was thirty-five. This means that a snowball sample can indeed grow rapidly. Specific methodological adaptations can be made to assure that no individual is interviewed twice and that specific quotas for sex, age or other social characteristics are met by the nomination procedure. To assure generalizability, a typical methodological adaptation is to select randomly a small fixed number of individuals to interview out of the mean number of thirty-five 'nominees' proposed by each interviewed drug user.

Hierarchically ascending classification analysis, often called 'cluster analysis', constructs successively more general classes or 'types' according to the similarities between the descriptive variables being analysed. Cross-classification analysis goes a step further by not only analysing similarity between variables for all individuals, but also similarity between individuals for all variables. These similarities are then combined or 'crossed' to form coherent blocks of individuals/ variables which are called 'polythetic classes' and described below.

The combination of snowball sampling and cross-classification analysis is well adapted to the study of hidden populations. This methodology does have certain problems with the calculation of general population estimates and the explanation of variance which are the subject of recently published research. Through the complementary combination of ascending and descending methodologies, recent work has largely resolved these problems, providing both a formal and operational tie between these two methodologies and an extremely useful tool in comparative sociological research.

Drug Abuse and the Analysis of Hidden Populations

In current sociology, there is an explicit association, on one hand, between the problem of studying social groups or types of social behaviour that are not 'easy to get to' or accessible by established institutional means of sociological survey research ('hidden populations'), and, on the other hand, the use of research methodologies based on intensive, detailed, data collection strategies and their associated methods of analysis, often referred to as 'qualitative research designs'. Implicitly, this identifies 'established institutional means of sociological research' with large-scale representative surveys ('quantitative research') and opposes them to 'qualitative' counterparts. Although there are real difficulties in studying hidden populations, the specific adequacy of intensive data collection strategies, such as snowball sampling for studying hidden populations, overcomes many of these obstacles.

In an important review article on the analysis of drug abuse, Kozel and Adams (1986) presented a critique of traditional medical epidemiological models, showing the inadequate nature of such descending methodology, though the authors do not use the term. Similarly, without using the terms of polythetic or monothetic classes which are developed below, they criticized the 'attempt to classify drug-using behavior into one of two apparently distinct categories' while noting that current research tends to study 'patterns of abuse'. Although the usefulness of surveys for monitoring trends and prevalence of drug use is clearly indicated, they conclude with the statement that 'drug epidemics often are localized and involve specific subpopulations that make surveillance based on national data systems difficult'. This is an explicit indication that descending methodologies have encountered serious problems with studying hidden populations. Ascending methodologies may be able to resolve some of them.

These authors present the American National Institute of Drug Abuse (NIDA) Household Survey as the 'single most important measure of drug abuse in our general population'. But they openly admit its limitations due to sample bias which missed an important hidden population: transient and non-residential groups or individuals. The President's Commission on Organized Crime (PCOC) has underlined the same: the Household Survey and the High School Senior Survey 'have been criticized because they do not include information from these populations that are frequently involved with drugs, high school dropouts and people without residence' (PCOC, 1986: 340). The PCOC also proposed a solution, 'over-sampling', that implies an ascending methodology. It recognizes that 'surveys of cocaine users demonstrated there is no "typical" cocaine user' (1986: 25) and that the concept of patterns of use must be employed. It also recognized that the necessary level of study, prevention, and treatment is the community (1986: 325).

The PCOC's specific criticism of descending methodology includes: the lack of data on the price and quantity of drugs purchased, on the sources of the funds, and on the source of the data (1986: 341); and the unreliable nature of 'analysis by negotiation' with final estimates of drug use 'resulting from a bargaining process among the member agencies' (1986: 343). As described by Hall (1988), these are the very lacunae that 'community epidemiology' attempts to fill by focusing on the consequences of abuse rather than the prevalence of use. 'For local purposes it is often more useful to determine answers to the questions "who" and "where" rather than "how many" so that limited resources may be most effectively applied to provide the greatest benefit' (1988: 2). 'The snowball methodology for tracking drug abusers is ideal because of its intensive results and the ability to present findings rapidly' (1988: 3). This may also be the specific methodology needed for monitoring the heterosexual spread of AIDS in the general population since it is now recognized that AIDS as an 'epidemic will be long and drawn out as it spreads through the different at-risk groups and in different localities over the coming decades' (Anderson and May, 1988).

In a recent European Communities study (Avico et al., 1988), we have shown that snowball sampling can quickly and efficiently survey a relatively large sample of current cocaine users. In two months of part-time fieldwork in three widely different cities (Rotterdam, Munich and Rome) a common instrument and sampling design was applied, resulting in 153 interviews with active cocaine users. This already is one of the largest samples of cocaine users ever collected in either Europe or America. In addition, approximately four times that number of cocaine users have been identified on socio-demographic variables by the interviewees through the nomination procedure involved in snowball sampling. These results weighted against the number of cocaine users known to each interviewee (in Munich and Rotterdam approximately thirty-five known users) raise the order of magnitude to the thousands that have been recognized.

The costs of a snowball sample are much less per case than other scientific sampling techniques such as a youth or household survey. Thus, if we assume that the current prevalence of cocaine is a high 1 per cent in the European population, we would have had to draw a sample of more than 15,000 Europeans to get the yield of 153 interviews produced by the snowball sample in two months of fieldwork. The methodology is also able to produce multiple kinds of data, including 'thick' descriptions of contexts and social relationships of networks of cocaine users. Thus, multiple scientific interests can be associated with a single snowball project. In so far as the fieldworker is also functioning in some capacity as an outreach worker, the conduct of research can be linked to the treatment system. The fieldwork involves the description and communication of problems with cocaine and therefore serves as a community needs assessment technique. Furthermore, the potential for information flow to the user group is also present, and, in careful coordination with treatment services, certain problematic users could be referred to appropriate treatment and counselling. In this way the epidemiological goal of intervention is joined to that of explanation.

Snowball Sampling and Drug Abuse in Rotterdam and Munich

In the context of this European Community study, we found that Emile Durkheim's concept of 'social milieu', instead of 'social strata', imposed itself as the means of describing drug users (Avico et al., 1988: III–7). Plotting the incidence curves of cocaine use (year of first use) in Munich and Rotterdam for the last fifteen years shows that cocaine is not at all a new drug in these cities. As the Munich data show, the supposed threat of a European cocaine epidemic, in this case, is the result of discrepancies between endemic cocaine use and changes in police strategies of seizure and arrest data. Similar discrepancies can also be found in official US government data. In both cases, it is the confrontation of results from ascending methodologies (snowball sampling or local data) and descending methodologies (official government statistics) that reveals such discrepancies.

The incidence curves of Rotterdam and Munich further suggest a certain convergence of cocaine consumption situations in these two cities with current levels tending towards the level of 15 to 20 per cent of the total drug-user population. However, the snowball sampling data show that the history of cocaine consumption is rather different. The first real cocaine epidemic in Rotterdam took place in the early 1970s when Munich had no noticeable consumption. As the epidemic in Rotterdam subsided, an epidemic in Munich began. Another such cycle followed before arriving at the current situation.

The study has produced clear estimates of the prevalence and distribution of certain patterns of use. Analysed according to job milieu, the data reveal some interesting similarities and differences. Although Munich is recognized as a 'cocaine glamour city', the prevalence among artists and actors in Rotterdam at 29 per cent is slightly higher than in Munich with 25 per cent, though this difference is not likely to be statistically significant. None the less, a quarter of cocaine users are artists, even in a workers' city such as Rotterdam, a statistic which poses an interesting question for further research. Common patterns were also found in the pimp and prostitute milieu (*c.* 5 per cent), the campus milieu (*c.* 15–18 per cent) and the blue-collar worker milieu (*c.* 20 per cent). The latter is particularly interesting in that it proves that cocaine is not only a luxury, high-status drug. As in the United States, cocaine use has spread to youth, working and lower classes, becoming more evenly distributed throughout the entire society of these two cities.

The differences between the two cities are also of interest. Munich, an entertainment and 'yuppie' city, has a much higher prevalence in the restaurant and café milieu (15 per cent) and the white-collar milieu (20) than Rotterdam (4 and 7 respectively). This hypothesis is further supported by the high prevalence of unemployed users in Rotterdam (18). This category does not even appear in the Munich data. Moreover, in Rotterdam, working- and lower-class use is indeed at least as prevalent as glamour use. This is consistent with the image of Rotterdam as a city of unintimidated, hard-working people.

Significantly enough, the data from Rome, which were obtained by a classic descending survey methodology, were incapable of furnishing the detailed statistics given above. Similarly, the snowball sampling technique in Rotterdam and Munich generates specific figures of 'cost per gramme', which is a major lacuna mentioned by the PCOC in general survey data. In Rotterdam, 75 per cent of the sample pay less than Fl200, while in Munich the proportion is merely 25 per cent. Most Munich users pay between Fl200–250 per gramme, while only 11 per cent of Rotterdam users pay that equivalent price. This pattern continues beyond the Fl250 per gramme level. The explanation of this price differential is complex, but it probably has to do with the different 'character' of each city's workforce and the relatively lower demand in Rotterdam in terms of lower absolute numbers of active cocaine users.

This ascending methodology has revealed that both cities have a pattern of problems engendered by cocaine use. The majority of users in both cities reported some kind of problem. Most of these were restricted to private difficulties in social life and at work. However, the prevalence of non-problematic use is higher in Rotterdam (39 per cent) than in Munich (25). An interesting hypothesis to explore would be to see if problem usage is related to the job milieu and cost factors.

Classification Analysis

In the case of classification analysis, there is a very clear distinction between ascending and descending methods. The latter construct classes (or 'clusters') by starting with the entire population and successively dividing it in order to obtain a descending hierarchy of classifications: the first level will have the entire population included in one single class; the second level will have the population divided into two (or possibly more) classes; the third and following levels will each have at least one new division resulting in a new class. This process continues until it arrives at an optimum classification or until it arrives at the zero level with each individual in its own unique class. Inversely, hierarchically ascending classification starts at the zero level (each individual in its own unique class) and constructs successive levels of classification by bringing together into the same class similar individuals (Lerman, 1981).

The classes obtained by hierarchically ascending classification are called 'polythetic classes', as opposed to 'monothetic classes' (Lerman, 1981: 169). A class of individuals is defined as monothetic if it is characterized by one, and only one, characteristic. This means that an individual belongs to the class if, and only if, that individual has the given characteristic. A class G is defined as polythetic if, and only if, each individual belonging to G has an important (but not fixed) proportion of a certain subset B of characteristics, and if each characteristic belonging to B is present in an important (but not fixed) proportion of the individuals in G. A corollary to this definition is that an individual with many characteristics in B is not necessarily a member of G, and there may be members of G that have an important proportion of characteristics not in B. This formal definition of a polythetic class is the generalization of a Weberian ideal type and also that given by the World Health Organization for a syndrome in the context of drug and alcohol abuse (Van Meter et al., 1987; WHO, 1981).

Those methods of classification analysis that are hierarchically ascending formally construct polythetic classes. 'Hierarchically ascending' in this case implies that resemblance between individuals is used to form classes. Therefore, the first classes formed are composed of those individuals who resemble one another the most. The later the class is formed – that is to say, the higher in the hierarchy – the less its members will resemble one another. This also means that for hierarchically ascending methods, each level in a tree of classifications corresponds to a particular and distinct classification of the entire population under investigation with successively fewer but larger classes of individuals. The final classification or level in the hierarchy, of course, is composed of one unique class including the entire population.

A specific type of hierarchically ascending classification analysis, called 'automatic classification' (Lerman, 1981), applies minimal criteria to reduce the number of descriptive variables figuring in a data set. This provides a formal systematic means of reducing or summarizing the often considerable list of variables or dimensions involved in typical ascending strategies of data collection. In automatic classification analysis, proximity between individuals or entities analysed is measured by a similarity index calculated over all variables taken into consideration (Prod'homme et al., 1983). It allows us to construct classes based on the 'maximum likelihood of association' between two individuals that emphasizes the resemblance between two classes more than the distance which separates each of them from nearby large classes of individuals (SAS, 1985).

The classifications based on inter-individual resemblance are then arranged in an ordered hierarchy or tree. The method also establishes, for each level of the hierarchy, the statistical probability or likelihood of the occurrence of each particular classification. This probability is calculated on the basis of the original null hypothesis that all characteristics are normally distributed. The evolution of this local statistic, associated with each level of the hierarchy of classifications or classification tree, permits the construction of a graph and the identification of local minima on the graph. These are by definition improbable occurrences and, therefore, where significant classifications are situated. By this means, one can identify, within the successive classifications, the more significant groups of subjects or nodes which, by their construction, form polythetic classes. Moreover, this same process reveals the development and evolution of such significant groups throughout the hierarchical tree of classifications. It follows them, starting with the first and most detailed classification (each individual constitutes his or her own class), and continues all the way to the final and roughest classification (everyone in one single class).

Cross-classification analysis is the Cartesian crossing of two automatic classification analyses of the same data. It reorganizes a two-dimensional data set (individuals by variables) by projecting on to the set the results of an automatic classification analysis of the individuals (or rows of figures) and of the descriptive variables (or columns of figures). In this manner, all initial data can be directly presented along with the organization of that data due to the cross-classification analysis. This unique form of presentation permits other researchers to carry out comparative and critical analysis of the same data. This method was employed in research on social deviance (Faugeron and Van Meter, 1990) in order to find the significant nodes or polythetic classes mentioned above.

It also provided a means of extending, in an unlimited fashion, the application of classification analysis to any finite population, no matter how large. This latter result is of a certain significance due to the fact that classification analysis of large data sets has been inhibited up until now by its heavy requirements in computer time and memory capacity. Furthermore, the groups or units of individuals/variables found by cross-classification analysis meet the same criteria as the blocks obtained by block modelling methods in social network analysis (Van Meter, 1986). Cross-classification analysis was used in our sociological survey of cocaine use in three Western European cities in order to determine and define types of cocaine use (Kaplan et al., 1985).

Applications of Cross-classification Analysis

These groups or units of individuals/variables mentioned above are of course polythetic classes and are rather stable units of analysis. This stability allows the construction of classification grids which characterize the most pertinent subset of variables for each group. It also permits the use of these groups in further cross-classification analyses where the initial results concerning a 'condition' of behaviour (the initial blocks of individuals/variables) are then submitted to a cross-classification analysis over a certain length of time. Thus, one can construct a polythetic class corresponding to a 'syndrome' which would be a stable block generated by the cross-classification analysis of individual 'conditions' crossed with chronological time. In turn, the individual 'conditions' will have resulted from an initial cross-classification analysis of individuals crossed with descriptive variables. This particular adaptation of cross-classification analysis, along with the experience sampling technique of gathering repeated measurements of behaviour and mental 'condition', as mentioned above, at randomly selected moments in the daily life of an individual, form the ascending methodology of a current research project at the

University of Limburg, Maastricht, the Netherlands, on anxiety and drug abuse (Van Meter et al., 1987).

Ascending and Descending Methodologies

The difficulty of studying hidden populations does reveal a significant difference between extensive survey methodologies and intensive data-collection methodologies. This difference distinguishes between what we have called 'descending methodology' and 'ascending methodology' (Van Meter, 1985; DSP, 1986; Kaplan et al., 1987). Moreover, this difference can be found both in data collection and methods of statistical analysis. Descending methodology involves strategies elaborated and executed at the level of general populations. They therefore necessitate highly standardized questionnaires and rigorous population samples, and, for historic and economic reasons more than methodological considerations, usually involve traditional statistical analysis. This methodology has been typically used by national governments in order to make statistical inferences and decide future social policy. The strict scientific rigour of this methodology, even in its most exemplary use, can be easily criticized (Guttman, 1984), but this does not reduce the usefulness of its results.

Ascending methodologies involve research strategies elaborated at a community or local level and specifically adapted to the study of selected social groups; for example, a hidden population. In order to be efficient, the means of data collection are usually selective and intensive. Snowball sampling, life histories and ethnographic monographs are typical forms of data collection in ascending methodology. Methods of analysis in this type of methodology must also be adapted to the specific form of data furnished and also to the specific objectives of the research. Typical forms of ascending data analysis are social network analysis and classification analysis.

However, the specific adaptation of ascending methodology is not obtained without the loss of easy generalizability. In exchange, descending methodology cannot reach hidden populations without specific adaptations. Indeed, that is exactly what the President's Commission on Organized Crime (PCOC, 1986: 340) was proposing when it recommended 'oversampling' high-school dropouts and people without residence in the National Institute on Drug Abuse annual High School Senior Survey and bi-annual Household Survey of drug use. Similarly, ascending methodology, such as network analysis, can be employed in the study of large populations, though at great material cost and rigorous standardization; the best example being Joel H. Levine's *Atlas of Corporate Interlocks* that covers the entire world population of corporations (Levine, 1988).

Problems of Extrapolation

Questions of bias are always present in any data-collection strategy, and are particularly acute in the study of hidden populations. Random error (or 'sampling error'), sample bias and response bias are the major sources of inaccuracy in data collection. The first is usually dealt with by increasing the sample size: in accordance with well-known statistical formulas, the larger the sample, the smaller the random sampling error. But this may vary with the type of data collection. Response bias is also dealt with through traditional means such as split samples, rearrangements of the same question-naire or in-depth interviews. Sample bias is often considered a more serious problem. Indeed, much of the criticism mentioned above related to descending methodologies concerns sample bias. Descending strategies of data collection can often miss an entire hidden population, such as blue-collar cocaine users in Rotterdam, for example, thus, in this case, rendering accurate estimation of drug use extremely difficult.

If ascending strategies, and snowball sampling in particular, offer a solution to the problem of data collection for hidden populations, the formalization of their sample bias seems to be beyond the reach of current statistics, though admirable attempts have been made (Rapoport, 1979; Frank, 1979, 1981). But these formal treatments of the question usually require further general information on the population, such as the mean number of ties between individuals, the distribution of ties throughout the population, including the number of triads and the number of diads. Once again we find that the solution being proposed is to revert to better descending strategies of data collection instead of directly addressing what we have called 'the limitations of this technique (of snowball sampling) that involve an uncontrollable selection bias that limits the external validity of the sample' (Kaplan et al., 1985: 3).

In snowball sampling, selection can be modelled as a stochastic process which permits the calculation of sample weights that are inversely proportional to the probabilities of selection and can generate unbiased estimates (Avico et al., 1988: I–14). Sample selection bias formulated in this manner offers a reliable sampling frame, particularly when data from initial respondents, other than selections of other respondents, are not recorded, and following respondents are selected at random (Kaplan et al., 1987). Another complementary manner of selection is to choose respondents according to the quota system of sampling, thus assuring an unbiased coverage of a hidden population.

This strategy was used in recent research in France (Pollak and Schiltz, 1988). Moreover, this snowball sample (N=300) was used as a control for a general descending survey of male homosexuals (N=1557) who read gay periodicals. The snowball sample was constrained to respect standard quotas for age, class, size of town of residence corresponding to the French male population from 18 to 55 years of age. The only significant difference found was that readers of homosexual literature changed their sexual behaviour due to the threat of AIDS earlier than non-readers by an average of six months. The same authors have published other works in this field, using astute combinations of descending and ascending methodologies (Pollak and Schiltz, 1987). In this latter case, a general typology of male homosexuals and their attitudes toward AIDS, typology based on hierarchically ascending classification analysis and factoral correspondence analysis, was complemented by numerous in-depth, extensive, semi-directive interviews.

Discussion: Towards Comparative Research

Different subpopulations of very difficult access, 'hidden populations', were encountered in Rotterdam in the snowball sampling of cocaine users. Indeed, significant blue-collar consumption of cocaine had not even been envisaged before the research began. None the less, the methodology employed furnished clear and coherent results. When a culturally and socially different city such as Munich was researched, a very robust and 'neutral' methodology was necessary in order to obtain results of similar quality. Not only was this the case, but the results were of such a homogeneous standard that it was quite possible to do a comparative analysis of cocaine use in these two very distinct social environments. However, the structure of the data gathered in Rome on cocaine use was largely determined by a traditional descending census-type methodology and, in spite of important institutional backing, and probably because of it, the Rome data could only furnish classic incident rates with little or no information on the 'milieu' of use and on the different types of cocaine use. Therefore, within a common empirical problematic, the ascending methodology performed effectively and, compared to traditional methods, proved both its adaptability and stability as a research tool in differing social contexts.

Conversely, when different empirical problematics are associated with a common empirical procedure, in the case of ascending methodology, researchers quickly discovered they could map out major differences and establish zones of comparability. Indeed, an initial Italian survey of cocaine use employing descending methodology directly inspired from American studies failed to find significant cocaine consumption. However, a brief survey with ascending methodology inspired from snowball sampling quickly found that, contrary to the American model, high schools were not a major 'milieu' of cocaine users but that the better-educated adult population was. Quite clearly, descending methodologies can encounter great difficulty in being applied outside the social framework in which they were created and adapted. Large-scale drug-use surveys in one country are often not valid in another.

These two contrasting examples show that as an empirical tool for comparative research, ascending methodology based on snowball sampling and cross-classification analysis is 'context-sensitive', coherent and stable, permitting identification of major differing aspects of surveys carried out in different nations and cultures, and zones of similarity where detailed comparisons can be pursued. For example, comparative research of abortion in a Protestant culture, a Catholic culture, and a Muslim culture could certainly not rely on official data produced by descending methods. In such a case, snowball sampling would appear to be one of the very few valid methods to provide sufficient systematized data to permit a formal analysis and comparison of this social phenomenon in different cultures.

Another example would be comparative research on how high-level cadres obtain their first professional positions in Western Europe, Eastern Europe and the Third World. Still another example would be cheating in school in different countries. The more a survey targets a sensitive social phenomenon, the more the survey population is a 'hidden population' and the more essential ascending methodology becomes as an empirical comparative research tool.

When research concerns socially 'accepted' behaviour, ascending and descending methodologies produce results which, when compared, offer less discernible distinctions. However, ascending methodology plays an important role in such research by offering an independent verification procedure. For example, it can address the question of whether or not, when West Germans speak of 'quality of life' or 'confidence between people', they are referring to the same social attitudes as Italians or Spaniards using these same terms. Even at the level of general population studies, certain research problematics require ascending methodology. Indeed, the most recent US census, for the first time, included individual friendship network information. A comparative survey in any other country would also be obliged to adopt an ascending methodology to obtain such information.

These various projects using ascending methodology have, until now, been carried out in rather specifically delimited empirical research programmes confronted with the problems, such as the analysis of hidden populations, that are major obstacles to the use of descending methodology. It is quite significant that in most of the cases mentioned above a form of ascending methodology has been developed as an original solution to overcome these problems of data collection and analysis.

The dispersed character of these specific research programmes, which have found ascending methodological solutions, largely explains why knowledge of these developments has not yet reached mainstream sociology. Only a year ago in an important work on cross-national and comparative research C. Ragin, noting 'the gulf between small-N and large-N research' (1989: 61), described the pressures 'that push research designs in comparative social science toward the two extremes of sample size – very small or as large as possible' (1989: 61), attributing this to the lack of a coherent and adapted methodology able to function between these two extremes. Indeed, his discussion of bridging this gulf between 'intensive (small-N) and extensive (large-N) work' (1989: 64) lays out the basic attributes of ascending methodology (without using the concept or the term) which can 'preserve the intensity of the case-oriented approach' (1989: 69) but can carry out formalized 'extensive, variable-oriented work . . . across a large number of cases' (1989: 69).

Perhaps a major contribution of the work you have in your hands is to bring into mainstream sociology under the concept and the term of ascending methodology those diverse original solutions to this traditional 'gulf' between large-N and small-N research that in many ways run parallel to the out-dated distinction between 'qualitative' and 'quantitative' methodologies, which is no longer tenable in concrete research efforts.

Even if ascending methodologies are well adapted to 'small-N research', and in particular to the study of hidden populations, as in the case of snowball sampling and cross-classification analysis, problems do exist with the 'large-N' pole of research, specifically with handling sample bias, estimates at the level of the general population, and variance explanation (Van Meter, 1990), which are traditional concerns of 'large-N', 'extensive' or descending methodologies. Examples of recent research employing complementary combinations of ascending and descending methodologies show ways to 'bridge the gulf', resolve these problems and suggest promising new perspectives in an integrated methodological approach to social science research.

References

Anderson, R.M. and R.M. May (1988) *Nature*, 6173 (9 June).
Avico, U., C.D. Kaplan, D. Korczak and K.M. Van Meter (1988) 'Cocaine

epidemiology in three European Community cities: A pilot study using a snowball sampling methodology'. Research report, Cocaine Steering Group, Health Directorate, Commission of the European Communities, Brussels (Feb.).

DSP (Department of Social Psychiatry) (1986) 'Cross-classification analysis'. Experience Sampling Symposium, University of Limburg.

Faugeron, C. and K.M. Van Meter (1990) 'Analysis of Deviance and of Social Class: The Impact of Methodological Research', *Quality and Quantity*.

Frank, O. (1979) 'Estimation of Population Totals by Use of Snowball Samples', in P.W. Holland and S.L. Leinhardt (eds), *Perspectives on Social Network Research*. New York: Academic Press, pp. 319–47.

Frank, O. (1981) 'A Survey of Statistical Methods for Graph Analysis', in S.L. Leinhardt (ed.), *Sociological Methodology*. London: Jossey-Boss, pp. 110–55.

Guttman, L. (1984) 'What is Not What in Statistics: Statistical Inference Revisited – 1984', *Bulletin de Méthodologie Sociologique*, 4: 3–35.

Hall, J.N. (1988) 'The Community-based Drug Epidemiology Network', Health Directorate of the Commission of the European Communities, Brussels (10 May).

Kaplan, C.D., D. Korf and C. Sterk (1987) 'Temporal and Social Contexts of Heroin-Using Populations: An Illustration of the Snowball Sampling Technique', *Journal of Nervous and Mental Disease*, 175(9): 566–74 (Sept.).

Kaplan, C.D., K.M. Van Meter and D. Korczak (1985) 'Estimating Cocaine Prevalence and Incidence in Three European Community Cities', Commission of the European Communities, Luxembourg (19 Sept.).

Kozel, N.J. and E.H. Adams (1986) 'Epidemiology of Drug Abuse: An Overview', *Science*, 234: 970–4 (21 Nov.).

Lerman, I.C. (1981) *Classification et analyse ordinale des données*. Paris: Dunod.

Levine, J.H. (1988) 'The methodology of the *Atlas of Corporate Interlocks*', *Bulletin de Méthodologie Sociologique*, 17: 20–58 (Jan.).

PCOC (President's Commission on Organized Crime) (1986) *America's Habit: Drug Abuse, Drug Trafficking, and Organized Crime*. Washington, DC: US Government Printing Office.

Pollak, M. and M.A. Schiltz (1987) *Une épidémie autogérée: les homosexuelles face au SIDA*. vol. 1, and *Annexes techniques et statistiques*. vol. 2. Paris: EHEES.

Pollak, M. and M.A. Schiltz (1988) 'Does Voluntary Testing Matter? How It Influences Homosexual Safer Sex', IVth International Conference on AIDS, Stockholm (13 June).

Prod'homme, A., L. Breton and L. Guenneguez (1983) 'Note méthodologique sur l'utilisation de l'algorithme de vraisemblance des liens en sciences humaines', in *Actes des journées de classification*. Brussels: Société francophone de Classification, pp. 367–83.

Ragin, C. (1989) 'New Directions in Comparative Research', in M.L. Kohn (ed.), *Cross-national Research in Sociology*. London: Sage, pp. 57–76.

Rapoport, A.A. (1979) 'A Probabilistic Approach to Networks', *Social Networks*, 2(1): 1–18.

SAS (1985) *User's Guide: Statistics*. Version 5 edition, Cary, SAS Institute.

Van Meter, K.M. (1985) 'Block-modelling and Cross-classification Techniques for Estimating Population Parameters for Network Data'. Workshop on the Methodology of Applied Drug Research. Luxembourg: European Community Health Directorate.

Van Meter, K.M. (1986) 'Basic Typology and Multimethod Analysis in the Social Sciences'. New Delhi: ISA World Congress.

Van Meter, K.M., M.W. De Vries, C.D. Kaplan and C.I.M. Dijkman (1987) 'States, Syndromes, and Polythetic Classes: The Operationalization of Cross-classification

Analysis in Behavioral Science Research', *Bulletin de Méthodologie Sociologique*, 15: 22–38 (July).

Van Meter, K.M. (1990, in press) 'Methodological and Design Issues: Techniques for Assessing the Representatives of Snowball Samples', in W. Wiebel (ed.), *Hidden Populations*, Rockville, MD: NIDA (US National Institute on Drug Abuse).

WHO (World Health Organization) (1981) 'Nomenclature and Classification of Drug and Alcohol Related Problems: A WHO Memorandum', *Bulletin of the WHO*, 59(2): 225–42.

11

Data Archives as an Instrument for Comparative Research

Jan-Erik Lane

Comparative sociology is based upon the interaction between theory and data, theoretical concepts and empirical indicators. Empirical information is as vital as theoretical argument when the frontiers of knowledge about social systems are to be advanced by means of a comparative perspective. Both research strategies – the *deductive* mode and the *inductive* mode – are essential to comparative social inquiry aiming at a balance between a strong theoretical structure and a wealth of empirical information. The collection of large amounts of data in data archives in several countries is of special interest and relevance for comparative sociology. For example, what can we reasonably expect from the employment of massive data archives for comparative inquiry in political sociology?

When the reciprocity between social theory and data is underlined, then it is natural to focus on the establishment of national data banks. National data archives may provide comparative research with a badly needed empirical information base which serves a number of purposes. First, there is the *test function*: the model implications derived from comparative theory could be tested against information stored in data banks. Second, national archives may serve a vital *heuristic function*, because empirical information in these archives may guide the conduct of comparative theoretical research in fruitful directions. Third, there is the *cumulation function* in that a central storing of large amounts of information means an opportunity to employ the data for re-analysis.

At the same time a word of caution must be raised, as there is the severe danger of *crude empiricism*. The use of data in archives has to be based on theoretical considerations derived from social theory. The employment of large data archives is neither a necessary nor a sufficient condition for interesting and relevant comparative research. And the conduct of a comparative inquiry may have to start from the beginning collecting its own data base outside of existing data at national archives. Moreover, a case study of a single country may be entirely based on data from a large data archive.

The relationship between comparative social research and the establishment of large data archives is evident, but complex.

Logic of Comparative Inquiry

It is not clear what comparative social inquiry amounts to – that is, what distinguishes this type of social science analysis from other kinds of inquiry (Przeworski and Teune, 1970; Dogan and Pelassy, 1984). According to a *thin* definition, social research is comparative in so far as it focuses on several objects of analysis in order to identify similarities and differences. However, each social inquiry contains at least some comparison in space or over time. The *thick* definition argues that comparative social inquiry involves the analysis of properties of various kinds of *spatial units*: countries, states, societies and sub-national government entities. This definition is to be preferred as comparative sociology focuses on how various kinds of spatial social systems vary, be it political systems (Weber, 1978), states (Wilensky, 1975) or civilizations (Eisenstadt, 1978).

In a trivial sense all kinds of social injury are comparative. How could there be an analysis of a single phenomenon without some tacit or implicit comparison with other phenomena, similar ones or dissimilar ones? Comparative inquiry in sociology constitutes much more than this thin definition involves. Comparative sociology is based on the comparison of behaviour and institutions in different spatial units. Typical of comparative social inquiry is the study of a cross-sectional spatial variation.

Social researchers have to have access to data in order to test and develop hypotheses derived from models or hypotheses. The establishment of large national data archives is of tremendous help here as they may provide comparative research with necessary information. The build-up of large data archives in several countries means that comparative research has become more feasible, at the same time as a comparative focus is increasingly considered theoretically relevant in classical fields of sociology. The establishment of national data banks has often originated within political sociology in attempts at systematizing election data of various kinds.

Comparative analysis in sociology has also attracted a growing interest in recent decades, as reflected in the number of publications and journals. New study programmes dealing with different areas of the world have emerged. Area specialists claim that cross-national studies are a legitimate concern, although area studies are more oriented towards *case study analysis* than the use of the *comparative method* proper. There tend to be two types of comparative social inquiry overlapping within this distinction, one employing as few cases as possible ('empirically intensive') and the other using a large number of cases ('empirically extensive') (Ragin, 1989). But while this tension between the case-study method and the comparative method proper still lingers on, the interest in all forms of comparative analysis has grown substantially. Modern comparative analysis is dfferent from what used to be designated the traditional approach. An integral part of this reorientation is the growth of major national data archives.

In the 1950s it was argued that comparative sociology was descriptive, parochial, static and monographic. It displayed a heavy bias towards the major Western countries and lacked an adequate methodology for the conduct of systematic empirical inquiry. The rejection of the traditional approach changed the course of comparative sociology. Comparative sociology carried the claim that the institutions of a country could be better understood if its institutions were related to social forces (Lipset, 1959; Lipset and Rokkan, 1967; Allardt and Rokkan, 1970). The emerging visibility of the Third World stimulated a whole new approach to the explanation of the differences between politics and society in rich and poor countries – the modernization theme (Eisenstadt and Rokkan, 1973).

The new comparative approach necessitated a systematic collection of large amounts of data about various countries. As data without theory would be *blind*, the comparative revolution implied the explicit elaboration of concepts, models and hypotheses. Since theory without data would be *empty*, genuine comparative theory had to be put to more severe empirical tests, now through the abundance of new data in the large national data archives. The attack on the traditional approach was no doubt successful. The reorientation of comparative analysis resulted in an expansion of comparative sociology in terms of theoretical depth and empirical scope, as attempts were made to integrate a growing but disparate body of knowledge by means of theory. Case studies of a single country were interpreted in terms of comparative frameworks for analysis and several attempts at employing the comparative method proper were made.

Build-up of Major National Archives

It is not accidental that the reorientation of sociology towards a distinct comparative emphasis took place at the same time as several countries started to build up large national data archives for social science data. Often the very same persons who spoke in favour of more truly comparative research also participated in the build-up of the data archives (Rokkan, 1970). With the advent of the new computer technology and the ease with which such information can be transmitted across national borders it became possible to create a central storage building for large amounts of social science data. The advantages in terms of increased accessibility for the scholars to data that would otherwise have remained in oblivion need not be underlined. At the same time the dangers of too strict a reliance on data banks must be stated.

It may be predicted that existing data archives will grow and that new ones will be founded in the 1990s. The increasing internationalization of social science research favours the idea of comprehensive data banks. At present the archives are of value mainly for research on the OECD countries, but this will change as more and more countries adopt the strategy of creating central storage buildings for social science data. No doubt the access to national data banks has greatly stimulated the research on West European politics and societies. Often advances in theory and the cumulation of empirical information have gone hand in hand here. In the United States there has been a similar beneficial, mutual interaction between developments in comparative theory and the emergence of large data archives. However, their existence should not be taken for granted. The case for allocating scarce resources to the establishment of data banks needs to be argued in terms of benefits and costs.

Pros and Cons of Archives

The value of information or documentation centres is always dependent upon the theoretical context in question or the problem and hypothesis being posed. Only advances in social science theory can guide the development of national data archives. A national data archive cannot be constructed from a non-theoretical starting point. Ideally, decisions as to how to collect social data in a data archive must be based on theoretical deliberations derived from hypotheses in social theory.

Advantages
The central storage of large amounts of social data has several advantages that seem to outweigh the disadvantages by a large margin. A good national archive is characterized by: (1) *quantity*: comprehensive data as well as of data of various kinds; (2) *quality*: a fairly precise elaboration of different variables and how they have been measured; (3) *access*: easily retrievable information at one central site stored by means of modern computer technology; (4) *overview*: knowledge about where to go in order to find relevant

data, including what is available at other locations outside the central archive; (5) *communication*: improved transmission of data for research purposes from one central site to places elsewhere; (6) *development*: the detection of lacunae in existing data is facilitated by the centralization of available information; (7) *re-analysis*: the central storage of various data bases assembled in connection with special projects by different groups of scholars opens up an opportunity for other scholars to use the same data for renewed analyses in terms of others' questions or approaches. To sum up, a national data archive leads to more (quantity) and better organized (quality) empirical information.

Disadvantages
There is the severe danger involved in the efforts at building up national data archives of *empiricism*. Data do not present themselves to the archives, because they have to be selected and processed. There is the constant hazard that data considerations govern the conduct of comparative inquiry instead of theoretical deliberations.

The selection problem: A large number of variables are conceivably of interest to the social scientist. But deciding criteria of selection is a profoundly difficult problem that cannot be resolved without that rare species which no data archive possesses; namely, good social science theory.

The processing problem: Information may be handled in a number of alternative ways and be stored by different techniques. Which processing technique is the proper one can only be decided in relation to a certain theoretical reasoning which is not self-evident. Data do not exist in a manner that is independent of social science theory. Information has to be manipulated in various ways before it becomes data. Before the data can be brought to bear on the evaluation of alternative hypotheses, it may have to be rendered in certain specific ways that could not be predicted at the time when the data were originally collected.

The measurement problem: There is always a bias in national data archives towards certain types of information that are readily stored. Quantitative data may not always be relevant to ongoing comparative research. Certain types of data may be collected simply because they are readily handled by quantitative measurement techniques. Or data may be rendered in a special form just because quantitative indicators suit available measurement techniques in the archive.

The contextual problem: Data that have been assembled for certain research problems may not be suitable for other research questions. The empirical information could have been assembled by indicators that are dependent for their validity on the problems at hand. Or a new framing of the problem may require that additional variables be added or already existing ones be measured by different indicators.

It must be emphasized that if these fallacies in the use of archives are not confronted openly and explicitly, then substantial costs will be incurred as steps are taken towards the enlargement of national data archives. The problem of empiricism for the establishment of archives is simply that the data collected may be useless for certain valid research purposes, meaning that the entire collection of data would have to be redone. This difficulty is nicely demonstrated in the move from an active to a passive strategy of assembling data.

Strategies

When the first steps towards the erection of national data archives were taken in the 1960s and 1970s an *active strategy* was often adopted. This meant that variables and indicators were identified by the archives themselves and huge amounts of data were collected and stored, often political sociology data about election turnouts, voter attitudes or political ecology information. However, once the problems of crude empiricism were recognized, a *passive strategy* was adopted, meaning that data were transferred to the archives after they had been collected and used by the researchers themselves. The passive strategy is superior to the active strategy, because it means that the information stored is theoretically relevant, at least for some problems identified by some parts of the research community.

Use of Data Archives in Political Sociology

There exist two fundamentally different species of comparative inquiry in political sociology. The *semi- or quasi-comparative* type is the informative, accurate, detailed analysis of one country. The *truly comparative* type is the theoretical comparison of a number of countries on the basis of an explicit model structuring the data in a systematic fashion (Armer and Grimshaw, 1973; Ragin, 1982). Although we must acknowledge that most of what is done in the field of comparative political sociology belongs to the semi-comparative mode which is close to the case study method, there is a spectrum of comparative approaches from the one polar type of highly sophisticated comparative modelling to the other polar type of narrow case studies. Behind the organization of the data in case studies there is an implicit theoretical framework focusing on relationships between properties of the social system analysed. In case studies the empirical findings tend to turn out stronger than the true comparative findings, because of the lack of a set of theoretical concepts and models with which to build true comparative hypotheses. Recent studies in political sociology indicate the whole range, from genuine comparative modelling to semi-comparative work with comparative implications, even though they all employ data stored somehow in national data archives. Let us examine a few of these in more detail.

Quasi-comparative research
Often the case study technique is employed in the fields of electoral behaviour and political party research which employ national data archives, meaning that the implications for comparative theory and concepts remain implicit. The standard image of government in a representative democracy is that of an electoral choice between party ideologies expressed in the form of electoral manifestos and election-day promises to be kept when the party(ies) get a majority of the vote. This Schumpeterian model of democracy has been challenged from two different angles: big government resulting in overload politics and implementation deficits, and the new model of democracy as participation rejecting the claim of party government.

Recent comparative work has evaluated the competitive model of party government using large-scale data-assembling techniques. *Ideology, Strategy and Party Change: Spatial Analyses of Post-war Election Programmes in Nineteen Democracies* (Budge, Robertson and Hearl, 1987) contains case studies of party election programmes in several countries. The analysis of a rich body of data about party programmes was conducted on the basis of a rather advanced statistical methodology. The tool for understanding the variety of information about party platforms was factor analysis based on an intricate system of coding the information. Two fundamental dimensions in the party platform data were identified for each country: the traditional left–right dimension, and a second dimension that may differ according to the national party system studied.

The left–right dimension turned out to be the most basic cleavage dimension in these party ideologies, although not to the same extent in every country studied. Perhaps this is not a truly astonishing finding, but it warrants attention in a comparative perspective for the future development of national data archives when searching for information about political parties. The work done on collecting the individual country data may benefit later comparative work as there is the possibility of re-analysis of the data from another theoretical perspective.

Party Systems in Denmark, Austria, Switzerland, the Netherlands and Belgium (Daalder, 1987), exemplifying the semi-comparative method, focused on the extent to which political parties performed the traditional functions allocated to them by democratic theory: interest articulation and aggregation, policy-making and system legitimation. Under test was the hypothesis that parties and party systems were in a state of crisis due to increased volatility, the bureaucratization of party organization and the expansion of corporatist patterns of policy-making and implementation.

The separate country studies in the volume present a wealth of empirical information that may be employed for true comparative analysis. Yet the volume lacks a comparative assessment of the implications of the country findings. The concepts of party crisis and party system challenge and response are ambiguous and need to be assessed in a comparative perspective as the conduct of party functions depends on other properties of the political system as well as the history of the party system. How come there was so little party crisis observed in Austria and Switzerland, but so much in Denmark, Holland and Belgium? Case-study findings on separate countries must be integrated in the light of genuine comparative theory.

The potentialities of national data archives for comparative research were demonstrated in *How Ireland Voted: the Irish General Election 1987* (Laver, Mair and Sinnott, 1987). The study analysed the Irish party system before and after the 1987 watershed election, based on a new data archive at the newly formed election study centre at Galway. A quasi-comparative analysis of the policy context of Irish political parties showed that the policy issues were no different in Ireland than elsewhere in Western Europe. The distinctions between, on the one hand, conservative corporatism versus social democracy and, on the other hand, between welfare politics versus markets, seemed to capture the realities of Irish politics much more than the myth of the civil war cleavage.

The examination of the electoral outcome displays that the new Dail derives its freshness from its radically different political composition, not because of any major change in its social composition. To make a comparison with the 1987 net volatility we must go the Danish 1973 earthquake election. The first survey of the Irish electorate finds that the decisive vote is cast by middle-class voters who have become much more volatile, seeking a new party identity in the Progressive Democrats. Despite the right-wing turn of the policy profile of the Fianna Fail, it still has a large backing within the working class to the detriment of the declining Labour Party under attack from the new Workers' Party. The choice of the voter seems to express more of discontent with established practice than a real understanding of the issues involved or an attachment to party leaders. Yet, the lessons from the case studies in the volume may make sense if one resorts to genuine comparative concepts like the Westminster model properties in the Lijphart senses (Lijphart, 1984). That Irish politics is different is less true after 1987 than before, but it is not incomprehensible, comparatively speaking.

The analysis of political parties from the standpoint of a party system perspective is without exception about *change* and *durability*, particularly with regard to the West European countries. Two basic questions are involved, one of which is how to *describe* whether a party system is characterized by continuity or transformation, whereas the other deals with how to *account* for a certain level of stability or instability in terms of a set of explanatory factors. *Parties and Party Systems in Liberal Democracies* (Wolinetz, 1988) exemplifies the semi-comparative mode of approaching political party systems.

The first step in party system research is to classify party systems longitudinally, preferably by means of a number of case studies. The second step is to model the relation between independent variables and the dependent variable measuring the extent of party system durability, either in terms of an explicit comparative model or on the basis of country-specific observations pertaining to some implicit comparative model. Political sociology studies tend to cover the first step and sometimes the second step, but few if any handle the various party systems in terms of an explicitly comparative model.

The study of differences and similarities between national party systems faces two difficult research questions, the answer to which guide the search for data. First, there is the problem of relevant party system properties and, second, we have the identification of a causal perspective on the set of variables that account for the variation in the set of standard properties of party systems. Progress has been made only with regard to the second methodological problem.

At first, the party system was viewed as determined by the structure of social cleavages in the environment, party systems locked into a long-term, rigid cleavage structure – Western Europe – or as freely floating above a cross-cutting system of cleavages – the United States. Now party system continuity is seen as conditioned by both forces of persistency or change in the social environment and the adaptive capacities of parties. A number of strategies are available for political parties: the mobilization of an electoral niche, the turn to a catch-all strategy or the use of the state power structure to create a symbiosis between party and public authority. The probability of success for an adaptive strategy depends not only on the environment of the social structure but also on the choice of strategy by the other remaining parties in the system. Party system instability may also be due to internal party processes which are unrelated to changes in the social cleavage structure. The likelihood of party system durability is high when there is adaptive party change in an uncertain environment. When the strategies of parties are fixed in relation to social change, then there will be considerable party system instability.

The basic question about the fundamental properties of party systems has not been resolved in any definitive way. Which variables remain stable or change when party systems develop over time: the number of parties, their social ties, the degree of polarization between the parties on the left and the right? As long as these questions remain unanswered, case studies about party system development in a single country may differ substantially in the kind of empirical information searched for. This is a frustrating predicament not only for comparative analysis, but also for the establishment of data archives.

A framework for comparative inquiry

The comparative method aims at the analysis of the *genus* and the *differentia specifica* of a social system: that is, similarities and differences. A model is searched for that may explain why and how there are similarities and differences between spatial entities by a number of independent factors. Often comparative research only reaches out to a description of similarities and differences, as was true of the so-called functional approach in sociology (Parsons, 1966, 1971).

Explicitly designing a comparative framework is a step ahead towards genuine comparative inquiry. In *Opposition in Western Europe* (Kolinsky, 1987), the validity of true comparative work besides all the case studies is recognized. What is *similar* in patterns of government–opposition interaction in Western Europe is the desertion of the dualistic model of opposition. Political opposition is no longer the strict Westminster model of political competition between two monolithic groups in parliament, nor the system struggle between the right and the left classes in continental Europe. Action complexity and party tactics prevail with consensus on the legitimacy of the rules of political opposition.

What is *different* in West European styles of opposition is the location of the centre in the country patterns. In some countries like the United Kingdom, the Netherlands and Italy opposition comes from the left of the centre whereas the opposite holds true in France and Spain. In other countries like the Federal Republic of Germany there are considerable extra-parliamentary movements of political opposition.

A comparative model could account for these country patterns, but that would require moving beyond merely a comparative framework for analysis. Often national data archives contain information about the social environment of political behaviour, entailing that explanatory hypotheses focusing on social forces may be tested in a comparative perspective.

The distinction between a comparative framework and a comparative model is not a sharp one. Often the intent behind the formulation of a framework for the analysis of country similarities and differences is the testing of a more profound hypothesis or model. In *Representatives of the People: Parliamentarians and Constituents in Western Democracies* (Bogdanor, 1985), it is argued that there is some kind of relationship between parliamentary roles and constituency characteristics.

There is found a cross-country variation in the two basic entities: three types of constituencies, including single-member, multi-member and one single national constituency, as well as four kinds of roles of parliamentarians covering constituency, partisan, interest and policy roles. In order to test this comparative model a number of cases of national country systems are analysed at length, but does the use of this comparative framework succeed in establishing a genuine comparative model?

Single-member constituencies without choice of candidates, like the British system, are conducive to a partisan role of the parliamentarian. When single-member constituencies are combined with a selection mechanism between candidates, like the primary or the second ballot system, the constituency role takes precedence. This is even more emphasized in multi-member constituencies which employ the single transferable vote. On the other hand, multi-member constituencies with the usual proportional methods tend to move towards the partisan role where party discipline is strong, as well as towards the interest role where the party system is highly segmented in terms of a few salient social cleavages.

Other factors, such as political culture, must be added to the simple model, but the case studies derive theoretical meaning when the findings are interpreted in terms of an explicit comparative model. The future development of national data archives may be of help here, as they come to consist of more diverse and qualitative data including information about the political elite.

In *Coalitional Behaviour in Theory and Practice: An Inductive Model for Western Europe* (Pridham, 1986) the aim is a balance between comparative theory and case-study empirical analysis. To trade model simplicity against model realism offers a route to a renewal of coalition theory, at present stuck in a cave of only two alternatives: the rational choice theories of Riker's size hypothesis and of the de Swaan's distance principle. The case studies describing patterns of government formation in West European countries are held together by a comparative framework for the analysis of dimensions of coalition behaviour: national histories, institutions, motivations, horizontal and vertical relationships, internal party configurations, socio-political as well as environmental/external dimensions are here the most important variables. The country analyses provide much empirical information about West European politics, and the findings may be employed for stating the limits of established coalition theory. Yet, the new theoretical vistas offer a new conceptual structure for the analysis of government formation in multi-party systems, but no genuine comparative theory in the sense of true comparative models is in sight.

Comparative modelling
The study of electoral behaviour has benefited tremendously from the erection of major data archives at a time when this brand of political sociology typically was conducted by means of the case-study technique: elections at various points of time in separate nations. However, the various country studies of election outcomes have comparative implications, as shown in *Elections and Voters: A Comparative Introduction* (Harrop and Miller, 1987). Due to the abundance of data in easily accessible form in national data archives, it has become possible to compare the electoral systems in a number of countries, rich and poor, democratic and non-democratic. A wealth of data has been organized in terms of a few models, indicating that true comparative analysis replaces a large number of case studies, because comparative modelling of election behaviour is a short-cut to insight into the cross-country variation in national voting systems.

If there is a field within political sociology where a strong paradigm for the conduct of inquiry may be fruitful, then that would be the comparative analysis of electoral systems. A number of so-called lawlike statements have been suggested in this area like Duverger's law, the cube law of seat allocation and of assembly size. Taagepera and Shugart (1989) make a major attempt to integrate the present comprehensive literature on how electoral frameworks function in practice in *Seats and Votes: The Effects and Determinants of Electoral Systems*, presenting the analysis in terms of a clearly structured formal system.

Taagepera's and Shugart's model comprises a simple set of properties: electoral district magnitude (M), allocation rules in terms of deviation from proportionality (D), the number of effective parties (N) and the number of issue dimensions (I). They formulate a few basic principles that govern these fundamental properties: the larger M is, the less D is; the larger D is, the lower N is; the larger N is, the larger I tends to be. They support these electoral laws by a wealth of comparative information.

Taagepera and Shugart reformulate and generalize the well-known cube law derived from data about elections in the United Kingdom as a quantitative law for the relation between votes received by a political party and its seat allocation. Thus, for two parties, K and L, with votes, v, and seats, s, we have:

(1) $s_K/s_L = (v_K/v_L)^n$, where
(2) $n = \log v/\log e$, with e as the number of electoral districts with plurality rule.
(3) $n \to 1$, if proportional representation is used.

A number of electoral formulas have behaved in such a way that the relationship between seats allocated and votes received may be *described* by manipulations of the parameters in the cube law. However, this finding cannot serve as the basis for *predicting* how electoral formulas will behave in the future, because there is no guarantee that the parameter n will be stable. In any case, *Seats and Votes* is an example of true comparative modelling, scoring high on theoretical criteria.

Conclusion

A new approach to comparative social research was initiated in the late 1950s and early 1960s due to both substantial and methodological criticism. The volume of cross-national studies has risen sharply, particularly the number of area studies. This has happened at the same time as large national data archives have been established in several countries. The efforts at more genuine comparative analysis have enhanced model-building and model-testing on the basis of data covering a large number of countries. As sociology is moving towards comparative research, the trend is going towards more explicit cross-country analysis using, *inter alia*, the large amount of information gathered in national data archives. However, much more needs to be done in order to bridge the gap between theory and data in the employment of the large data banks in order to obtain true comparative modelling of areas such as political behaviour and political institutions. The allocation of large sums of money to the foundation and development of huge national data archives has to be done on an explicit consideration of the dangers of empiricism. The search for information to be stored at a central site must be done from theoretical starting points.

Appendix

Below are some of the new national data archives.

AUSTRIA
Wisdom
Maria Theresienstrasse 9/5
A–1090 Wien

BELGIUM
Belgian Archives for the Social Sciences
  (BASS)
Bâtiment SH 2 J. Leclerc
Place Montesquieu 1
B–1348 Louvain-la-Neuve

DENMARK
Danks Data Arkiv (DDA)
Campusvej 55
DK–5230 Odense M

FRANCE
Banque de Donnes Socio-Politiques
  (BDSP)
Institut d'Etudes Politiques
BP 34
F–38401 St Martin d'Heres

IRELAND
Centre for the Study of Irish Elections
University College
Galway

ITALY
Archivo Dati e Programmi per la
  Scienze Sociali (ADPSS)
Istituto Superiori di Sociologia
Via G. Cantoni 4
I–20144 Milano

NETHERLANDS
Steinmetz Archive (STAR)
Social Science Information and
  Documentation Centre
Herengracht 410–412
NL–1017 BX Amsterdam

NORWAY
Norsk Samfunnsvitenskapelig
  Datatjeneste (NSD)
Universitetet i Bergen
Hans Holmboesgate 22
N–5014 Bergen

SWEDEN
Svensk Samhållsvetenskaplig Datatjänst
  (SSD)
Box 5048
S–402 21 Göteborg

UNITED KINGDOM
Economic and Social Research Council
  Data Archive
University of Essex
Wivenhoe Park
Colchester
Essex CO4 3SQ

AUSTRALIA
Social Science Data Archive (SSDA)
Australian National University
Post Office Box 4
Canberra ACT 2600

CANADA
Machine Readable Archives – Public
  Archives Canada
395 Wellington
Ottawa, Ontario
K1A 0N3

Social Science Data Library (SSDL)
Department of Sociology
Carleton University
Colonel By Drive
Ottawa, Ontario
K15 5B6

University Data Library (UDL)
University of British Columbia
Room 206
6356 Agricultural Road
Vancouver, British Columbia
V6T 1W5

USA
Data and Program Library Service
  (DPLS)
University of Wisconsin
4452 Social Science Building
Madison, Wisconsin 48106

Inter-University Consortium for
  Political and Social Research (ICPSR)
University of Michigan
PO Box 1248
Ann Arbor, Michigan 48106

National Opinion Research Center
  (NORC)
University of Chicago
6030 South Ellis Avenue
Chicago, Illinois 60637

Social Science Data Library (SSDL)
Institute for Research in Social Science
University of North Carolina
Chapel Hill, North Carolina 27514

The Roper Center (RC)
University of Connecticut
Box U–164
Storrs, Connecticut 06268

References

Allardt, E. and S. Rokkan (eds) (1970) *Mass Politics: Studies in Political Sociology*. New York: Free Press.

Armer, M. and A.D. Grimshaw (eds) (1973) *Comparative Social Research: Methodological Problems and Strategies*. New York: John Wiley.

Bogdanor, V. (ed.) (1985) *Representatives of the People? Parliamentarians and Constituents in Western Democracies*. Aldershot: Gower.

Budge, I., D. Robertson and D. Hearl (eds) (1987) *Ideology, Strategy and Party Change: Spatial Analyses of Post-war Election Programmes in Nineteen Democracies*. Cambridge: Cambridge University Press.

Daalder, H. (ed.) (1987) *Party Systems in Denmark, Austria, Switzerland, the Netherlands and Belgium*. London: Pinter.

Dogan, M. and D. Pelassy (1984) *How to Compare Nations: Strategies in Comparative Politics*. Chatham: Chatham House.

Eisenstadt, S. (1978) *Revolution and the Transformation of Societies*. London: Macmillan.

Eisenstadt, S.N. and S. Rokkan (eds) (1973) *Building States and Nations*. 2 vols. Beverly Hills, CA: Sage.

Harrop, M. and W.L. Miller (1987) *Elections and Voters: A Comparative Introduction*. Basingstoke: Macmillan.

Kohn, M.L. (ed.) (1989) *Cross-national Research in Sociology*. Newbury Park: Sage.

Kolinsky, E. (ed.) (1987) *Opposition in Western Europe*. London: Croom Helm.

Laver, M., P. Mair, and R. Sinnott (eds) (1987) *How Ireland Voted: The Irish General Election 1987*. Dublin: Poolbeg.

Lijphart, A. (1984) *Democracies: Patterns of Majoritarian and Consensus Government in Twenty-one Countries*. New Haven, CT: Yale University Press.

Lipset, S.M. (1959) *Political Man*. Garden City, NY: Doubleday.

Lipset, S.M. and S. Rokkan (eds) (1967) *Party Systems and Voter Alignments: Cross-national Perspectives*. New York: Free Press.

Parsons, T. (1966) *Societies: Evolutionary and Comparative Perspectives*. Englewood Cliffs, NJ: Prentice-Hall.

Parsons, T. (1971) *The System of Modern Societies*. Englewood Cliffs, NJ: Prentice-Hall.

Pridham, G. (ed.) (1986) *Coalitional Behaviour in Theory and Practice: An Inductive Model for Western Europe*. Cambridge: Cambridge University Press.

Przeworski, A. and H. Teune (1970) *The Logic of Comparative Social Inquiry*. New York: Wiley.

Ragin, C. (1982) 'Comparative Sociology and the Comparative Method', *International Journal of Comparative Sociology*, 22: 110–20.

Ragin, C. (1989) 'New Directions in Comparative Research', in M.L. Kohn (ed.), *Cross-national Research in Sociology*. Newbury Park: Sage.   ·

Rokkan, S. (1970) *Citizens, Elections, Parties: Approaches to the Comparative Study of the Process of Development*. Oslo: Universitetsforlaget.

Taagepera, R. and M.S. Shugart (1989) *Seats and Votes: The Effects and Determinants of Electoral Systems*. New Haven, CT: Yale University Press.

Weber, M. (1978) *Economy and Society*. 2 vols. London: University of California Press.

Wilensky, H. (1975) *The Welfare State and Equality*. Berkeley: University of California Press.

Wolinetz, S. (ed.) (1988) *Parties and Party Systems in Liberal Democracies*. London: Routledge & Kegan Paul.

12

The Use of Time Series in International Comparison

Rudolf Andorka

The Research Problem

The statement from Stein Rokkan that the big questions of sociology, like the evolution of the industrial sociology and of democracy, are still essential, and that the best way to study them is through international comparison across countries and time, and that Europe is the ideal place for this comparative research, continues to be valid (Rokkan, 1964; quoted also in Flora, 1986). European countries might be classified along several dimensions; for example, following Haller (1987), into more or less developed countries, countries belonging to the German Protestant, the Roman Catholic, the Slavic Orthodox and other cultural circles, capitalist and socialist countries. By comparing research findings from countries belonging to different types it would be possible to ascertain the influence of the level of development, of the cultural background and of the political and economic system on social phenomena and processes.

Several important cross-sectional international comparative studies were performed in selected European countries to analyse the influence of the capitalist and the socialist system, or of the multi-party, democratic and the one-party system, on selected characteristics of these societies, like the use of time of the population (Szalai, 1972) and the openness of the society in terms of social mobility chances (Erikson and Goldthorpe, 1987a, 1987b). These comparative studies were based on surveys carried out and analysed by identical methods in a given year or at least in neighbouring years. In the following an attempt will be made to analyse time series of social indicators demonstrating, if possible, the more general development of societies.

This comparative study was stimulated by a very real and intriguing research problem in Hungary. The economic, social and political history of Hungary in the nineteenth and twentieth centuries might be conceptualized as a series of unsuccessful or half-successful attempts at modernization; that is, at catching up with the more advanced societies of Western Europe (Janos, 1982). Recently also the post-1945 period, earlier interpreted as the building of a socialist society, was conceptualized as a new attempt at modernization (Kulcsár, 1984). However, in the last two years severe doubts have been expressed among Hungarian social scientists concerning the results of this last period of modernization. Economists as well as sociologists consider the reforms more a failure than a success, and maintain that the 'socialist way' has been altogether unsuccessful. One way to verify these hypotheses would obviously be to compare the development of Hungary since 1945 with the development of more market-oriented countries in similar positions in Europe during the first half of the twentieth century. Austria, Greece and Finland, being in a similar semi-peripheral position in Europe in the nineteenth century, seem to be obvious candidates for such a comparison. In the present study Finland was selected for practical reasons; namely, the availability of data in Finland and the several earlier comparative analyses of the Hungarian and Finnish societies (for example, Andorka, Harcsa and Niemi, 1983; Alestalo, Andorka and Harcsa, 1987; Harcsa, Niemi and Babarczy, 1988).

Although the study has the above mentioned immediate relevance for the self-interpretation of the Hungarian society, it might be conceptualized in more theoretical terms; namely, whether the capitalist versus socialist economic and political system makes a difference in medium- and long-term social development. Three alternative hypotheses might be found in the world-wide literature concerning this question, namely:

- the 'industrial society' hypothesis, according to which the techno-logical and economic imperatives are stronger than the peculi-arities of the economic and political institutions, therefore all industrializing societies develop more or less along similar lines;
- the opposite hypothesis, propagated on the one hand by orthodox Marxists, on the other hand by conservative social scientists, that capitalist and socialist societies are completely different, one being superior to the other;
- the intermediate hypotheses according to which the Western and the Eastern European societies represent two different models of the industrial society, differing in several aspects, but characterized also by important common features and eventually converging towards a more similar economic, political and social system (for example, Solenius, 1983).

Hungary and Finland are in a certain sense ideal candidates for such a comparative study. Not only did they both belong to the semi-periphery of the European system, and were at the beginning of the twentieth century at similar levels of development. In addition, they also have important cultural similarities and were therefore classified by Haller into the 'Other cultural circle' (both originating in very ancient times from the Finno-Ugrian people). Therefore, it might be assumed that the difference in social development we find in this study might be due at least to a certain degree to the economic and political institutions of the two countries.

In order to avoid in the following the simplified use of the 'capitalist' and 'socialist' labels, the following characteristics of the two countries are specified: Hungary had till 1989 an economy which was predominantly centrally planned, in which the productive assets were predominantly in state ownership and where the political system was dominated by one party. Finland has a predominantly market-oriented economy, most of the productive assets are in private ownership, and the country has a multi-party, democratic political system. In consequence, the characteristics of the two countries are not 'black boxes', in the sense of the term given by Scheuch (Chapter 2). Rather, the two countries might be considered systems, as defined by Teune (Chapter 3). Therefore, it can be justified to compare the social phenomena and processes that have taken place within the two countries in the past decades.

In terms of the typology of Kohn (1987), this Hungarian–Finnish comparison has the relatively modest aim of comparing nations as objects of the study, parallel to the earlier Finnish–Polish comparison (Allardt and Wesolowski, 1978). The study might be further developed, however, into a comparison of nations as units of analysis, by analysing more deeply the interrelations of the economic and political system and the characteristics of social development in Hungary and in Finland.

The novelty of the present comparative analysis, as compared, for example, to the above mentioned Finnish–Polish comparison, is the investigation of time series. For this purpose the approach of the social indicators movement of the late 1960s and the 1970s is utilized. Important aspects of level of living, way of life and quality of life were defined, and indicators of these dimensions were selected and combined with indicators based on time series. Preference was given to those time series which allow breakdown by social class and strata. In the present analysis only those social indicators which were available for both countries were selected. The indicators, as constructed and compiled for Hungary (Andorka and Harcsa, 1988) and for Finland (Niitamo, 1971; Allardt, 1973), partly came from official statistical publications, partly from large social surveys, and partly from the comparative analyses of the Hungarian and Finnish time-budget surveys. The analysis ought to be considered as a first attempt to use time series to compare the social development of two countries and can in no way be considered a comprehensive and definite comparative analysis of the changes in these two societies.

Comparative Analysis

Economic development

The level and the rate of economic development in the two countries has been compared in several previous studies, using different methods. As measured by the percentage of the active population employed in agriculture – that is, by a very *crude* indicator – Finland might have been at a similar or even lower economic level of development than Hungary in the pre-1914 years (Alestalo, 1986). However, the economic growth rate in the interwar period was higher in Finland, and at the beginning of World War II Finland had already attained a higher level of economic development than Hungary (Maddison, 1976). According to a recent estimate by a Hungarian economist (Ehrlich, 1988, 1990), based on nineteen indicators in 'natural' terms, the per capita GDP in Hungary in 1937 attained 21 per cent, and that of Finland 38 per cent, of the level of the United States at the same time. Finland suffered less from the war than did Hungary. From 1945 to the end of the 1950s, however, the economic growth rate of Hungary seemed to have been similar to that of Finland. In 1960 Hungary was still at 21 per cent and Finland at 38 per cent of the level of the United States. In the 1960s, and even more so in the 1970s, the economic growth rate increased more rapidly in Finland. By 1980 the per capita GDP in Hungary reached 32 per cent of the level of the United States, while Finland reached 73 per cent. In the 1980s the Hungarian economy more or less stagnated, while the Finnish economy continued to grow. By 1986 Hungary fell back to 29 per cent of the level of the United States, while Finland increased the per capita GDP to 77 per cent of the level of the United States (Ehrlich, 1988). The Income Consumption Parity (ICP) comparisons of per capita GDP showed similar differences: in 1980 Hungary was estimated to be at 41 per cent of the level of the United States and Finland at 76 per cent.

Apart from the different impact of the wars experienced by the two countries, it can be seen that the relapse of the Hungarian economy as compared to the Finnish economy happened mainly in the inter-war period, when Hungary had a capitalist economic system – and after the shock of the steep increases in the price of oil in 1973, when Finland was able to adapt much more successfully than Hungary to the changing world market conditions.

Table 12.1 *Sectoral distribution of the economically active population, Hungary and Finland, 1949–80*

		Percentage employed in		
		Agriculture, forestry, fishing	Manufacture, construction	Services, transport and other
Hungary	1949	54	22	24
	1960	39	34	27
	1970	25	43	32
	1980	20	42	38
Finland	1950	46	27	27
	1960	35	31	34
	1970	20	34	46
	1980	13	33	54

Source: Alestalo, Andorka and Harcsa, 1987

Despite the overall similarity of the growth rate from 1945 to the 1970s, however, important differences can be observed in the sectoral distribution of the economically active populations (Table 12.1). In both countries the share of the population employed in agriculture declined, the share employed in manufacture and construction increased till 1970 before it began to decline slightly, while the share of those employed in the tertiary sector increased. However, the percentage of employment in manufacturing in Finland never attained the high levels of that in Hungary, as the percentage of employment in the tertiary sector increased to a much higher level in Finland. Thus, Hungary achieved its industrial growth with much higher labour inputs, paralleled by a lower level in the development of services. The latter can be assumed to have influenced in a negative way the non-material dimensions of the living conditions and the quality of life in Hungary, as compared to Finland.

Income differences by socio-economic strata
It could be expected that a market-oriented economic system might produce socio-economic strata and income differences that are different from a centrally planned system. The Hungarian economy, which was almost completely centrally planned in the first half of the 1960s, underwent important changes towards a more market-oriented system beginning from the second half of the 1960s. Both countries have regular income surveys. Since 1962 the Hungarian

Central Statistical Office has carried out family income surveys every five years. The Finnish Central Statistical Office has made similar surveys since 1966, the last one in 1985 (Uusitalo, 1989). Both surveys use the concept of the household disposable income. The Finnish data are published in terms of income per OECD consumption unit, but not in per capita terms. The Hungarian data are mostly published in per capita terms, and some of the data are also presented in per consumption unit terms. The data per consumption unit are rather different from the per capita data, when the averages of the income deciles are used, but do not show much difference when the averages of socio-economic strata are used. Therefore it might be justified to compare the Hungarian data in per capita terms (Table 12.2) with the Finnish data in per consumption unit terms (Table 12.3).

Table 12.2 *Relative per capita income by socio-economic strata, Hungary, 1962 and 1987*

Socio-economic stratum of household head	Per capita income, as % of national average	
	1962	1987
Upper white collar worker	154	125
Medium white collar worker	128	117
Lower white collar worker	119	93
Skilled worker	109	102
Semi-skilled worker	95	88
Unskilled worker	82	81
Peasant	87	90
Pensioner and other inactive	84	94
National average	100	100

Sources: Andorka and Harcsa, 1988; CSOH, 1988

Although the socio-economic classifications are not completely identical, it is remarkable how similar the income differences and their tendencies of change are. Upper white collar workers are at the top of the income distribution, while non-skilled workers and peasants are found at the bottom in both countries. The average income level of pensioners and others not participating in the labour market is more advantageous in Hungary than in Finland, but below the level of those in the labour force.

The differences between the socio-economic strata are somewhat

Table 12.3   *Relative per consumption unit income by socio-economic strata, Finland, 1966 and 1985*

Socio-economic stratum of the household head	Per consumption unit income, as % of national average	
	1966	1985
Upper white collar worker	174	134
Lower white collar worker	127	109
Self-employed outside agriculture	119	95
Manual worker	95	97
Self-employed in agriculture	68	91
Pensioner and other inactive	84	81
National average	100	100

Source: Uusitalo, 1989

smaller in Hungary, but the tendency in both countries is towards more equality. This tendency seems to have prevailed both in capitalist Finland and the changing economic structure of Hungary. It is especially notable that the cooperative peasants in Hungary and the self-employed farmers in Finland were situated very similarly in the income hierarchy. The landless farm workers in Finland have a somewhat lower income. The self-employed outside agriculture (that is, artisans and merchants – 2.4 per cent of the households in Hungary, and 4.8 per cent in Finland), attained a higher income level (122 per cent of the average in 1982).

Similarly, the hierarchy of occupational prestige is nearly identical in both countries (Kulcsár, 1985: Alestalo and Uusitalo, 1978) and rather strongly correlated with the International Occupational Prestige Scale (Treiman, 1977). Thus, it might be concluded that the functional requirements of industrial societies produced similar occupational hierarchies in Hungary and Finland.

Income inequality
Because socialist countries can be expected to be more egalitarian than capitalist countries, it seems important to include social indicators covering this issue. There are several ways in which income inequalities can be measured. Here the share of the lowest and of the highest income decile, and the ratio of the share of the highest and of the lowest decile are used to analyse the changes of income inequalities. In Hungary the decile distributions of *persons*

by per capita income were published at the time of each survey (Table 12.4). According to these data the income inequalities were relatively moderate in 1962 and tended to decline further with some fluctuations, till 1982. In the 1980s the inequalities increased slightly.

Table 12.4   *The share of the lowest and of the highest income decile of persons in total household income, Hungary, 1962–87*

	Lowest (%)	Highest (%)	Highest/ lowest
1962	3.9	20.2	5.2
1967	4.1	18.0	4.4
1972	4.0	19.9	5.0
1977	4.5	18.6	4.1
1982	4.9	18.6	3.8
1987	4.5	20.9	4.6

Sources: Andorka and Harcsa, 1988; CSOH, 1988

From the Finnish surveys the data on the decile distribution of *households* by total households income can be compared to similar Hungarian data from the surveys of 1967, 1977 and 1982 (Table 12.5). Income inequalities in Finland were more pronounced than in Hungary in 1967, but declined strongly in the subsequent 10 years, where the data from the surveys in 1982 seem to indicate an almost identical degree of income inequalities in the two countries. As the inequalities in terms of per capita income increased in

Table 12.5   *The share of the lowest and of the highest income decile of household in the total household income, Hungary and Finland, 1967–87*

Hungary	Finland	Hungary			Finland		
		Lowest (%)	Highest (%)	Highest/ lowest	Lowest (%)	Highest (%)	Highest/ lowest
1967	1966	2.2	20.8	9.5	2.1	24.9	11.9
	1971	–	–	–	2.4	23.4	9.8
1977	1976	2.3	20.5	8.9	2.7	20.9	7.7
1982	1981	2.6	20.5	7.9	2.6	20.8	8.0
1987	1985	–	–	–	2.7	21.4	7.9

Sources: Andorka and Harcsa, 1988; CSOH, 1988; Uusitalo, 1989

Hungary after 1982, it may be assumed that at present the income inequalities are somewhat larger in Hungary than in Finland.

What might be the explanation of the only slightly different trends in the development of inequality in the two countries? Certainly, it does not seem to be warranted to distinguish clearly between socialist versus capitalist inequality patterns. The Finnish welfare state, which is based on a predominantly market-oriented and privately owned economy, produced similar levels of inequality to the socialist system in Hungary, which is based on a partly market-oriented and predominantly state-owned economy. In Finland the enhanced redistribution by the welfare state explains most of the decrease of income inequalities (Uusitalo, 1989). In Hungary, contrary to expectations, the market-oriented reforms did not produce more, but less inequality, so that in 1982 the level of inequality was probably lower than in the 1950s; that is, in the 'golden age of socialist ideology'. Only the economic depression of the 1980s brought a slight increase of income inequalities.

Social mobility and the openness of society

Another indicator of inequality is the distance between the different social strata in a society. Chances of social mobility might be an indicator of inequality, as well as an indicator of the openness of a society, traditionally considered to be a desirable goal of capitalist societies.

Three national mobility surveys were made in Hungary, in 1962–64, 1973 and 1983, and two national mobility surveys were made in Finland, in 1972 and in 1981–82 (Pöntinen, 1983; Pöntinen, Alestalo and Uusitalo, 1983). Neither the samples, nor the social classifications are completely identical for the two countries, but it is nevertheless possible to construct some selected outflow and inflow rates which can be compared.

General inter-generational mobility of men increased in both countries from the 1960s to the 1980s. One of the main components of the observed mobility was in both countries the outflow from the peasant stratum (in Hungary all persons doing manual work in agriculture, in Finland self-employed peasants and agricultural workers). This outflow increased in both countries and was almost identical in percentage terms (see table on next page). This high and growing outflow rate from the peasantry was in both countries predominantly determined by the decrease of the number of persons employed in agriculture, which was itself a consequence of the changes of the economic structure. The opposite flow, from other strata into the agricultural strata, was somewhat higher in Hungary than in Finland, due to the different agrarian structure in

| Hungary | Finland | Sons of peasants who belonged to other social strata (percentages) | |
		Hungary	Finland
1962–64	–	49	–
1973	1972	57	58
1983	1980–81	75	72

Hungary. Here the collectivization of agriculture created an increased number of work-places of industrial character in the large state farms and cooperatives.

Similarly, the outflow from the manual strata (self-employed artisans, merchants and small entrepreneurs here included into the manual category) increased in both countries:

| Hungary | Finland | Sons of manual workers who belonged to the non-manual strata (percentages) | |
		Hungary	Finland
1962–64	–	13	–
1973	1972	16	19
1983	1980–81	19	26

The higher outflow rates in Finland can be explained by the higher level and the faster rate of economic development in Finland.

The opposite flow, from the non-manual strata into the manual strata, similarly increased in both countries:

| Hungary | Finland | Sons of non-manual workers who belonged to the manual strata (percentages) | |
		Hungary	Finland
1962–64	–	30	–
1973	1972	42	32
1983	1980–81	46	38

The somewhat higher outflow rate in Hungary might be explained by the slower growth of the non-manual strata in Hungary, a consequence of the slowdown of economic growth in general. The percentage of persons originating from the manual strata and now in the most privileged social category – namely, managers and professionals, or upper white-collar workers – was almost identical in both countries, and no clear tendency of change can be ascertained:

| Hungary | Finland | Male managers and professionals of manual origin (percentages) | |
		Hungary	Finland
1962–64	–	68	–
1973	1972	60	59
1983	1980–81	64	60

The overall openness of the Hungarian society (measured by the log-linear method based on the odds-ratios) increased to a considerable degree since the inter-war period, but did not show unidirectional significant changes after the 1960s (Andorka, 1989a). The international comparison of inter-generational mobility in the framework of the CASMIN-Project demonstrated that the inter-generational fluidity of men in 1973 in Hungary was rather similar in terms of the odds-ratios to the Western European countries, with some minor exceptions, and most notably as a consequence of the higher fluidity of the outflow and inflow mobility of the agricultural classes (Erikson and Goldthorpe, 1987a, 1987b).

Thus it might be conjectured that in the field of income inequalities and of the openness of the society, Hungary performed more or less similarly to Finland, as well as compared to other more advanced European societies. Taking into consideration that in the inter-war period Hungary was much more unequal both in terms of income and of mobility chances, the proximity to the levels attained in the more advanced European societies might be evaluated as a rather interesting development.

Time budget, and way of life
When we move to the analysis of the 'softer' indicators of the way of life, larger differences are visible. Time-budget data can be used to investigate the framework of the way of life. Three time-budget surveys were performed in Hungary in 1963, 1976/77 and 1986/87. As the samples were somewhat different, the results of the surveys can be compared only pairwise (Tables 12.6 and 12.7). Two surveys were performed in Finland in 1980 and in 1987/88. Both the Finnish

surveys were compared with the Hungarian surveys using rigorously exact comparative techniques; that is, identical samples, social classifications and definitions of activities (Andorka, Harcsa and Niemi, 1983; Andorka and Harcsa, 1986; Harcsa, Niemi and Babarczy, 1988; Harcsa and Niemi, 1989).

Table 12.6 *Time budget of men and women aged 18–60, Hungary, 1963 and 1976/77, minutes per day*

	Men		Women	
Activity	1963	1976/77	1963	1976/77
Work in first job	420	328	162	203
Second economy in agriculture	30	46	42	42
Building, repairing	18	38	6	11
Household chores	66	51	330	249
Care for children	12	14	48	33
Travel	60	74	24	55
Free time, incl. learning	198	254	174	195
Physiological needs	636	635	654	639
Total	1440	1440	1440	1440

Source: Andorka, Falussy and Harcsa, 1982

Table 12.7 *Time budget of men and women aged 15–69, Hungary, 1976/77 and 1986/87, minutes per day*

	Men		Women	
Activity	1976/77	1986/87	1976/77	1986/87
Work in first job	279	231	172	150
Second economy	67	96	54	58
Building, repairing	23	28	3	4
Household chores	53	58	248	236
Other work	19	6	9	2
Care for children	12	13	26	35
Travel	72	70	55	54
Learning	18	19	16	17
Free time	228	251	187	217
Physiological needs	669	668	670	667
Total	1440	1440	1440	1440

Source: Andorka, 1989b

Table 12.8 *Time budget of men and women aged 15–64, Hungary and Finland, minutes per day*

	Hungary		Finland	
Activity	1976/77	1986/87	1980	1987/88
Men				
Work in first job	317	254	223	233
Second economy	62	98	42	39
Building	16	23	13	11
Household chores	85	81	94	97
Travel	76	69	70	81
Learning	18	23	40	33
Free time	238	245	338	338
Physiological needs	628	647	620	608
Total	1440	1440	1440	1440
Women				
Work in first job	201	170	170	180
Second economy	52	53	21	18
Building	3	4	1	1
Household chores	280	272	222	208
Travel	58	55	60	72
Learning	18	20	47	39
Free time	196	219	299	312
Physiological needs	632	647	620	610
Total	1440	1440	1440	1440

Sources: Andorka, Harcsa and Niemi, 1983; Harcsa and Niemi, 1989

Total contracted and committed time, here defined as time spent in activities which might be broadly considered as obligatory, (namely, all the activities listed in Tables 12.6–12.7, except free time and tending to physiological needs), was much longer in Hungary than in Finland (Table 12.8). During the period of observation the amount of 'obligatory' time spent declined relatively slowly in Hungary, while it remained almost unchanged in Finland. Women were overburdened in both countries as compared to men. The workload of women diminished in Finland, but remained almost unchanged in Hungary from the 1970s to the 1980s.

The reason for the longer hours committed to daily routines in Hungary is the longer working hours spent in the first and the second economy, as well as in building activities, and (for the women) the longer hours taken up by household chores. ('Building' here means the construction of dwellings, mostly of one-family houses in rural areas, by the manpower of family members, kin and friends.) It might be concluded that most members of the Hungarian society in the 1960s and in the first half of the 1970s tried to improve their level of living by undertaking extra work efforts, such as labouring on household plots, in order to supplement their family income. After the onset of the economic depression in 1978 when the real wage level began to decline, the immediate goal of these extra efforts was increasingly simply to avoid the deterioration of standard of living of the family.

As the length of the contracted and committed time spent was strongly differentiated by social strata (Andorka and Falussy, 1982), it might be concluded that the willingness of the lower strata to engage in extra efforts to work was an important factor in the diminution of income inequalities. These efforts also had an impact on the inequalities of mobility chances as the extra income to a large extent was used to help the schooling and the early careers of the children. In other words, the overburdening of the majority of the population was the price paid for the relatively favourable achievement in the field of income inequality and fluidity in social mobility.

Mortality
Some of the most widely used indicators on the quality of life of a population are rates of life expectancy and mortality. Here the development of life expectancy at birth shows striking differences in Hungary and in Finland. Around 1960 life expectancy was quite similar in the two countries. In Finland life expectancy continued to improve for both sexes, while in Hungary the life expectancy for men attained a maximum in 1966 (68.0 years) and then began to decline, reaching the lowest point in 1984 (65.1 years). Life expectancy for women did not decline, but stagnated around 73 years (Table 12.9). However, mortality for women increased in the age groups between 30 and 64 years.

It is assumed that the main factor for explaining increased mortality is found in the growth of age-specific mortality caused by circulatory diseases. It is well known that social differences in mortality are quite large. The underlying causes of this disadvantageous tendency are not clearly known, but Józan (1989), the leading expert on mortality in Hungary, argues that a social maladaptation syndrome, manifested by high alcohol consumption and smoking, unhealthy nutrition, a high level of stress in everyday life and the malfunctioning of the health-care system, are important factors.

Some forms of deviant behaviour
The alarming increase in some forms of deviant behaviour, first of

Table 12.9   *Expectancy of life at birth, Hungary and Finland, 1956–88*

	Male		Female	
	Hungary	Finland	Hungary	Finland
1956–60	65.2	64.9	69.7	71.6
1961–65	67.0	65.4	71.7	72.6
1966–70	67.2	65.9	72:5	73.6
1971–75	66.5	66.7	72.4	75.2
1976–80	66.2	68.5	72.7	77.2
1981	65.5	69.5	72.9	77.8
1982	65.6	70.1	73.2	78.1
1983	65.1	70.2	73.0	78.0
1984	65.1	70.4	73.2	78.8
1985	65.1	70.1	73.1	78.5
1986	65.3	70.5	73.2	78.7
1987	65.7	–	73.7	–
1988	66.2	–	74.0	–

Sources: CSOH, 1989; CSOF, 1988

all suicide, alcoholism and mental disorder, stimulated intensive research in Hungary. The suicide rate, being the highest in the world, is the best-documented of these problems. Since the turn of the century Hungary has shown a high suicide rate. In the 1950s, however, the suicide rate was similar in Hungary and Finland. Since then the Hungarian rate has increased continuously till 1987, while the Finnish suicide rate has shown only a slight increase (Table 12.10).

Table 12.10   *Suicide rates, Hungary and Finland*

	Number of suicides per 100,000 population	
	Hungary	Finland
1931–35	32.9	20.6
1955	20.5	19.9
1971–75	37.7	23.9
1976–80	42.7	25.4
1980–85	45.1	24.4
1986	45.2	26.6
1987	45.0	–
1988	41.3	–

Sources: Andorka and Harcsa, 1988; CSOF, 1988

Alcoholism, measured either by the mortality rate by liver cirrhosis or by the per capital alcohol consumption, similarly showed a high rate of growth in Hungary, and a much slower rate of growth in Finland (Tables 12.11 and 12.12).

Table 12.11   *Death rate by cirrhosis of the liver, Hungary and Finland*

| | Number of deaths by liver cirrhosis per 100,000 population | |
	Hungary	Finland
1955	5.5	–
1964	8.7	3.5
1971	13.8	4.2
1977	20.1	5.4
1982	32.2	5.8
1985	43.1	7.4
1986	42.8	10.8
1987	44.2	–
1988	43.9	–

Sources: CSOH, 1989; CSOF, 1988

Table 12.12   *Per capita alcohol consumption*

| | Total alcohol consumption per capita expressed in % alcohol content, litres | |
	Hungary	Finland
1971–75	9.6	5.6
1976–80	11.3	6.3
1981–85	11.5	6.4
1986	11.4	6.9
1987	10.7	7.1
1988	10.5	–

Sources: CSOH, 1989; CSOF, 1988

It is difficult to point precisely to the causes of these unfortunate tendencies, but it might be hypothesized that the stress of everyday life plays a role in inducing persons to drink heavily and to commit suicide in extreme situations. What might cause the stress of everyday life in Hungary? We do not have any comparable research which might point to possible causes. The overburdening of the members of the society by the very long working hours in the first and second economy might be one of the factors. Other possible causes might be sought in the deficits in the 'loving' and 'being' dimensions of Hungarian quality of life (Allardt, 1975), or in the domains to which the sociological concepts of happiness, anomie, '*Entfremdung*' and social disorganization refer.

The modernization process in Hungary

If we are to draw conclusions from what has been found so far, it can be said that the attempt to modernize the Hungarian economy and society since 1945 – namely, the 'socialist way' – has been neither completely successful nor completely unsuccessful. In addition, neither the achievements nor the failures are to be found in the dimensions which are often quoted publicly as successes and failures.

The performance of the Hungarian economy seems to have been poorer than that of the Finnish economy, in particular since the mid-seventies – that is, in a period when the conditions of the world economy changed into the 'third industrial revolution', and the Hungarian economy already had attained a moderately high level of development. Thus, it seems that the economic system based on the state ownership of productive assets and on central planning became rather inefficient at a relatively higher level of development. Under these circumstances the rigidity caused by state ownership and by central planning was a hindrance to the rapid adaptation of the economic institutions. It might be hypothesized that without the reforms that were introduced after 1966, aiming at a greater role for the market forces and encouraging the development of a small private sector, the economic crisis in the 1980s might have been worse. In order to throw a better light on this hypothesis other socialist countries ought to be included in the comparison.

In terms of income inequalities and the openness of the society Hungary seems to have approached the advanced welfare states, but certainly no special 'socialist' pattern of equality and openness was developed. It is surprising that both the level of equality and the degree of openness could be maintained under the critical economic conditions (with an almost stagnating GDP and declining relative wages).

The serious problems in Hungary within the 'softer' fields of way of life and quality of life are clearly visible from the time-budget surveys. It might be hypothesized that the relatively good performance of the Hungarian economy after the first economic reforms in 1966 and the avoidance of a deeper economic crisis have to be attributed to the willingness of the population to work for very long hours both in the first and in the second economy.

If the suicide rate and alcoholism are conceptualized as indicators of quality of life, and if we assume that the deterioration of adult mortality in Hungary is also at least partly a consequence of negative developments in quality of life, it might be concluded that the 'costs' of the socialist way of modernization seem to be high in this respect. Further studies would be necessary to find out how much of the deterioration in quality of life might have been caused by the economic and social factors discussed here, and how much of the deterioration is due to the characteristics of the political system and to changes of values in the population.

Some Lessons for International Comparison

This preliminary and short comparison of Hungary and Finland with a combination of social indicators derived from social statistics and from repeated sociological surveys shows that it is worth while to develop further this type of comparative research. The conclusions that can be drawn from these fairly simple comparisons are interesting, at least for a better understanding of the recent economic, political and social development of Hungary. It is obvious, however, that in order to obtain more valid conclusions, it is necessary to carry out more sophisticated comparative research (Scheuch, 1967; Kohn, 1987), more countries must be included, a wider spectrum of indicators ought to be taken into consideration and the indicators must also be defined by social strata and other relevant categories.

At present there are serious obstacles in carrying out combined cross-country and cross-time analyses. The social indicator movement was almost halted in the 1980s, partly due to methodological criticism. There are few new comprehensive national compendia of time series of social indicators, and the concepts and classifications used by the national archives are far from unified. The existing time series are almost all based on 'hard' indicators, and time series on 'soft' indicators relating to subjective satisfaction and quality of life are scarce, the Federal Republic of Germany being one of the few exceptions (Zapf (1987), and the *Datenreports* released since 1983). Social indicators by social categories are only available for a few countries, as repeated surveys are needed to produce such time series. The annual level of living survey conducted by the Swedish Bureau of Statistics is an outstanding exception (Vogel et al., 1988).

If progress is to be made in this area it is necessary to revitalize the work on internationally comparable social statistical data and social indicators, and to publish time series of social indicators. Such time series can be used in combination with historical and quantitative comparative studies of social phenomena. In addition to statistical data, standardized social surveys repeated in given countries and carried out in a parallel fashion in several countries could be a very important data source (Duncan, 1969). Nevertheless, the surveys of different countries are comparable *only* if additional bilateral or multilateral efforts are invested into comparability, the Hungarian–Finnish time budget comparisons being good examples.

Along with the development of data sources, new advances in sociological theory are desirable. The social indicator movement was largely based on a multi dimensional theory of well-being (Allardt, 1973; Zapf, 1987; Glatzer and Zapf, 1984). This theory was useful in defining the dimensions to be measured by the social indicators and in emphasizing that human well-being cannot be reduced to the level of per capita income. In addition to this theory a theoretical framework of the interrelations of economic, political and social development, including the development of well-being, would be necessary to select the social phenomena and processes that ought to be included into international and inter-temporal comparative studies of social development.

Last, but not least, such comparative studies are impossible to carry through without the intensive cooperation of social scientists from the countries compared. Although the present chapter is authored by one person, it would not have been possible to write it without the earlier intensive cooperation with Finnish sociologists – among others, M. Alestalo, I. Niemi, S. Pöntinen and H. Uusitalo.

References

Alestalo, M. (1986) *Structural Change, Classes and the State. Finland in an Historical Perspective*. Research Group for Comparative Sociology, University of Helsinki, Research Reports, no. 33.

Alestalo, M., R. Andorka and I. Harcsa (1987) *Agricultural Population and Structural Change: A Comparison of Finland and Hungary*. Research Group for Comparative Sociology, University of Helsinki, Research Reports, no. 34.

Alestalo, M. and H. Uusitalo (1978) *Occupational Prestige and its Determinants: The Case of Finland*. Research Group for Comparative Sociology, University of Helsinki, Research Reports, no. 20.

Allardt, E. (1973) *About Dimensions of Welfare: An Exploratory Analysis of a Comparative Scandinavian Survey*. Research Group for Comparative Sociology, University of Helsinki, Research Reports, no. 1.

Allardt, E. (1975) *Dimensions of Welfare in a Comparative Scandinavian Study*. Research Group for Comparative Sociology, University of Helsinki, Research Reports, no. 9.

Allardt, E. and W. Wesolowski (eds) (1978) *Social Structure and Change: Finland and Poland in Comparative Perspective*. Warsaw: Polish Scientific Publishers.

Andorka, R. (1989a) 'Half a Century of Trends in Social Mobility in Hungary'. Paper presented at the Conference Sociale Reproduktie in Oost en West Europa, University of Groningen.

222 Rudolf Andorka

Andorka, R. (1989b) 'Recent Changes of the Hungarian Society, Measured by Social Indicators'. Paper presented at the Conference on Social Reporting and Social Indicators, Wissenschaftzentrum für Sozialforschung, West Berlin.

Andorka, R. and B. Falussy (1982) 'The Way of Life of the Hungarian Society on the Basis of the Time Budget Survey of 1976–1977', *Social Indicators Research*, 11: 31–73.

Andorka, R., B. Falussy and I. Harcsa (1982) *Idömérleg. Részletes adatok*. Budapest: Central Statistical Office of Hungary.

Andorka, R. and I. Harcsa (1986) 'Economic Development and the Use of Time in Hungary, Poland and Finland', in *Time Use Studies: Dimensions and Applications*. D. As, A.S. Harvey, E. Wnuk-Lipinski and I. Niemi (eds), Helsinki: Central Statistical Office of Finland, pp. 7–35.

Andorka, R. and I. Harcsa (1988) *Modernization in Hungary in the Long and Short Run Measured by Social Indicators*. Karl Marx University of Economic Sciences, Department of Sociology, Sociological Working Papers, no. 1.

Andorka, R., I. Harcsa and I. Niemi (1983) *Use of Time in Hungary and in Finland*. Helsinki: Central Statistical Office of Finland.

Central Statistical Office of Finland (CSOF) (1988) *Suomen tilastollinen vuosikirja 1988*. Statistical Yearbook of Finland. Helsinki: Central Statistical Office of Finland.

Central Statistical Office of Hungary (CSOH) (1988) *A lakosság jövedelmi rétegzödése 1987–ben*. Budapest: Central Statistical Office of Hungary.

CSOH (1989) *Statisztikai Évkönyv 1988*. Statistical Yearbook. Budapest: Central Statistical Office of Hungary.

Duncan, O.D. (1969) 'Social Forecasting: The State of the Art', *Public Interest*, 17: 88–118.

Erhlich, E. (1988) *Gazdasági fejlettségi szintek, arányok, szerkezetek, iparositási utak*. Doctor of Sciences thesis, Hungarian Academy of Sciences.

Erhlich, E. (1990) 'Országok versenye, 1937–1986', *Közgazdasági Szemle*, 37: 19–43.

Erikson, R. and J.H. Goldthorpe (1987a) 'Commonality and Variation in Social Fluidity in Industrial Nations. Part I: A Model for Evaluating the "FJH Hypothesis"', *European Sociological Review*, 3: 54–77.

Erikson, R. and J.H. Goldthorpe (1987b) 'Commonality and Variation in Social Fluidity in Industrial Nations. Part II: The Model of Social Fluidity Applied', *European Sociological Review*, 3: 145–66.

Flora, P. (ed.) (1986) *Growth to Limits: The Western European Welfare States since World War II*, vol. 1. Berlin: Walter de Gruyter.

Glatzer, W. and W. Zapf (eds) (1984) *Lebensqualität in der Bundesrepublik*. Frankfurt: Campus.

Haller, M. (1987) 'Grenzen und Variationen gesellschaftlicher Entwicklung in Europa – eine Herausforderung und Aufgabe für die vergleichende Soziologie'. Paper presented at the Conference of the Austrian Sociological Association.

Harcsa, I. and I. Niemi (1989) 'The Use of Time in Hungary and Finland, 1986–1987'. Manuscript.

Harcsa, I., I. Niemi and A. Babarczy (1988) *Use of Time in Hungary and in Finland II: Life Cycle and Time Use*. Helsinki: Central Statistical Office of Finland.

Janos, A.C. (1982) *The Politics of Backwardness in Hungary 1835–1945*. Princeton, NJ: Princeton University Press.

Józan, P. (1989) 'Contrasts in mortality trends', in *International Population Conference New Delhi 1989*, vol. 3, pp. 231–45.

Kohn, M.L. (1987) 'Cross-national Research as an Analytic Strategy', *American Sociological Review*, 52: 713–31.

Kulcsár, K. (1984) *Contemporary Hungarian Society*. Budapest: Kossuth.

Kulcsár, R. (1985) 'Az elsö magyar országos presztizsvizsgálat eredményei', *Statisztikai Szemle*, 63: 1115–26.

Maddison, A. (1976) 'Economic Policy and Performance in Europe 1913–1970' in C.M. Cipolla (ed.) *The Fontana Economic History of Europe. The Twentieth Century – 2*. London: Collins/Fontana, pp. 442–508.

Niitamo, O.E. (1971) 'Social Indicators – Instruments of Modern Social Policy' in *Yearbook of the Finnish Society for Economic Research 1971*. Helsinki, pp. 35–45.

Pöntinen, S. (1983) *Social Mobility and Social Structure: A Comparison of Scandinavian Countries*. Helsinki: Societas Scientiarium Fennica.

Pöntinen, S., M. Alestalo and H. Uusitalo (1983) *The Finnish Mobility Survey 1980: Data and First Results*. Helsinki: Suomen Gallup Oy Report, no. 9.

Rokkan, S. (1964) 'Comparative Cross-national Research: The Context of Current Efforts', in R.L. Merritt and S. Rokkan (eds), *Comparing Nations: The Use of Quantitative Data in Cross-national Research*. New Haven, CT: Yale University Press, pp. 3–25.

Scheuch, E.K. (1967) 'Society as Context in Cross-cultural Comparisons', *Social Science Information*, 6: 7–23.

Scheuch, E.K. (1988) 'Theoretical Implications of Comparative Survey Research', Paper presented at the Conference of the ISA Research Council, Ljubljana.

Solenius, J. (1983) *Bridge-Building in Social Theory*. Stockholm: Almquist & Wicksell International.

Szalai, A. (ed.) (1972) *The Use of Time: Daily Activities of Urban and Suburban Populations in Twelve Countries*. The Hague: Mouton.

Teune, H. (1988) 'Comparing Countries: Lessons Learned'. Paper presented at the Conference of the ISA Research Council, Ljubljana.

Treiman, D.J. (1977) *Occupational Prestige in Comparative Perspective*. New York: Academic Press.

Uusitalo, H. (1989) *Income Distribution in Finland*. Helsinki: Central Statistical Office of Finland.

Vogel, J., L.-G. Andersson, U. Davidsson and L. Häll (1988) *Inequality in Sweden: Trends and Current Situation*. Stockholm: Statistics Sweden.

Zapf, W. (ed.) (1987) 'German Social Report: Living Conditions and Subjective Well-being, 1978–1984', *Social Indicators Research*, 19: 1–171.

Index